全国教学型本科院校商务英语系列规划教材

国际贸易实务

（双语版）

International Trade Practices

主编　徐　凡

对外经济贸易大学出版社
中国·北京

图书在版编目（CIP）数据

国际贸易实务：双语版／徐凡主编．—北京：对外经济贸易大学出版社，2013

全国教学型本科院校商务英语系列规划教材

ISBN 978-7-5663-0906-8

Ⅰ.①国…　Ⅱ.①徐…　Ⅲ.①国际贸易－贸易实务－高等学校－教材　Ⅳ.①F740.4

中国版本图书馆 CIP 数据核字（2013）第 259979 号

国际贸易实务（双语版）

International Trade Practices

徐　凡　**主编**

责任编辑：戴　菲

对 外 经 济 贸 易 大 学 出 版 社

北京市朝阳区惠新东街 10 号　　邮政编码：100029

邮购电话：010－64492338　　发行部电话：010－64492342

网址：http://www.uibep.com　　E-mail：uibep@126.com

北京市山华苑印刷有限责任公司印装　　新华书店北京发行所发行

成品尺寸：185mm×230mm　　16.5 印张　　332 千字

2013 年 12 月北京第 1 版　　2013 年 12 月第 1 次印刷

ISBN 978-7-5663-0906-8

印数：0 001－3 000 册　　定价：30.00 元

出 版 说 明

随着经济全球化浪潮的日益高涨，中国与世界各国之间的经贸往来日益密切，既掌握娴熟英语又具有扎实商务专业知识的复合型人才已成为市场的主要需求。根据教育部发布的《国家中长期教育改革和发展规划纲要》，“建立高校分类体系，实行分类管理”的要求，对外经济贸易大学出版社专门针对教学型本科院校组织编写了这套“全国教学型本科商务英语系列规划教材”。

现时，我国的高等院校分为大致可分为研究型、教学研究型、教学型三大类。不同类型高等院校在人才培养类型、创新贡献和服务社会方面都应有各自的定位；与之相应，其适用教材也各有不同。教学型高校作为我国高等教育的主力，量大面广、层次多、类型多，是培养应用型高级人才的主要力量。教学型高校以培养应用型、复合型人才为出发点，按“基础扎实，知识面宽，应用能力强，素质高，有较强的创新精神”的要求，以人为本，使学生“会学习”、“会创新”、“会做人”；既加强通识教育，同时也为终身教育作准备，打基础。

本系列教材面向全国教学型本科院校，目标群体明确，教材选题和内容均根据全国教学型本科院校课程设置而定，作者队伍也拟联合全国教学型本科院校的优秀一线师资，适用于全国教学型本科院校商务英语专业、财经专业和英语专业校商务/应用/外贸外语方向的学生。

本套“全国教学型本科商务英语系列规划教材”适用于全国应用型本科院校商务英语专业、英语专业的商务/应用/外贸英语方向以及财经类专业的学生，内容包括《商务英语综合教程 1-4 册》、《商务英语听说》、《商务英语阅读》、《商务英语写作》、《商务英语函电》、《商务英语翻译》、《商务英语口译》、《商务知识导读》、《英语财经报刊阅读》、《跨文化交际基础》、《国际商务礼仪》、《进出口贸易实务》、《国际商务制单》、《国际贸易实务》、《国际贸易理论与实务》等。

本系列的编撰者们不仅具有丰富的语言教学经验，而且具备商务活动的实践经验，他们集教学经验和专业背景于一身，这是本套商务英语系列教材编撰质量的有力保证。

此外，本套教材配有辅导用书或课件等立体化教学资源，供教师教学参考（可登录我社网站 www.uibep.com 下载）。

对外经济贸易大学出版社

外语图书事业部

2013 年 6 月

前　言
Preface

“国际贸易实务”是我国高等院校商务英语专业的必修课程之一，其名称历经“进出口业务”、“商品进出口业务”、“进出口贸易实务”等变化，最终由国家教委统一定名为“国际贸易实务”。

随着我国社会主义市场经济的发展与完善，我国的对外经济与贸易活动更加活跃。只有掌握了国际贸易实务知识，才能在进出口业务活动中正确贯彻我国对外贸易的方针政策，按国际规则办事，确保最佳经济效益。因此，本课程以科学发展观等重要思想为指导，培养通晓国际贸易基本知识和实务，具有较强沟通能力、应用能力和较高综合素质的复合型商务英语专门人才。本课程旨在使学生了解和掌握国际贸易的基本理论知识、相关交易流程与操作技能等。内容涉及国际贸易的基本概念、国际贸易术语和惯例、商品运输与运输保险、货款结算、贸易中的争议，贸易流程，贸易形式等，具有较强的实践性。

鉴于本课程实践性强的特点，在实际教学过程中，其教学方法需服从于培养学生掌握国际进出口业务的基础理论与知识、提高其使用英语从事进出口贸易知识学习和进行贸易实践的能力这一总目标。具体而言，教学目标和要求可分为以下几点：

1. 使学生了解国际贸易业务的基本理论和基本知识，熟悉相关英文术语；

2. 使学生能针对进出口业务的各个环节进行实际操作，通过课堂教学、课后练习、到企业及相关部门调查实习，加强基本技能的训练，培养学生对于业务的实际操作能力；

3. 训练学生分析商务英语语篇并探讨其结构背后的社会文化因素和心理、认知因素等，培养其跨文化交流技能；

4. 培养学生自主学习、探究学习、发现和体验式学习的能力，为其今后的英语和商务知识学习打下坚实的基础。

鉴于国际贸易实务知识体系兼具专业性与实践性，与对外经济贸易的发展与时俱进，本书在编写过程中具有如下特点：

1. 术语规范，选材兼顾经典性与新颖性；在参考国外著名专家、学者的原版著作，使学生掌握国际贸易领域的常用词汇、句型、文本格式等，熟练阅读并领会其语言和文字魅力的同时，突出介绍本领域的最新规定与趋势，以与国际接轨；此外，部分内容的双语注释帮助学生更深入准确地了解相关概念。

2. 本教材由对外经济贸易大学多年从事商务英语及国际贸易教学研究的一线教师精心编撰完成。此外，还特邀该领域的著名学者修改审阅，并聘请具有丰富国际贸易实战经验的行业专家担当编写顾问。

3. 整本教材按主题划分为若干单元，重在帮助学生了解该领域的基础知识，还增加了一些能反映最新国际贸易活动趋势及理论变化的全新选题，以增强时效性、完善内容覆盖面、拓宽学生的知识面；同时，根据本学科特色，对各领域的基本原理、基础知识及历史沿革做补充，目的在于帮助学生完成从基础到专业领域的过渡，为其今后的商务知识学习打下坚实的基础。

4. 全书编写主题突出、内容覆盖全面，包括商品及其属性、常见国际贸易条款、国际支付、争端解决、国际贸易流程等，涵盖了广义上的商务、经济学、贸易等领域，具有丰富的知识性，可培养学生的商务英语认知和理解能力。

5. 教材的配套练习以培养学生的英语综合能力及实际开展国际贸易业务能力为目标，实用性强、形式多样，辅以对贸易等商务知识的深层次解读和系统介绍，以增强训练效果。

6. 本教材的附录部分配有练习答案、词汇释义和参考阅读书目，并辅以多媒体课件等，以利于教师授课和学生对照自学，培养学生自主和探究式学习的能力，从而达到举一反三、触类旁通的教学效果。

7. 单词释义准确——全部参照最新权威工具书（如《国际贸易术语解释通则 2010 版》，INCOTERMS 2010），并采用英汉两种方式，以培养学生的理解、记忆能力和查阅原文词典的能力。

8. 全面遵循 ESP（English for Specific Purposes）的教学理念，教材编写注重时代气息、使学生感兴趣，练习的编排也注重培养学生的思考能力，并注意令其反复操练以形成良好的学习习惯与能力等，体现了以学生为主的理念。

本教材的使用对象为全国高等院校商务英语专业本科层次的学生，也适用于对外经贸、财经、金融、工商管理等专业的学生，更可供从事国际商务、经贸实际工作人员进修、提高和社会各界人士自学之用。

本书借鉴、吸收了国内外专家学者的理念和最新研究成果。然而，随着国际经济和科学技术的发展，贸易活动亦日趋复杂化，各种新贸易政策和理论不断推陈出新，因此，本书的缺点和不妥之处在所难免，敬请使用本书的教师、学生和读者批评指正。在编写过程中，也得到了国内外有关专家学者和出版单位的支持与帮助，在此谨致谢意。

编　者

目　录
Contents

Chapter 1　Introduction ········ 1
绪论

1.1　Basics of International Trade ········ 2
国际贸易基础

1.2　Basics of Contract ········ 6
合同的基础

Chapter 2　Object of Contract ········ 13
合同的标的

2.1　Name of Commodity ········ 14
商品的品名

2.2　Quality of Commodity ········ 16
商品的品质

2.3　Quantity of Commodity ········ 23
商品的数量

2.4　Packing of Commodity ········ 27
商品的包装

Chapter 3　International Trade Terms and Customs ········ 37
国际贸易术语和惯例

3.1　Foundation of International Trade Customs ········ 38
国际贸易惯例概述

3.2 Foundation of International Trade Terms ······ 39
国际贸易术语概述
3.3 Main Trade Terms in International Trade ······ 42
国际贸易中的主要贸易术语
3.4 More Kinds of Trade Terms ······ 56
其他贸易术语
3.5 Choosing the Proper Trade Terms ······ 62
选择恰当的贸易术语

Chapter 4 Delivery of Commodity ······ 69
货物的交付
4.1 Transportation of Commodity in International Trade ······ 70
国际贸易货物的运输
4.2 International Transportation Insurance ······ 92
国际运输保险
4.3 Forwarding Agency in International Trade ······ 104
国际贸易中的货物运输代理业务
4.4 Customs Service for Merchandise Export and Import ······ 105
进出口货物的报关

Chapter 5 Payment of Commodity ······ 113
货款的支付
5.1 Instrument of Payment ······ 114
结算工具
5.2 Remittance and Collection ······ 122
汇付与托收
5.3 Letter of Credit（L/C） ······ 123
信用证

5.4 Bank Guarantee and Standby Letter of Credit ········· 127
银行保证书及备用信用证

Chapter 6 Precaution and Settlement of Disputes ········· 133
争议的预防与处理

6.1 Inspection of Commodity ········· 134
商品的检验

6.2 Claim ········· 138
索赔

6.3 Arbitration ········· 139
仲裁

6.4 Force Majeure ········· 143
不可抗力

Chapter 7 Procedure of International Trade ········· 147
国际贸易程序

7.1 Arrangements before Trade ········· 147
交易前的准备

7.2 Negotiation ········· 148
磋商

7.3 Implementation of the Contract ········· 155
合同的履行

7.4 Breach of Contact ········· 161
违约

Chapter 8 Methods of International Trade ········· 165
国际贸易的形式

8.1 Distribution, Exclusive Sales, Agency ········· 165
经销、包销、代理

8.2 Auction, Consignment, Fairs and Sales ································· 169
拍卖、寄售、展卖
8.3 Invitation to Tender and Submission of Tender ························ 171
招标和投标
8.4 Countertrade ··· 172
对销贸易
8.5 Futures Trading and Hedging ··· 173
期货交易与套期保值
8.6 Processing Trade and Leasing Trade ··································· 177
加工贸易与租赁贸易
8.7 Electric Commerce and Paperless Business ···························· 179
电子商务与无纸化办公

Appendix ··· 185
Key to Exercises ·· 185
Glossary ·· 190

References ··· 249

Chapter 1

Introduction

绪　论

The twenty-first century is an age of unprecedented globalization. As one of the most important economic activities, international trade is playing a more and more important part in the development of a country's economy and in the acceleration of globalization.

For the convenience of studying the following chapters, this opening chapter sets the stage by discussing the basic concepts of international trade and contracts.

☞ **Learning Objectives:**

After learning this chapter, you are expected to:

→ Understand the basic concepts of international trade;

→ Understand the fundamental concepts of contract;

→ Outline the reasons why countries are engaging in international trade;

→ Remember the principles of a contract.

1.1 Basics of International Trade 国际贸易基础

1.1.1 Definition 定义

International trade, also as world trade, foreign trade or overseas trade, is the fair and deliberate exchange of goods and services across national boundaries. It concerns trade operations of both import and export and includes the purchase and sale of both visible and invisible goods.

Import means the purchase of goods or services from another country, while export means the sale of goods or services to another country.

国际贸易（International Trade）是指不同国家和/或地区之间的商品、服务和生产要素交换的活动。国际贸易是商品、服务和生产要素的国际转移。国际贸易也叫世界贸易。国际贸易是各国之间分工的表现形式，反映了世界各国在经济上的相互共存。从国家的角度可称对外贸易；从国际角度可称国际贸易。

国际贸易由进口贸易（Import Trade）和出口贸易（Export Trade）两部分组成，故有时也称为进出口贸易。

1.1.2 Characteristic of International Trade 国际贸易的特点

The fundamental characteristic that makes international trade different from domestic trade is that international trade involves activities across national boundaries. Special problems may arise in international trade that are not normally experienced when trading at home. In particular:

- Deals might have to be transacted in foreign languages and under foreign laws, customs (cultural shocks) and regulations.
- Information on foreign countries needed by a particular firm may be difficult to obtain.
- Foreign currency transaction will be necessary, e.g. USD, EURO etc.
- Exchange rate variations can be very wide and create many problems for international trade.

使国际贸易区别于国内贸易的最根本特点是其相关活动的跨国界性质。国际贸易会产生许多国内贸易不会遇到的问题。国际贸易的特点主要是：

1. 交易可能会使用外语，在外国法律、惯例（文化冲击）和规则下进行。

2. 个别企业所需的外国信息可能难以获得。

3. 外币交易在所难免，如美元、欧元等。

4. 汇率大范围的变化将给国际贸易带来很多问题。

- Risk level might be higher in foreign markets. The risks include political risks (of the imposition of restrictions on imports etc.); commercial risks (market failure, products not appealing to foreign customers, etc.); financial risks (of adverse movement in exchange rates, high rates of inflation reducing the real value of a company's working capital, and so on); and transportation risks.
- International managers need a broader range of management skills than managers who are only concerned with domestic problems.
- Large amount of important work might have to be left to intermediaries, consultants and advisers.

5. 国外市场风险水平可能更高。这些风险包括政策风险（如进口限制等）；商业风险（如市场判断错误，产品对于外国消费者无吸引力等）；金融风险（如汇率的不利变化，高通胀减少了企业的实际价值等）以及运输风险。

6. 国际贸易管理者们比国内贸易管理者需要范围更广的管理技能。

7. 可能会有大量重要工作需要中间商、咨询、顾问来完成。

1.1.3 Reasons for International Trade 国际贸易产生的原因

There are many reasons why nations trade goods, with the most obvious being that they can get products from abroad that are cheaper or of higher quality than those that can be produced at home.

Besides, the reasons may also be to acquire resources and/or benefit, to achieve diversification, and/or to expand sales.

1. 获得更便宜/质量更好的产品
2. 获取资源/获利
3. 产品多样化
4. 扩大销售

1.1.4 Benefits from International Trade 国际贸易的好处

The benefits that countries gained from trading internationally are great, which partly explains the increasing volume involved in international trade. Generally, countries are likely to get the following benefits from trading with each other:

- To get cheaper goods or services. As has been mentioned above, the major reason for countries to trade with one another is that there is a cost advantage. And it is this cost advantage of the supplying countries that enables the demanding countries to buy certain goods or services of the same quality or higher quality at lower prices as the cost involved in producing them in their own countries is much higher. Furthermore, the ever developing technology in various fields and the ever escalating competition in the world market in the new millennium have been making prices of the goods even lower, which benefits consumers to a larger degree. Consumers thus are able to enjoy goods at much lower price.

1. 获得更便宜的商品和服务，即上节所述国际贸易的主要原因—成本优势。供给国的成本优势使需求国以比本国更低的价格买到质量相同甚至更高的产品或服务。此外，不通领域技术的发展和竞争的激烈化使新世纪的世界市场产品价格更低廉，使得广大消费者受益。

- To get larger economic growth. By trading with other nations, nations can gain more market share on its exported goods and take advantage of economies of scale. Economies of scale characterize a production process in which an increase in the scale of the firm causes a decrease in the long run average cost of each unit. In other words, when economies of scale are realized, the average cost of each unit is reduced, more profits are able to be generated from selling more units to more markets.

2. 获得更大的经济增长。通过与其他国家的交易，出口商品将占据更大的市场份额并从规模经济中获益。规模经济（Economics of scale）是指企业生产规模的扩大会降低单位产品的长期平均成本。即，达到规模经济时，单位产品平均成本下降，将更多产品销售至更多市场会获取更高利润。

- To get greater variety. No nation can produce all the commodities or services that it needs, which makes the international trade possible. And the different tastes and preferences of the consumers urge international trade to go even further. Undoubtedly, as a result, international trade makes it possible for a nation to provide

3. 产品更加多样化。没有哪个国家能生产其所需的所有商品或服务，这也导致了跨国贸易的可能性。消费者偏好的不同更是促进了国际贸易。毫无疑问，国际贸易使各国为消费者提供更多样化的产品，并因此提高了人民生活水平。

a wider variety of products for its consumers and thus help to improve the living standards of its people.

1.1.5 Forms of International Trade 国际贸易的类型

Generally, the forms of international trade can be summarized into two types:

- Merchandise Exports and Imports
  - → Exporting
    1) Direct exporting
    2) Indirect exporting
  - → Importing
- Service Exports and Imports
  - → Travel, Tourism, and Transportation
  - → Performance of Activities Abroad
  - → Use of Assets From Abroad

1. 商品出口
(1) 出口
① 直接出口
② 间接出口
(2) 进口
(1) 旅游业、交通运输业
(2) 国外商务活动
(3) 国外资产的运用

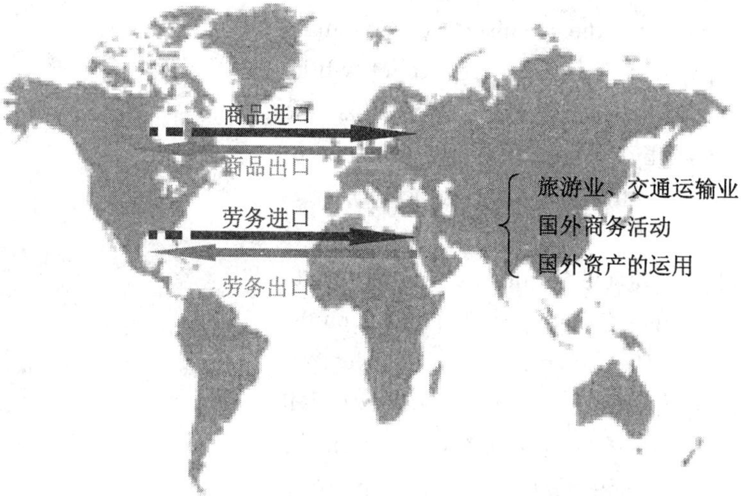

1.2 Basics of Contract 合同的基础

1.2.1 Concept of Contract 合同的定义

Contract, also known as a covenant, has various concept statements according to different scholars and many different regulations based on domestic or international laws. The earliest contract definition derived from Roman law. In accordance with the provisions of the Roman law: contract is consensus（合意） between the two parties on debitor and creditor's right. The France Civil Code article 1101 regulates contracts to be consensus, which are mutually satisfactory, the person or persons for any other person or other persons make payment, act or omission of the debt. Countries that adopt the common law consider the essence of the contract is the promise made by mutual parties. If contrary to the promises, legal relief will be provided. The fulfillment of the promise is the obligation confirmed by the law. The basic principles of bourgeois countries: "freedom of contract, contract first."

合同（Contract），又称契约，对其概念或定义，中外学者有众多不同的表述，国内外法律也有种种不同的规定。最早合同的定义来源于罗马法。按照罗马法的规定：合同为双方当事人间发生债权债务关系的合意。《法国民法典》第1101条规定合同为一种合意，彼此合意，一人或数人对于其他一人或数人负担给付，作为或不作为的债务。采用英美法的国家则认为合同的实质在于双方当事人之间做出的诺言，允诺。违反该允诺，将有法律给予救济，履行该允诺是法律所确认的义务。资产阶级国家资本原则："契约自由，契约至上。"

In September 1998, the fourth session of the Ninth China National People's Congress (NPC) agreed on the new "Contract Law". The 2nd article stating: "agreements about establishing, changing, and termination of civil rights and obligations of the partnership between the equality bodies of natural persons, juridical persons, and/or between other organizations."

我国1998年9月全国人大九届四次会议通过新的《合同法》。第2条表述："平等主体的自然人、法人，其他组织之间设立、变更、终止民事权利、义务关系的协议。"

1.2.2 Nature of Contract 合同的性质

Generally, the natures of contract can be summarized into four parts:

- Contract is an act in civil law. The meaning expression is the element. It represents the content which leads to the appropriate legal consequence.
- Contract parties' behavior of the civil law is on a voluntary and equal basis. It means that a contract must be true and voluntary.
- Contract is a bilateral civil legal act.
- Contract is an agreement that will definitely produce legal consequence.

合同的性质:

- 合同是一种民事法律行为,合同以意思表示为元素,按意思表示内容赋予其相应的法律后果,故为民事法律行为。
- 合同的当事人在平等、自愿的基础上产生的民事法律行为。意思表示必须真实、自愿。
- 合同是一种双方民事法律行为。
- 合同能够产生法律后果。

1.2.3 Features of Contract 合同的特征

The features of contract are showed as following:

- Body with equality. Article Ⅲ in the General Principles of Contract Law of People's Republic of China writes, "The parties to a contract shall have equal legal status; a party shall not impose its will on the other party."
- Contractual relationship is agreeable. The contract itself is a kind of agreement between the parties.
- Contract validity. Article Ⅶ in the General Principles of Contract Law of People's Republic of China writes, "The performance of the contract shall base on the legal foundation, the parties shall observe laws, administrative regulations, respect social ethics, not to disturb the social and economic order, not to cause any detriment of the public interest."

合同的特征:

- 主体具有平等性。《中华人民共和国合同法》总则第三条:"合同当事人的法律地位平等,一方不得将自己的意志强加给另一方。"
- 合同的关系具有协议性。合同本身是当事人之间的一种协议。
- 合同的内容具有合法性。《中华人民共和国合同法》总则第七条:"当事人订立、履行合同,应当遵守法律、行政规定,尊重社会公德,不得扰乱社会经济秩序,损害社会公共利益。"

- Contract sanction for the parties. Article Ⅷ in the General Principles of Contract Law of People's Republic of China writes, "The contract established by law, legally binds on the parties. The parties shall, in acceptance with the convention, fulfill their obligations, and without authorization, shall not alter or rescind the contract. Contract established by law shall be protected by law."

- 合同的效力具有约束性。《中华人民共和国合同法》总则第八条："依法成立的合同，对当事人具有法律约束力。当事人应当按照约定履行自己的义务，不得擅自变更或者解除合同。依法成立的合同，受法律保护。"

1.2.4 The Principles a Contract Should Follow 合同遵守的原则

- Parties Freedom Principle (Freedom of Contact)

  The General Clauses Act 1.1 stipulates: "the parties have the right to establish a contract freely, has the right to determine freely the contract." The principle of freedom of the parties is a fundamental principle of Contract Law, and is also the cornerstone of the international economic activities.

自由原则

《通则》1.1 条规定："当事人有权自由订立合同，有权自由决定该合同的内容。"缔约自由原则是合同法的基本原则，也是国际经济活动的基石。

- Principles of Honesty

  The general rule of the contract regulates, "An effective contract has sanction to both parties. The parties only modify or terminate the contract under the terms of the contract or agreement or pursuant to the provisions of general rules." China has consistently emphasized on following contract regulation and keeping promise, which is consistent with the principles.

诚信原则

《合同通则》中规定合同必须信守原则，《通则》中规定："有效订立的合同对当事人均有约束力。当事人仅能根据合同条款或通过协议或根据通则规定，修改或终止合同。"

- Principles of Honesty and Fair Trade

  The general contract establishes the basic principle, which includes the principle of good faith and trade concepts. Article 6 of China Contract Law

诚信和公平交易原则

《合同原则》确立了上述基本原则，该原则包含了诚实信用和公平交易两个概

states: "a party shall follow the principle of good faith in exercising their right and obligation."

念，我国合同法第六条规定："当事人行使权力、履行义务应当遵循诚实信用原则。"

1.2.5 Law and Practices Applicable to International Trade Business 国际贸易中运用的法律和惯例

To sign a sales contract, we need to base on the international trade practices, international treaties and related legislation. Therefore to understand and be familiar with the relevant conventions, treaties and laws are significantly important for people who are dealing with international business.

如何签订买卖合同，我们所依据的就是有关的国际贸易惯例、国际条约和有关的法律。我们从事国际贸易的业务实际上就是要了解和熟悉有关的惯例、条约和法律。

➢ Application of the Law

China Contract Law No. 126 stipulates that parties to a contract involving foreign interests can choose the applicable law to process the contract dispute except as otherwise stipulate by law. If parties to a contract involving foreign interests have not made such a choice, the most connected country laws shall apply to the contract, such as the United Nations Convention on Contract for the International Sale of Goods. Act hereinafter referred to as the Convention, the lesson of each section of the terms of the contract must be related to the Convention.

我国合同法第 126 条规定：涉外合同的当事人可以选择处理合同争议所适用的法律，但法律另有规定的除外。涉外合同的当事人没有选择，适用于合同有最密切联系的国家的法律。

《联合国国际货物销售合同公约》(United Nations Convention on Contract for the International Sale of Goods)，以下简称《公约》，本课讲述的每一个章节有关合同的条款都要涉及该公约。

Relevant international trade practices in international trade evolved and developed on the basis of long-term practicing are the norms and standards that shall be followed by those who are engaged in the international sales of goods and economic activities, and relevant international practices are also a source of international law.

有关的国际贸易惯例是在国际贸易长期实践的基础上逐步形成和发展起来的，是人们从事国际货物买卖经济活动的行为规范和应当遵守的准则，有关的国际贸易惯例也是国际贸易法律的渊源之一。

➢ The Application of International Trade Practices

International trade practices law, is not legally

国际贸易惯例不是法律，没有法律强制性、约束力，但当它援引入合同时就具

mandatory, binding, but when it refers to the contract, it is then legally binding.

→ When in conflict with the practice of contract, the contract shall take precedence over the convention.

→ General Principles of the Civil Law of the People's Republic of China stipulates:"If any international treaty concluded or acceded to by the People's Republic of China contains provisions differing from those in the civil laws of the People's Republic of China, the provisions of the international treaty shall apply, unless the provisions are ones on which the People's Republic of China has announced reservations."

有法律的约束力。

《中华人民共和国民法通则》第一百四十二条规定："中华人民共和国缔结或者参加的与合同有关的国际条约同中华人民共和国法律有不同的规定，适用该国际条约的规定。"同时规定："中华人民共和国声明保留的条款除外。"

Notes

1. International trade
   国际贸易是指不同国家和/或地区之间的商品、服务和生产要素交换的活动。国际贸易是商品、服务和生产要素的国际转移。
2. Contract
   合同，又称契约，我国 1998 年 9 月全国人大九届四次会议通过的《合同法》第 2 条表述："平等主体的自然人、法人，其他组织之间设立、变更、终止民事权利、义务关系的协议。
3. United Nations Convention on Contract for the International Sale of Goods
   《联合国国际货物销售合同公约》
4. General Principles of the Civil Law of the People's Republic of China
   《中华人民共和国民法通则》

Exercises

1. Translate the following into Chinese or English.

purchasing power
domestic markets
trade discrimination
finished goods
诚信原则
劳务进出口
recession
portfolio investment
trade intermediary
visible exports and imports
商品进出口

2. Match each one on the left with its correct meaning on the right.

1. motivation	A. to make continual efforts to gain something
2. pursue	B. the action of obtaining, esp. by efforts of careful attention
3. mark up	C. which by is its nature cannot be known by senses, not clear and certain, not real
4. procurement	D. the goods (freight) carried by a ship, plane or vehicle
5. intangible	E. the amount by which a price is raised
6. cargo	F. profit, interest
7. royalty	G. the net value of assets or interest, invest.
8. equity	H. not needing other things or people, taking decisions alone
9. yield	I. a share of the profits
10. independent	J. need or purpose

3. Fill in the following blanks with proper terms.

1) __________ are tangible goods sent out of countries.

2) __________ are international earnings other than those derived from the exporting and importing of tangible goods.

3) __________ are tangible goods brought in.

4) __________ is all business transactions that involve two or more countries.

5) __________ is used primarily as financial means for a company to earn more money on its money with relative safety.

4. Translate the following passages into English.

1）世界上没有任何一个国家能生产它所需的所有产品，所以各国参与国际分工，进行有效的生产和再生产。有时一个国家能够以易货方式从国外购买产品和服务，易货是指以一种货物交换另一种货物，而不是用钱交易。易货贸易本身并不足以满足一个国家的进口需要。但作为一种贸易方式，它对于外汇短缺、外资流入远远无法满足外贸需求的发展中国家来说具有一定的吸引力。

2）世界各国的贸易千差万别，错综复杂，有形贸易和无形贸易并存。大多数国家对出口的依赖，都大于对其他活动的依赖。出口所赚取的外汇用来支付需要进口的货物。一个国家的国际收支就是这些错综复杂交易的记录。通过用货币来反映所有这些交易，一个国家能够把比如出口、外国游客的花费和移民汇款的收入汇总在一起。这些收入汇总起来，便可支付诸如购买其他国家的制成品，本国居民到其他国家旅游和雇用建筑工人的费用等。

Chapter 2

Object of Contract

合同的标的

Business can't be done without commercial contract. An international sales contract is an agreement, made by two or more parties that from different countries, towards the transfer of ownership of the subject matter. According to CISG Article 35 (1), the seller must deliver goods which are of the quantity, quality and description required by the contract and which are contained or packaged in the manner required by the contract. Therefore, specific standards must be made for the stipulation of commodity. This chapter mainly deals with subject matter of the international sales contract, including the name, quality, quantity and packing clauses etc. of the object.

Basically, a contract includes: the full name and address of the buyer and the seller, the commodities involved, all the terms and conditions agreed upon, indication of the number of original copies of the contract the language used and the term of validity and possible extension of the contract.

国际货物买卖合同的标的物条款一般都要订明合同标的物的品名、品质、数量与包装条款，通过本章的学习，认识在合同中约定这些条款的法律意义及其规定方法，以利于合同的商订与履行。

标的物条款是对货物的说明，在具体合同中可分别写成几个条款。主要订明货物的名称、质量或规格、数量、包装等。标的物条款在法律上的重要意义在于，它是合同双方当事人履行货物交付与接受义务的主要依据，在实际履行中最容易发生争议。如卖方所交的货物短量、不符规格等问题都是最常见的争议问题。

☞ **Learning Objectives:**

After learning this chapter, you are expected to:

→ Understand the concepts and importance of different terms of commodity;

→ Distinguish name, quality, quantity and packing clauses properly;

→ Describe different methods of stipulating quality of commodity;

→ Remember different ways to calculate quantity of commodity;

→ Outline different types of export packing.

2.1 Name of Commodity 商品的品名

The name of commodity clause is a main component of the description of goods when signing an import-export contract. Generally, this clause is relatively simple, the parties to the contract just specify the name of the product that in the offer or counter-offer under the article of name of commodity. And sometimes we only write several sentences showing the two parties' agreement on the business of some commodity at the beginning of a contract.

合同中的品名条款（The name of commodity clause），通常比较简单，一般只是在“商品名称”或品名（Name of Commodity）的标题下，列明交易双方成交商品的名称。有时为了省略起见，也可不加标题，只在合同的开头部分，列明交易双方同意买卖某种商品的文句。

However, being the basis of the delivery of the goods, name of commodity should concern the rights and obligations of the parties to the contract. If the goods delivered do not conform to the agreed name of commodity, the buyer is entitled to claim against the seller for compensation, reject the goods or even cancel the contract. Therefore, it is of great importance to specify the name of commodity clearly in the contract.

When setting the clause of the name of commodity, the following points should be considered:

规定品名条款的注意事项:

- Be clear and specific. It is required by laws that each commodity of a transaction should be legal and uncontroversial. Meantime, there are different ways of naming commodities. Therefore, the name of commodity in the contract should be clear, specific and free from ambiguous expressions so as to avoid trouble in the execution of the contract.

  必须明确、具体表达品名条款时，必须能确切反映交易标的物的特点，避免空泛、笼统的规定，以利合同的履行。

- Be practical and realistic. The name of commodity stipulated in the contract must be in conformity with the goods that the seller is able to supply and the buyer requires. Exaggerated or unnecessary descriptions should not be used.

  针对实际做出实事求是的规定，使用正确的译名

- Try to adopt the name of commodity which is widely accepted internationally. Sometimes a commodity has different names in different areas. To avoid misunderstanding, both the seller and the buyer shall agree on the name.

  尽量使用国际通用名称，有些商品的名称各地称法不一，为了避免误解，应尽可能使用国际上通用的称呼。

- Select appropriate names of commodities to facilitate importing and reduce customs duties and freight charges. In international trade, sometimes a certain commodity has different names, and tariff rates and freight rates may be different for the same commodity with different names. Besides, there may be some import and export restrictions in such a case. Therefore, choosing an appropriate name as the name of commodity in the contract can be beneficial to both the exporter and the importer.

  注意选用合适的品名，以利于方便进口、降低关税和节省运费开支

2.2 Quality of Commodity 商品的品质

2.2.1 Concept and Significance 概念和意义

Quality refers to the intrinsic elements of commodities including the internal properties or ingredients as well as the external appearance. In the quality clause, the name and detailed qualities of commodities should clearly list. As commodities are various, the ways showing their qualities are not the same. So the terms of quality must be fit for the characteristics of commodities.

商品品质（quality），是商品的内在属性和外部形式的综合。前者包括货物的化学成分、物理和机械性能、生物特征等自然属性；后者包括货物的款式、结构、色泽、味觉和嗅觉等。在磋商交易中，买卖双方都要针对一定的商品，按质论价。

Quality of commodity

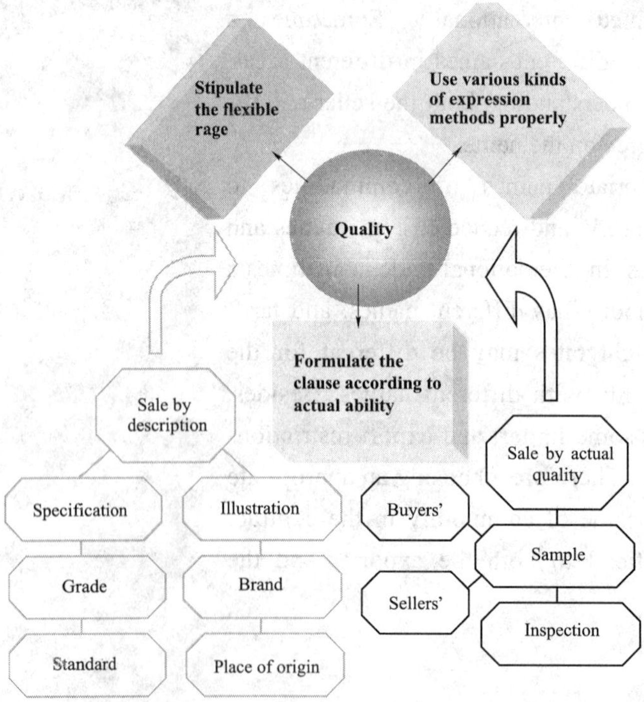

The quantity clause mainly includes the quantity and unit of commodity. To facilitate the performance of contract and avoid disputes, the quantity clause should be clear and detailed. In addition, it is improper to use those uncertain words like about, circa, approximate to define the quantity.

数量条款主要包括商品数量和计价单位。为促进交易，避免纠纷，数量条款应清晰具体。另外，不应使用诸如大致、大约这样模糊的词。

2.2.2 Methods of Stipulating Quality of Commodity 规定商品品质的方法

In international trade, buyers and sellers may be thousands of miles apart. It would be difficult for buyers to see the goods before they reach the port of destination. However, they should have known the quality of the commodities before buying them. Therefore, a number of methods have been developed to specify the quality of the goods. Overall, the common methods of stipulating quality of the commodities can be classified into two categories: sale by actual quality and sale by description.

由于在国际贸易中，买卖双方通常地处两国，在洽谈交易时，往往没有看到全部商品，因此，需要有某种说明品质的方法，作为洽谈和履行合同的依据。当前，国际贸易商品种类繁多，特点各异，用以说明品质的方法也就不可能一致。概括起来，国际贸易中常用来表示商品品质的方法基本上有两大类：实物表示法与说明表示法。

Sale by description is adopted to specify the quality of most commodities in international trade. It may take the form of sale by specification, sale by grade, sale by standard, sale by illustration or description, sale by brand or trademark, and sale by place of origin.

在国际贸易中，除了用样品外，凡是运用文字或图样表示商品品质的方法，均属说明表示法，具体又分为下列几种：凭规格、等级或标准的买卖（Sales by Specification，Grade or Standard）、凭图样（Illustrations）以及说明书（Descriptions）的买卖、凭牌号（Brand）或商标（Trade Mark）的买卖、凭产地名称（Place of Origin）买卖。

- Sale by specification, grade, standard
  - Specification: The specification of the goods refers to certain main indicators which indicate the quality of the goods, such as composition, content, purity, size, length, etc.

    规格（specification）泛指规定的标准、要求或条件。

  - Grade: The grade of the goods refers to the classifications of the commodity of the goods which is indicated by words, numbers or symbols. The classifications are usually decided

    等级（grade）指按某一标准区分的高低差别。

by different qualities, weights, compositions, appearances, properties, etc.

→ Standard: The standard refers to the specifications or grades which are stipulated and announced by the government or the chambers of commerce, etc.

标准（standard）是一种以文件形式发布的统一协定，其中包含可以用来为某一范围内的活动及其结果制定规则、导则或特性定义的技术规范或者其他精确准则，其目的是确保材料、产品、过程和服务能够符合需要。

➢ Sale by illustration or description

The quality of some commodities, such as technological instruments, electric machines, etc. cannot be simply indicated by quality indexes, instead it is quite necessary to explain in detail the structure, material, performance as well as method of operation. If necessary, pictures, photos, etc. must also be provided.

➢ Sale by brand or trademark

As to the goods whose quality is stable, reputation is sound and with which the customers are quite familiar, we may sell it by brand name or trademark.

➢ Sale by place of origin

It is suitable for some agricultural products and by-products whose origins are well-known all over the world.

Sale by actual quality, also called sale by actual commodity, means to form the condition of transaction according to the quality of the actual goods. It is usually adopted when the traders deal with goods that are already available at the time of contracting.

用实物表示（Sale by actual quality），也称看货买卖，是指在买卖双方洽谈时，以实际货物的品质作为质量依据。

Sale by inspection (凭验货销售) is concluded with the spot inspection by the buyers or their agents and the quality is determined thereof. This method is of special necessity for particular goods such as ornaments, jewels, paintings, artworks, etc. In many cases, the buyer may be advised to arrange for inspection of the goods before or at the time they are handed over by the seller for carriage (pre-shipment inspection, PSI). Unless the contract stipulates otherwise, the buyer would himself have to pay the cost for such inspection that is arranged in his own interest. However, if the inspection has been made in order to enable the seller to comply with any mandatory rules applicable to the export of the goods in his own country he would have to pay for that inspection.

Sale by sample means a sale made on the basis of a sample. A sample is a small quantity of a product, often taken out from a whole lot or specially designed and processed that is given to encourage prospective customers to buy the product. When the sample is accepted by the buyer, the seller is responsible for the delivery of the goods of the same quality as shown in the sample. Such transaction is called sale by seller's sample. In this case, the seller should keep some equivalent samples for himself before sending to the buyer. The sample kept by the seller is called a duplicate sample, which can serve as proof of quality if there is a dispute. Sometimes, the buyer may send a sample to the seller, who is asked to supply the commodity in accordance with it. This is called sale by buyer's sample. If the seller cannot do accordingly, he may send back a sample in similar quality, called return sample or counter sample, as a proposal for the buyer's consideration.

样品（Sample）通常是从一批商品中抽取出来或由生产、使用部门加工、设计出来的足以反映该批商品平均质量的少量实物。

凭样品买卖（Sales by Sample）是指买卖双方约定凭样品作为交货的品质依据的交易。标准样品一般多由卖方提供，但有时也可以由买方提供。前者称力“凭卖方样品买卖”（Sale by Seller's Sample），后者称为“凭买方样品买卖”（Sale by Buyer's Sample），不论样品由谁提出，一旦达成交易，卖方所交货物的品质均须与样品相符，这是必须遵守的一项基本原则，也是卖方的一项主要义务。如两者不符，除合同另有规定外，买方可以提出索赔，甚至可以拒收货物，撤销合同。

凡凭卖方样品的买卖，在出口对外寄送样品时，应留存复样（Duplicate Sample），以便作为日后交货或处理品质争议时的依据。

凡凭买方样品的买卖，即“来样成交”，当买方寄给卖方样品要求按样成交时，卖方也可以根据买方样品进行复制或提出与之相似的样品作为“回样”（Return Sample）或“对等样品”（Counter Sample），寄交对方确认，作为交货时的品质依据。

2.2.3 Quality Clause in Contract 合同中的品质条款

2.2.3.1 Basic Contents

The quality clause is one of the main conditions of

the contract. Both parties to the contract must agree upon the details covering the quality of the contracted commodity. Generally the name of commodity and specific quality should be indicated explicitly in the quality clause. However, as there are many ways to indicate the quality of commodities, the contents of the quality clause are also various.

In the case of a contract for sale by sample, it is necessary to indicate the number of the sample and the date of dispatch.

In the case of a contract for sale by description, it should be stipulated clearly the name of goods, specification, grade, standard, brand, trademark or place of origin. When it is a contract for sale by description, the name and number of illustration, drawing and the like should be also indicated in the contract.

2.2.3.2 Requirements of Quality

The quality of products related to the vital interest of the buyers and sellers, and the stipulation of quality is also an important clause in a sales contract. So, how do we define quality?

➢ ISO9000 Standard

ISO9000 standard is the quality standard of manufacturing enterprises established by International Organization for Standardization in 1987. With the certificate of ISO9000, export products will obtain permits to enter into international market.

The release of ISO9000 series of standards has unified the concepts, principles, methods and procedures of quality management and quality certification to an international standard, marking a new height of quality management and quality certification. Since ISO9000

国际贸易中，商品种类繁多，品质千差万别，因此，合同中的品质条款也有繁有简，须根据具体商品的特性和不同用途而定，不可能千篇一律，一成不变。

ISO9000 标准(ISO9000 Standard)，是国际标准化组织（International Standards Organization）在 1987 年制定的产品的生产企业的质量标准。出口产品如果能得到 ISO9000 的质量认定，就取得了进入国际市场的通行证。

ISO9000 系列标准的发布，使主要发达国家的质量管理和质量认证概念原则、方法和程序统一在国际标准的基础上，它标志着质量管理和质量保证走向规范化、程序化的新高度。自发布以来已有包括我国在内的 60 个国家和地区采用为标准，并在国际经济技术合作中被称作相互认可的技术基础和确认质量保证能力的依据。

series of standards were issued, they have been adopted by 60 countries and regions, including and confirming quality assurance capacity in international economic and technological cooperation.

➢ ISO14000 Environmental Standards

ISO14000 environmental standards were enacted by “ISO Technical Committee 207 on Environmental Management”, which was established in June, 1993. Some developed countries have taken them as one kind of “green barrier”. The developed countries will refuse the import of such goods without the certificate, with the aim of establishing implementing an effective environmental management system within the organization to regulate the environmental behavior of the organization, control and reduce damage to the environment caused by the production and management activities, encourage and promote enterprises to produce green environmental protection products so as to meet the demands for environmental protection and other related interests. Enterprises that meet the ISO14000 series of standards belong to green enterprises, and their products are recognized as environmental friendly products.

1993 年 6 月成立 ISO/TC207 “环境管理委员会” 制定 ISO14000 环境保护标准 (ISO14000 Environmental Standards)。目前一些发达国家以此作为一种 “绿色壁垒”。如果没有取得此证，则发达国家拒绝进口，其目的是为了通过在组织内部建立和实施一个有效的环境管理体系，来规范组织的环境.

➢ CE Mark

According to EU regulations, from January 1,1996, To enter the European market, electrical products must comply with the common safety standards(with CE Mark)identified by the EU.

根据欧盟规定，从 1996 年 1 月 1 日进入其市场的电器产品必须符合欧共体共同认定的安全标准——CE 标志（CE Mark）。

➢ UL Mark

It’s a mark of security certificate stipulated by the inspection agency subordinated to the Underwriters’ Laboratories. Electrical products exported to Canada and America should not be sold without UL mark.

美国保险人公会属下的检验机构所指定的安全认证标志。凡销往美国、加拿大的电器产品如无 “UL” 标志（UL Mark），不得销售。

2.2.3.3 Quality Latitude and Quality Tolerance

In international trade, the quality clause of goods in the contract is the cornerstone and basis of goods delivery. According to international trade laws and practices, the seller must deliver goods which are of the quality and description required by the contract. In case the quality of goods delivered does not correspond with the stipulation of the contract, the buyer will be entitled to lodge a claim against the seller or even cancel the contract. However, as certain commodities may be affected by some factors like natural losses in production, production capacity, and characteristics of commodities, the quality of delivered goods cannot be in full conformity with the stipulation of the contract. Therefore, when laying down the quality clause in the contact, it is necessary to add some flexible conditions, leaving enough room for deviation.

Quality latitude means that the seller and buyer agree that the quality of the delivered goods can vary with an agreed range. Three ways are commonly used in stating to quality latitude: flexible range, maximum & minimum and allowed deviation.

品质机动幅度（Quality Latitude），即对某些初级产品，由于卖方所交货物品质难以完全与合同规定的品质相符，为便于交货，往往在规定的品质指标外，加订一定的允许幅度。只要在允许的幅度内，买方无权拒收，但可根据合同规定调整价格。一般可以用三种方法标志品质机动幅度：规定范围，规定极限，规定上下差异。

Ways of Stating Quality Latitude	Example
➢ Flexible Range	Printed Shirting (width) 41″-42″ Plank (thickness) 3″-5″
➢ Maximum & Minimum	White Kidney Bean, 2007 Crop, F.A.Q Moisture (max.)17%
➢ Maximum & Minimum	Admixture (max.) 1% Imperfect Grains (max.):3%
➢ Allowed Deviation	Grey Duck Feather Down Content 90%, Allowing 1% More or Less

Some industrial products, as in the production process cannot be very accurate, in accordance with international practice or the agreement by the seller and the buyer of the contract quality indicators have allowed the "tolerance", which is the quality of tolerance (Quality Tolerance). In the quality of mobility within the range or quality of tolerance, if there are differences in the quality of delivery is generally calculated according to the contract price, rather than other adjustments.

品质公差（Quality Tolerance）指国际上公认的产品品质的误差，在公差的限度内，买方不得以质量不符拒收货物。由于这类商品在生产过程中，受科技水平或生产水平所限，往往会有一些误差。这些误差有的是国际上所公认的，有的是经买卖双方所同意的。国际贸易中，卖方交货的品质只要在公差范围内，则免负品质责任。商品品质的公差是不计算增价或减价的。

2.3 Quantity of Commodity 商品的数量

2.3.1 Concepts of Quantity 数量的概念

Goods in the contract for the international sale of goods are not only shown by a certain quality, but also a certain quantity. Quantity clause is one of the necessary conditions for the conclusion of an import-export contract. In international trade, the quantity of commodity is always shown as a specific amount in weight, length, width, area, volume, etc.

除了确定的品质，在国际贸易中，买卖双方必须以约定的货物数量作为履行合同的依据，商品数量是买卖合同中不可缺少的主要条件之一。货物的数量，是指以一定的度量衡单位表示的货物重量、个数、长度、面积、容积等。

2.3.2 System and Units of Measurement 计量制度和单位

In international trade, there are various units of measurements due to various natures and characteristics of the commodities. Basically, quantity of goods refers to the weight, number, length, volume, area, capacity, etc. which are indicated by different measuring units.

The mainly used units of measurement are tabled as follows:

Measurement	Used for the Goods Below	Common Measurement Units
Weight	general natural products and some industrial finished products, such as wool, cotton, grain, mineral products, etc.	kilogram, gram, ton, metric ton, pound, ounce, long ton, short ton, etc.
Length	textiles, metal cord, etc.	meter, centimeter, foot, mile, yard, inch, etc.
Area	textiles, building materials, animal by-products, plastic products, etc.	square meter, square inch, square foot, square yard, etc.
Volume	timber, natural gas, chemical gases, etc.	cubic yard, cubic meter, cubic foot, cubic inch, etc.
Capacity	liquid products, agricultural products, petroleum, etc.	litre, pint, gallon, bushel, etc.

在国际贸易中，由于商品的种类、特性不同以及各国度量衡制度不同，因此，计算数量的单位也不相同。

国际贸易中通常使用的计量单位有以下几类：

1. 重量（Weight）

如吨（公吨、长吨、短吨）、克、公斤、磅等。一般天然产品及其制品，如矿产品、钢铁、盐、农副产品等，均按重量买卖。

2. 长度（Length）

如米（公尺）、英尺、码等。一般多用于绳索、纺织品等货物。

3. 个数（Number）

如只、件、双、套、打、罗、令、台、架等。一般杂货及工业制品，均按个数买卖。

4. 面积（Area）

如平方米（平方公尺）、平方码、平方英尺等。多用于玻璃和纺织品等货物。

5. 体积（Volume）

如立方米（立方公尺）、立方英尺、立方码等。按体积单位成交的商品不多，仅应用于木材及化学气体等少数商品。

6. 容积（Capacity）

如公升、加仑、蒲式耳等。粮食及部分液体商品按容积计算。

2.3.3 Calculation of Weight 计算重量

Among the units of measurement, weight is definitely a very important concept. Proper interception of the weight will benefit both parties involving the contract. The commonly methods to measure the weight of goods are as follows:

国际贸易中的许多商品是按重量买卖的。按照一般商业习惯，计算重量的方法有以下几种：

- Gross Weight

  The gross weight refers to the weight of the cargo itself plus the tare, i.e., the weight of the cargo plus the weight of the packing material.

- Net Weight

  Net weight is the weight of the product itself, that is, after removing the packaging the actual weight of goods. Net weight is the most common international trade weight approach. However, some lower-value agricultural products or other goods, sometimes using the "gross for net" approach to weight.

- Conditioned weight

  The weight obtained by deducting actual moisture content and adding standardized moisture content high value, easily absorbs moisture.

$$\text{Conditioned weight}=\frac{\text{actual weight}\times(1+\text{standard regaining rate of water})}{1+\text{actual regaining rate of water}}$$

- Theoretical weight

  It assumes that the weight of each item is approximately the same.

  Theoretical weight = Unit weight×Quantity

- Legal weight

  It is the weight of the goods including the immediate, inner or direct packing of the goods, and it is usually adopted as the basis for tariff calculation.

  Legal weight = Net weight + Tare (immediate packing)

- Net net weight

  The net net weight of the goods refers to the weight of only the product itself, without any wrapping, packaging, etc.

- 毛重（Gross Weight）

  即商品本身的重量加包装的重量，一般适用于低值的商品。

- 净重（Net Weight）

  商品本身的重量，即除去包装后的商品实际重量。在国际贸易中，大部分以重量计量的商品，都是以净重计价。但是一些价值较低的农副产品，如粮谷、饲料等有时也以毛重计价。这种以毛重计价的办法称之为“以毛作净”（Gross for Net）。

- 公量（Conditioned Weight）

  即用科学方法除去商品中所含的实际水分，再另加标准水分，所求得的重量。这种方法经常用于水分含量不稳定、易受空气湿度影响的商品，如羊毛、生丝、棉花等。

  其计算公式为：

$$\text{公量}=\frac{\text{实际重量}\times(1+\text{标准含水量})}{1+\text{实际含水量}}$$

- 理论重量（Theoretical Weight）

  对于有固定规格和固定尺寸的商品，根据其数量经推算所得的重量。

  理论重量=单位重量×数量

- 法定重量（Legal Weight）

  纯商品的重量加上直接接触商品的包装材料，如内包装的重量，即为法定重量。法定重量是海关依法征收从量税时作为征税基础的计量方法。

  法定重量=净重+皮重（暂时包装）

- 净净重（Net Net Weight）

  又称实物净重，它是法定重量减去直接接触商品的包装重量，即纯商品的重量。净净重主要也为海关征税时使用。

2.3.4 Quantity Clause in Contract 合同中的数量条款

2.3.4.1 Basic Contents

The quantity clause of a sales contract is the foundation for effecting delivery of the goods. The basic contents of the quantity clause consist of two parts—the quantity to be delivered and the measurement to be used. If the goods are measured by weight, the way of calculating the weight should also be indicated. The contents of the quantity clause can be various depending on the characteristics of goods.

It is the buyer's basic obligation to deliver the goods based on the quantity stipulated in the sales contract. The business laws of certain countries stipulate that the quantity of goods delivered should be identical to that called for in the contract, otherwise the buyer is entitled to claim against the seller, and even reject the goods. According to United Nations Convention on Contracts of International Sale of Goods, the seller must deliver goods which are of the quantity required by the contract. If the seller delivers a quantity of goods greater than that provided for in the contract, the buyer may take delivery or refuse to take delivery of the excess quantity. The buyer also has the right to reject the goods if the quantity delivered is found to be less than that called for in the contract. Therefore due attention should be paid to the quantity terms during business negotiation.

合同中的数量条款（Quantity Clause）是买卖双方交接货物和处理争议的依据，因此，买卖双方签订合同时，必须对数量条款做出明确合理的规定。在买卖合同的数量条款中，一般须订明数量和计算单位。以重量计量的，还须明确计量的办法。

2.3.4.2 More or Less Clause & Approximate Quantity

Quantity allowance is the allowed deviation in quantity on delivery from that stipulated in the contract. The quantity clause in a sales contract usually specifies the quantity allowance. The purpose of the quantity allowance is to facilitate delivery, shipment or preparation of goods. Totally, the quantity allowance can be stipulated in two ways: by the more or less clause or using approximate quantity.

More or Less Clause is the number of terms in the contract specified the number of delivery can be increased or decreased, but the rates of increase in the percentage does not exceed the prescribed limit. Generally, more or less clause includes: the quantity allowance percentage; the party which determines the quantity allowance and the price of the exceeding quantity.

在农副产品和工矿产品的交易中，往往由于商品的特性、生产能力、船舶舱位、装载技术和包装等原因，比较难以准确地按合同规定的数量交货。因此，买卖双方在商订交货数量时应订有一定的机动幅度，即应在合同中明确规定溢短装条款（More or LessClause）。

Sometimes an approximate quantity clause can also be used to indicate the tolerance of the actual quantity to be delivered. In such a clause, the words like "about", "circa" and "approximately" are used to define the quantity of goods. In addition, it should be noted that different countries may interpret these words differently.

在少数场合，也有使用"约"数（Approximate or About）条款来表示实际交货数量可以有一定幅度的伸缩，即在某一具体数字前加"约"或类似含义的文字. 此外，我们应注意到"约"数的含义在国际贸易中有不同的解释，容易引起纠纷，如果买卖双方一定要使用"约"数条款时，双方应事先在合同中明确允许增加或减少的百分比，或在"一般交易条件"协议中加以规定，否则不宜采用。

2.4 Packing of Commodity 商品的包装

2.4.1 Concept of Packing 包装的概念

Packing normally refers to the process of packaging and labeling. It is one of the key terms in business communication and negotiation. In international trade, exporters usually have to take total steps from the design of the packaging to the choice of transport to protect the safety of cargo.

在国际贸易中，大多数商品都要有一定的包装，以保护商品在流通过程中的品质安全和数量完整。因此，凡买卖需要包装的商品时，交易双方必须在合同中对包装条件作出明确规定。包装条款，是买卖合同中的重要条款之一。

The major functions of packing of goods are:

- Protect the product;
- Make the product look appealing to the buyer;

- Provide information about the product, make it easy to carry and convenient to use.

Requirements of packing of goods are:

- Easy to identify
- Easy to display
- Easy to carry and use
- Artistically attractive

2.4.2 Transport Packing and Sales Packing 运输包装和销售包装

Transport packing, also called big packing or outer packing, is mainly to keep the goods safe and sound during transportation. It must not only be solid enough to prevent the packed goods from any damage, but also be pilferaged-proof, easy to store, convenient to load and unload. To stand long transportation of the ocean and rough handling of cargoes, and for other purposes, the outer packing of the cargoes should meet the

运输包装（Transport Packing），又称大包装（Big Packing）或外包装（Outer Packing），它的作用主要在于保护商品的品质和数量，便于运输、储存、检验、计数、分拨，有利于节省运输成本。

following requirements: be solid and durable, adaptable to the changing climates at the loading and unloading ports and transit areas; be uniform so as to convenience storage, stowing, calculation, cargo inspection and identification; have the least weight, volume and cost.

Packing Containers 包装容器	
Bags 袋	May be made of strong paper, linen, canvas, rubber, etc.可用硬纸、亚麻布、帆布、橡胶等制成。
Sack 麻袋	A large bag usually made of jute. 通常是黄麻制成的大袋。
Carton 纸箱	Made of light but strong cardboard, or fiberboard with double lids and bottoms, fixed by glue, adhesive tapes, metal bands or wire staples. Sometimes a bundle of several cartons is made up into one package, held by metal bands. 用轻且坚固的纸板或纤维板，双盖双底，用胶水、胶带、金属带或骑马钉固定。有时几个纸箱为一组用金属带绑起来形成一个包装。
Case 木箱	A strong container made of wood. For extra strength it may have "battens". Sometimes thinner wood may be used with metal bands or wires passed around the case. The inside of the case may be "lined" with various materials, e.g. damp resisting paper, tin foil, etc., to prevent damage by water, air or insects.用木材制成的坚固容器。为使其更为坚固，可加上板条。有时可用较薄的木材制成，并用金属带或金属丝缠绕箱子。箱内可用各种材料如：防湿纸、锡箔等加衬，以便保护商品免受水、空气或虫子造成的损坏。
Box 盒	A small case, which may be of wood, cardboard or metal, and may have a folding (hinged) lid. 小箱子，用木材纸板或金属制成，可带折叠盖。
Crate 板条箱	This is a case, but one not fully enclosed. It has a bottom and a frame, sometimes open at the top. Crates are often built for the particular things they have to carry. Machinery packed in crates needs a special bottom (a skid) to facilitate handling. 是一种没有完全封闭的箱子。它有一个底和一个框架，有时顶部敞开。板条箱通常是为运输某种特定的物品而制作的。用板条箱包装的机械设备需要一个特制的底（滑动枕木）以便于操作。
Drum 桶	A cylinder-shaped container for carrying liquids, chemicals, paints, etc. It is usually made of metal. Certain dry chemicals (non-inflammable) or powders are sometimes packed in wood or cardboard drums. 用来装运液体、化学品、油漆等的圆柱状容器。通常用金属制成。一些干燥的化学品（不易燃烧）或粉末有时用木制的或纸板桶包装。
Bale 包	A package of soft goods (e.g. cotton, wool, sheepskin) tightly pressed together and wrapped in a protective material. Usually sized 30×15×15 inches. May be strengthened by metal bands. 紧压在一起并用保护性材料包裹起来的柔软货物（如棉花、羊毛、羊皮）的包装。通常的尺寸是30×15×15英寸，可用金属带加固。

continued

Packing Containers 包装容器	
Can/Tin 罐/听	A small metal container in which small quantity of paint, oil or certain foodstuffs are packed. 一种小的金属容器，用于包装少量的油漆、油或特定的食品。
Carboy 玻璃瓶	A large glass container protected in a metal or wicker cage with soft packing between glass and cage. It is used for chemicals. 一种大的有金属或柳条罩防护的玻璃容器，玻璃与罩之间有软包装，用于装运化学品。
Bundle 捆	Miscellaneous goods packed without a container. A number of small carton fixed together could be called a bundle. 没有容器的混杂货物的包装。大量的小纸板箱放置在一起称之为一捆。
Container 集装箱	A very large metal box for transport of goods by road, rail, sea or air. Packing goods in a large container facilitates loading and unloading by mechanical handling; thus time is saved. 一种非常大的金属盒，用于公路、铁路、海运或航空运输货物。用大集装箱装运货物便于用机械来进行装卸，从而节省时间。
Pallet 托盘	A large tray or platform for moving loads (by means of slings) e.g. from a lorry into a train or onto a ship, and so save time for handling of separate items. 一种大的盘子或平台，通过吊索来转移货物，如从卡车上转送到火车或船上，这样能节省处理单个货物的时间。

Sales packing, also called small packing or inner packing, provides some necessary information about the quality, function, origin, usage and some other things about the commodities. With the development of consuming taste and science and technology, inner packing plays a more and more important part in sales promotion. Various forms of inner packing have been developed to meet the demands of consumers and marketing competitions, including suspensible packing, transparent packing, portable packing, window packing, gift packing, etc.

销售包装（Sales Packing），又称小包装（Small Packing）或内包装（Inner Packing）。它是指直接接触商品，随着商品进入零售环节和消费者直接见面的包装，实际上是零售包装。因此，销售包装除了要求具备保护商品的条件外，更重要的是要美化商品，宣传商品，便于销售和便于使用。在销售包装的造型结构、装潢画面和文字说明等方面都有较高的要求。

2.4.3 Nominated Brand and Neutral Packing 定牌和中性包装

Nominated Brand means using the brand name or

trademark designated by buyers on their manufactured goods.

Neutral packing refers to the packaging of goods and no production inside and outside the country and the name of the manufacturer. This is sometimes needed because the exporters want to break down the high tariff duties or to avoid the problems caused by the import quota imposed by the importing countries on their exports, or for some other marketing reasons. In China and other countries, the export quota of the commodity agreements should be strictly handled. Because re-exporting goods to the quota countries has a negative impact on those countries. Exporters should not be a result of plans to the detriment of their own benefits and interests of the country's reputation. Sometimes the importer may ask the exporter to use a specified brand. under such cases the contract should stipulate that the brand or trademark is to be supplied by the exporter and the exporter should answer in case all the disputes arising hereof.

定牌（Nominated Brand）是指在商品包装上卖方采用买方指定的商标或牌号。

中性包装（Neutral Packing）是指在商品上和内外包装上不注明生产国别、地名和生产厂名，也不注明原有商标和牌号，甚至没有任何文字。在国际贸易中，使用中性包装的目的主要是为了打破某些进口国家和地区实行的关税壁垒、配额限制和其他一些限制进口的歧视性措施。所以它是推销出口商品的一个手段。目前，其些出口商品使用中性包装已成为国际贸易中的一种习惯做法。

2.4.4 Factors Determining Proper Packing 决定合格包装的因素

In deciding what method of packing to use, we must take into account, for each shipment, a number of factors. The following guidelines should be followed when goods are packed:

- The goods are protected from rain, seawater and moisture.
- Large loads are sent whenever possible. Large loads are less likely to be damaged than small loads. Also most shipping companies offer a discount for "unitized" loads in which different

packages of goods are combined into one large unit, for example, by strapping to an expandable wooden pallet.

- The contents are packed tightly within the box, or crate in a way which gives the container wall added strength and prevents harmful shifting of goods.
- Heavy machinery and odd-shaped items should be boxed or crated and provided with skids for easier handling and storage.
- The weight should be distributed evenly within the container.
- The goods should be adequately protected against pilferage.
- The shipment should be clearly marked or labeled.
- If the cargo is liquid, do not fill containers completely but leave enough space to allow for variations in temperature.
- For liquid cargos, certain additional guidelines apply to shipment by air: the packing should be able to withstand air pressure; and air regulations require that airlines are informed and their permission obtained before shipping liquid or pressurized products.
- Extra care should be taken when packing hazardous goods and all regulations covering such materials should be observed.

2.4.5 Packing Clause in Contract 合同中的包装条款

In international trade, when consigning a sales clause, the seller and buyer usually specify the above details under the packing clause. They agree on who to pay for the packing, how to pack, how to mark or label.

When stipulating packing clause, attention should be paid to the following points:

- Ambiguous expressions should be avoided in the packing clause.
- The seller should adopt appropriate package according to different characteristics of goods and transportation.

Notes

1. Quality
   商品品质，商品的内在属性和外部形式的综合。前者包括货物的化学成分、物理和机械性能、生物特征等自然属性；后者包括货物的款式、结构、色泽、味觉和嗅觉等。
2. Sale by Inspection
   看货买卖，在国际货物买卖中，有些特殊商品既无法用文字说明描述其品质，也不宜提供质量完全相同的标准样品作为买卖双方交接货物的品质依据，如特制的工艺制品、古董、珠宝首饰、字画等。对于这类独具特性的商品，通常由买方或其指定代理人到货物所在地验看货物，根据所看到货物的实际品质（Actual Quality）达成交易。
3. Quality Latitude
   品质机动幅度是指对某些初级产品，由于卖方所交货物品质难以完全与合同规定的品质相符，为便于卖方交货，往往在规定的品质指标外，加订一定的允许幅度，卖方所交货物品质只要在允许的幅度内，买方就无权拒收，但可根据合同规定调整价格。
4. Quality Tolerance
   品质公差，即所谓品质公差是指允许卖方交货的品质可以高于或者低于合同规定的品质的幅度。
5. Conditioned Weight
   有些商品具有较强的吸湿性，其所含水分受客观环境的影响较大，其重量也就很不稳定，因而国际上有一种专门计算此类商品重量的方法，即用科学的方法除去其所含的实际水分，然后再加上国际公认的标准含水量。按此法求出的重量，称为公量。
6. More or Less Clause
   溢短装条款,也称为数量机动幅度，数量增减条款或是指允许卖方所交货物的数量指标可有一定幅度范围内的差异，只要卖方所交货物的数量没有超出机动幅度的范围，买方就无权拒收货物，这一方法主要适用于散装货物。

7. Nominated Brand Packing

定牌包装，是指卖方按买方要求在其出售的商品或包装上标明买方指定的商标或牌号。

8. Neutral Packing

中性包装，是指在商品的内外包装上不标明原产地、厂商、商标、牌号等有可能导致识别商品来源地的商品包装。

Exercise

1. Translate the following into Chinese or English.

quality latitude
quality tolerance
gross weight
sale by actual quality
more or less clause
neutral packing
nominated brand packing
复样
含水量
凭卖方样品买卖
凭买方样品买卖
理论重量
从价税
货样不符

2. Translate the following sentences into Chinese or English.

1) There is no marked qualitative difference between the two.
2) We sincerely hope the qualities are in conformity with the contract stipulations.
3) The quality and price of commodities should be taken into consideration in choosing the packing material and package designing.
4) We should take not only the quality and appearance of the goods into consideration, but also the customers' taste and preference.
5) For dangerous and poisonous goods, the explanation of the nature and the generally adopted symbol shall be marked obviously on each package.
6) 醒目的内包装一定有助于我们促销.
7) 高档商品配上高档的包装，以显其优质与名贵。
8) 要增强我国出口商品在国际市场的竞争能力，就必须提高出口商品的质量。

3. Decide whether the following statements are true (T) or false (F).

1) The more or less clause is mainly applicable to industrial finished products.
2) The goods of the best quality shall be chosen as the sample for sale.
3) The breach of the quality clause in the contract is regarded as a fundamental breach of contract.
4) When goods of higher quality than the contract quality are delivered, there will be no dispute arising thereon.
5) Generally, quality deviation within the quality tolerance or quality latitude will not result in an adjustment in price.
6) Quality difference within the agreed quality latitude or tolerance will not give rise to the increase or decrease in price unless stipulated otherwise.

4. Two columns are given for you to decide which method is best suited for a certain commodity. Please match them.

1) mineral ore	A. sample
2) ordinary garments	B. manual
3) fish	C. F.A.Q
4) Haier washing machines	D. G.M.Q.
5) medical apparatus	E. famous brand
6) wheat	F. specification
7) calligraphic works	G. origin
8) power plant generator	H. drawing or diagram

5. Calculation

1) Company A has a contract to export 10 metric tons of seafood, to be packed in cartons each of 40 lb. (1 lb. =0.45358 kg), with a 5% more or less allowed both in quantity and in amount.

① How many cartons of Seafood can Company A deliver at most?

② How many cartons of Seafood should Company A deliver at least?

2) 公司出口生丝，合同数量为 100 公吨，溢短装（more or less）5%，约定标准回潮率（standard regaining rate of water）为 11%。现有生丝 104 公吨，实际回潮率（actual regaining rate of water）9%。

问：① 这批生丝符合约定回潮率的重量为多少？

② 是否符合溢短装条款规定的重量？

③ 应取出多少回潮率为 9%的生丝？

6. **Case Analysis**

1) In 1990, a certain export company of China sent a group of businessmen to the United States for selling equipment. In New York both parties reached an oral agreement on such items as specifications, unit price, and quantity etc. Upon leaving, the group indicated to the other party that, when they got back to Beijing, they would draw a contract which would become effective after being signed by both parties. After going back to Beijing, the group found that the clients withdrew their import of the equipment, and thus the contract was not signed and the L/C was not opened, either. The US side urged the Chinese side to perform the contract; otherwise they would lodge a claim with the Chinese side in the US. Please analyze the case and give an opinion on how the Chinese export company was to deal with this case and why.

2) A Chinese export company sent an offer to a businessman living in Italy on June 1, asking for a reply to reach them before June 10. The Italian businessman cabled his acceptance of the offer on June 8. Because of the delay by the post office, the acceptance did not reach the Chinese company until the morning of June 11. Before receiving the acceptance, the Chinese company was informed that the prices of the said products were rising rapidly. What do you think is the best way for the Chinese company to deal with this case? Why?

Chapter 3

International Trade Terms and Customs

国际贸易术语和惯例

In the international trade, it is of great importance to determine the responsibilities and obligations of both the seller and buyer. In order to make definite the obligations, risks and costs of the two parties in the transfer of the goods, the buyer and seller, during business negotiation, must adopt a certain trade term, which is a dispensable part of the contract for the international sale of goods, because trade terms are directly related to the prices of commodities. Therefore, it is essential for the people engaged in international trade to understand and master various kinds of trade terms that are in universal use in international trade practices.

在国际货物买卖中，交易双方通过磋商，确定各自的权利和义务。为了明确买卖双方在货物转移过程中的责任、风险和费用的划分，在国际销售合同中必须使用特定的贸易术语。贸易术语和货物价格直接相关。因而贸易商应理解和掌握在国际贸易中广泛使用的贸易术语。

☞ **Learning Objectives**

After learning this chapter, you are expected to:

→ Understand the definition and contents of different trade terms;

→ Identify differences among eleven terms under the Incoterms 2010;

→ Outline determining factors when choosing trade terms;

→ Understand the basic concepts of customs.

3.1 Foundation of International Trade Customs 国际贸易惯例概述

3.1.1 Definition of Customs 国际贸易惯例的定义

International trade customs are universally recognized as the customary ways of doing business and explanation evolving in the long process of trade development and have been compiled by relative international organizations into rules and regulations which are acquainted, recognized and adopted by many trading organizations in most countries.

国际贸易惯例是在国际贸易的长期实践中逐步形成发展的具有普遍意义的一些习惯做法和解释，经过有关国际组织的编纂与解释成为规则、条文，并为较多的国家或贸易团体所熟悉、承认和采用。

3.1.2 Nature of Customs 国际贸易惯例的性质

- International trade customs are not compulsory since they are bot legislation or laws for all countries, neither legislations nor laws of a certain country.
- When both parties cite one international custom, it becomes legally valid and both parties are subject to it.
- Even if the contract does not indicate which custom the contract is subject to, the custom still has binding force.

它是各国的共同立法，也不是某一国的法律，不具有法律的强制性。

当买卖双方在合同中援引某项惯例时，则该惯例即具有法律效力，对双方均有约束力，有法律强制性。

合同中未引入某项惯例，惯例仍有约束力。

When disputes arise during the contract execution, court of justice or arbitration agencies usually make ruling according to the customs, thus the customs are influential

在执行合同中发生争议时，法院判决、仲裁机构仲裁往往以惯例作为准则进行裁

to some extent. Especially lately, some international convertibles and laws endow the customs legality. China's laws indicate what Tehran law fails to cover is subject to international trade customs. CISG stipulates that the commonly used and universally known customs which are not excluded from the contract are binding to both parties. Therefore, it is of great significance to get familiar with the customs and carry out trade practices.

决，因此这些惯例实际上有一定的影响力，特别是目前的新的趋势，某些国际公约或某些国家以立法的形式直接赋予惯例法律效力。如我国的法律规定：凡是中国法律没有规定的适用国际贸易惯例。《公约》规定：合同没有排除的惯例，已经知道或应当知道的惯例和经常使用反复遵守的惯例对双方当事人均有约束力。

- If the contract clauses conflict with customs, the contract to be followed is as a basic principle.

如果合同中的条款与惯例有冲突，将遵循合同优先惯例的原则。

- Both parties could make out some clause different from customs when signing a contract on the principle of contract first and contract freedom.

遵循契约至上、契约自由的原则，合同双方当事人在签订合同时也可以作出与惯例不同的规定。

3.2 Foundation of International Trade Terms 国际贸易术语概述

3.2.1 Concept and Significance of Trade Terms 贸易术语的概念和意义

Trade terms, also known as price or delivery terms, are standardized terms used in sales contracts that describe the place and manner for the transfer of goods from the seller to the buyer. It refers to the use of brief English concepts or abbreviations to indicate the formation of the unit price and determine the responsibilities, expenses and risks borne by two parties as well as the time of the passing of the property in the goods.

贸易术语（Trade Terms），又称为价格术语（Price Terms）或交割术语（Delivery Terms），是用来表示交易双方责任、费用与风险划分的专门用语。贸易术语来源于国际贸易惯例，是在国际贸易长期实践的基础上逐渐产生的。

The functions of international trade terms can be summarized as follows:

- Define the rights, obligations, risks and expenses

of both the seller and the buyer.

- Name the exact point at which the ownership of the merchandise is transferred from the seller to the buyer.
- Simplify the procedure of negotiations, and thus save time and cost.
- Offer rules to settle disputes in the fulfillment of contract.

3.2.2 International Conventions About Trade Terms 贸易术语的国际公约

Among the history of international trade, there are three sets of rules that influence the development of trade terms—*Warsaw-Oxford Rules 1932*, *Revised American Foreign Trade Definitions 1941* and *International Rules for the Interpretation of Trade Terms 2010*. In addition, there is one thing must be point out: the use of international trade terms are to some extent the result of customary practice, they do not have any legal binding forces unless they have been listed in the relevant contract as an integral part and are protected by relevant legal instruments.

需要强调的是，贸易术语是由国际组织将在国际贸易业务中反复实践的习惯做法，加以编纂与解释所形成的、非强制性文件。

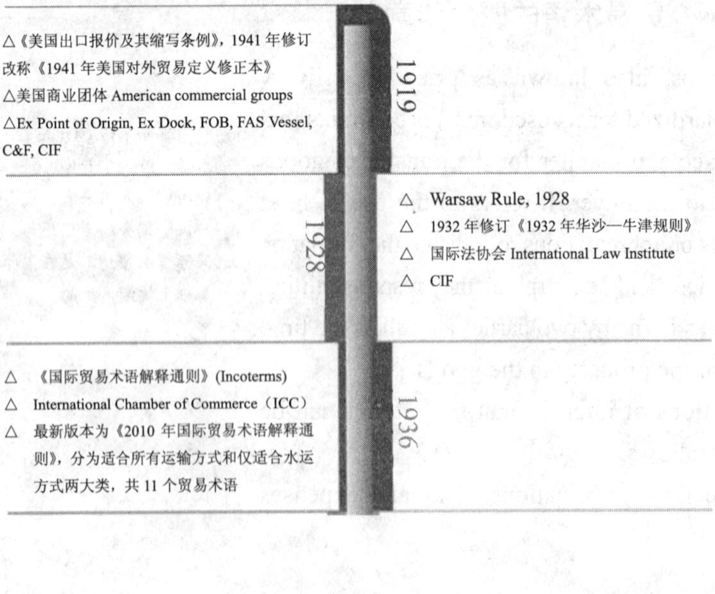

- Warsaw-Oxford Rules 1932 (**Still in use**)
  During the 1028 convention of the International Law Association held in the capital of Poland, Warsaw, a set of uniform rules were established—"Warsaw Rule, 1928". In 1930 and 1931, the Association held convention in New York and Paris discussing further amendment to the Rules. Then in the 1932 convention in Oxford, England, the rules were changed into the "Warsaw-Oxford Rules 1932". Moreover, it contains 21 clauses, which only stipulate the nature of CIF.
- Revised American Foreign Trade Definitions 1941 (Applicable in the USA, Canada and other countries in America.)
  In 1919, nine business communities in USA devised "the US Export Quotations and Abbreviations", which is aimed at clarifying and simplifying the terminology applied in international trade. Then at the 27th National Foreign Trade Conference in 1940, it was revised and on July 31st 1941, the "Revised American Foreign Trade Definitions 1941" was completed. This rule was made out by nine American commercial organizations in 1941. It is a set of foreign trade terms which are considered obsolete(过时的), but still sometimes used in U. S domestic trade.
- International Rules for the Interpretation of Trade Terms 2010
  In 1936, the International Chamber of Commerce (ICC), a world business organization based in Paris, first published the International Commercial Terms (Incoterms). To keep pace with the changes in trade practice, ICC revised and updated the rules

1928 年由国际法协会在华沙制定，1930 年、1931 年、1932 年在牛津作了修订后使用至今，故称《1932 年华沙——牛津规则》(Warsaw-Oxford Rules1932)。需要指出的是，该协议是国际法协会专门对 CIF 制定的。

1919 在美国举行泛美贸易会议时所制定的出口报价定义，原称为《美国出口报价及其缩写条例》，1941 年经美国商会、进口商协会、外贸协会三个民间团体所组成的联合委员会修订后，改称为《1941 年美国对外贸易定义修订本》(Revised American Foreign Trade Definition 1941)。它在美洲国家有较大影响，合同双方可以自愿采用。

国际商会(ICC，International Chamber of Commerce)是世界性的民间经贸商会组织，成立于 1919 年，总部在巴黎。

贸易术语通则是国际商会为了统一对各种贸易术语的解释而制定的，最早产生与 1936 年，六次修改与补充沿用至今，合同双方可自愿采用。其最新版本即为《2010 年国际贸易术语解释通则》(International Rules for the Interpretation of Trade Terms

for several times. Significant updates happened in 1953, 1967, 1976, 1980, 1990, 2000 and 2010. The latest version, International Rules for the Interpretation of Trade Terms 2010, was amended in 2010 and came into force on 1st January, 2011.

2010, IN-COTERMS 2010）.

The Incoterms® 2010 rules take account of the continued spread of customs-free zones, the increased use of electronic communications in business transactions, heightened concern about security in the movement of goods and consolidate in transport practices. And it is also the first version of the Incoterms rules to make all references to buyers and sellers gender-neutral（中立）.

3.3 Main Trade Terms in International Trade 国际贸易中的主要贸易术语

3.3.1 Basic Concepts for Incoterms 2010 2010 国际贸易术语解释通则的基本概念

Incoterms are international rules that are accepted by governments, legal authorities and practitioners worldwide for the interpretation of the most commonly used terms in international trade. They either reduce or remove altogether uncertainties arising from differing interpretations of such terms in different countries. The newly published 2010 version take into account issues such as developments in cargo security and the need to replace paper documents with electronic ones. Moreover, it made several important changes to the previous version.

Incoterms 1990 consists of 13 trade rules. Incoterms 2000 groups the 13 rules into 4 categories. Incoterms 2010 updates and consolidates the 'delivered' rules, reducing the total number of rules from 13 to 11. The Incoterms 2010 rules, DAF, DES, DEQ and DDU are replaced by two new Incoterms rules DAT and DAP. Incoterms 2010 present 11 rules in two distinct classes: Rules for any mode or modes of transportation, EXW, FCA, CPT, CIP, DAT, DAP and DDP; Rules for sea and inland waterway transportation, FAS, FOB, CFR and CIF.

1990 年修订时主要内容包括 13 个贸易术语。《2000 通则》保留了这 13 个贸易术语，并把贸易术语分成 4 组。《2010 通则》改为 11 个贸易术语，删去了原来 D 组的 DAF、DES、DEQ、和 DDU，新增加了 DAT 和 DAP。2010 年版通则把这 11 个贸易术语分成两组。一组是可以适用于任何运输方式或多种运输方式的术语：EXW、FCA、CPT、CIP、DAT、DAP 与 DDP。另一组为适用于海运及内河水运的术语：FAS、FOB、CFR 与 CIF。

➢ Scope of Governance

适用范围

Incoterms 2010 does not apply to all the duties which all parties may wish to include in a typical transaction. It has a strictly defined scope of governance. As stated in the introduction of Incoterms 2010, the scope of this document is limited to matters relating to the rights and obligations of the parties to the contract of sale with respect to the delivery of tangible goods sold. The following issues are defined:

→ It is the parties with which it is concerned. That is, during the whole process of international trade a lot of parties may get involved: sellers, buyers, carriers, insurers, customs, brokers, etc. But as far as Incoterms 2010 are concerned, the relation between only two parties—sellers and buyers, no others—will be dealt with.

只涉及买卖双方。

→ It is the document in question. Among all the contracts needed in fulfilling an international sales transaction—contract of sale, contract of carriage, contract of insurance and contract of financing—

只限于销售合同中与买卖货物（有形货物）有关的部分事宜。

Incoterms relate to only one of them, the contract of sale.

→ It is the specific aspects of the contract of sale governed. A contract of sale can be considered the foundation of a transaction. It should include all basic and important factors of sale. Incoterms, however, settle matters only with respect to the delivery of goods sold.

只限于销售货物过程中的交货环节。

In a word, Incoterms tell to what extend both sellers and buyers should bear the obligations, costs and risks of the goods under a contract of sale.

➢ Obligation

责任

One aspect that needs clarification between sellers and buyers under Incoterms is the division of obligation. Obligation is a forceful word which implies a legal duty to do something according to a certain agreement. Concerning the delivery of goods under a contract of sale, obligation of the two parties refers to all the necessary handling procedures. Some obligations are universally accepted and fulfilled, even without any written explanations. While other obligations, however, may differ under different circumstances.

➢ Cost

费用

Cost is another important element that the two trading parties need to settle under a particular transaction. Major cost involved in international trade may include local and overseas transportation and insurance cost. Other detailed costs may refer to goods supervision and inspection expenses, customs clearance charges like expenses for obtaining export or import licenses, and loading and unloading charges of the goods at some particular transport points.

- Transfer of risks

风险转移

Explaining how the risk of loss and damage to goods would be transferred between the sellers and buyers during a transaction is an important contribution Incoterms made to the global trade. Unlike Revised American Foreign Trade Definitions 1941, Incoterms 2010 explicitly defines the critical point of transfer of risk under each case.

- Categorization of Terms

术语分类

Incoterms 2010 divides the eleven trade terms into two classes. The availability with the transport modest is the basis of classification. The seven terms—EXW, FCA, CPT, CIF, DAT, DAP and DDP can be used in any mode of transport, while the other four terms—FAS, FOB, CFR and CIF can only be applicable to sea and inland waterway transport.

适用于任何运输方式		
EXW	Ex Works	工厂交货
FCA	Free Carrier	货交承运人
CPT	Carriage Paid To	运费付至
CIP	Carriage and Insurance Paid To	运保费付至
DAT	Delivered At Terminal	指定终端交货
DAP	Delivered At Place	指定目的地交货
DDP	Delivered Duty Paid	完税后交货
仅适用于水运方式		
FAS	Free Alongside ship	装运港船边交货
FOB	Free On Board	装运港船上交货
CFR	Cost and Freight	成本加运费
CIF	Cost, Insurance and Freight	成本加运保费

术语缩写	术语全称	适用运输方式
EXW	Ex Works 工厂交货（……指定地点）	所有运输方式
FCA	Free Carrier 货交承运人（……指定地点）	所有运输方式
CPT	Carriage Paid To 运费付至（……指定目的地）	所有运输方式
CIP	Carriage and Insurance Paid To（……指定目的地）	所有运输方式
DAT（新）	Delivered At Terminal 终点站交货（……指定终点站）	所有运输方式
DAP（新）	Delivered At Place 指定地点交货（……指定地点）	所有运输方式
DDP	Delivered Duty Paid 完税后交货（……指定目的地）	所有运输方式
FAS	Free Alongside Ship 船边交货（……指定装运港）	水运方式
FOB	Free On Board 船上交货（……指定装运港）	水运方式
CFR	Cost and Freight 成本加运费（……指定目的港）	水运方式
CIF	Cost, Insurance and Freight 成本，运费加保险价格（……指定目的港）	水运方式

Incoterms 2010 买卖双方权利义务一览表						
序号	贸易术语	交货地点	风险转移界限	出口报关责任、费用由谁负担	进口报关责任、费用由谁负担	适用的运输方式
1	EXW	商品产地、所在地	买方处置货物后	BUYER	BUYER	任何方式
2	FOB	装运港口	货交装运港船上后	SELLER	BUYER	水上运输
3	FCA	出口国内地、港口	承运人处置货物后	SELLER	BUYER	任何方式
4	FAS	装运港口	货交装运港船边后	SELLER	BUYER	水上运输
5	CFR	装运港口	货交装运港船上后	SELLER	BUYER	水上运输
6	CIF	装运港口	货交装运港船上后	SELLER	BUYER	水上运输
7	CPT	出口国内地、港口	承运人处置货物后	SELLER	BUYER	任何方式
8	CIP	出口国内地、港口	承运人处置货物后	SELLER	BUYER	任何方式
9	DAP	进口国国内	买方处置货物后	SELLER	BUYER	任何方式
10	DAT	进口国国内	在指定目的港或目的地的运输终端上货交买方后	SELLER	BUYER	任何方式
11	DDP	进口国国内	买方在指定地点收获后	SELLER	BUYER	任何方式

3.3.2 Three Trade Terms Suitable for Water Transport 适用于水运的三种贸易术语

The three commonly used trade terms suitable for water transport are FOB, CIF, and CFR.

3.3.2.1 FOB (Free on Board,...named port of shipment)

FOB means that the seller delivers the goods on board the vessel nominated by the buyer at the named port of shipment or procures the goods already so delivered. The risk of loss of or damage to the goods passes when the goods are on board the vessel, and the buyer bears all costs from that moment onwards.

船上交货（……指定装运港），FOB (Free on Board,...named port of shipment)。FOB是指当卖方在指定的装运港将货物运至买方指定的船上或取得已按此送交的货物，即完成交货。当货物已运至船上时，货物灭失或损坏的风险发生转移，买方自那时起承担一切费用。

The seller is required either to deliver the goods on board the vessel or to procure goods already so delivered for shipment. The reference to "procure" here caters for multiple sales down a chain ('string sales'), particularly common in the commodity trades.

卖方必须将货物运到船上或取得已按此送交准备发运的货物。这里的"取得"适合于多层次链条式销售（线性销售），在商品销售中尤为普遍。

FOB may not be appropriate where goods are handed over to the carrier before they are on board the vessel, for example goods in containers, which are typically delivered at a terminal.

FOB requires the seller to clear the goods for export, where applicable. However, the seller has no obligation to clear the goods for import, pay any import duty or carry out any import customs formalities.

FOB要求在需要办理海关手续时由卖方负责货物出口清关。然而，卖方并没有义务办理货物进口清关、负担任何进口关税或办理任何进口海关手续。

➢ The sellers' obligations 卖方义务

1) The seller must provide the goods and the commercial invoice in conformity with the contract of sale and any other evidence of conformity that may be required by the contract. Any document referred to in A1-A10 may be an equivalent electronic record or procedure if

卖方必须提供符合销售合同规定的货物和商业发票以及按照合同约定必需的有同等作用的其他任何凭证。以及经当事人同意或根据交易习惯在A1-A10中提到的任何有同等作用的电子记录或程序的凭证。

agreed between the parties or customary.

2) Where applicable, the seller must obtain, at its own risk and expense, any export licence or other official authorization and carry out all customs formalities necessary for the export of the goods.

在需要办理清关手续时，卖方必须承担风险和费用获得任何出口许可或其他官方授权，办理货物出口所需的一切海关手续。

3) The seller has no obligation to the buyer to make a contract of carriage. However, if requested by the buyer or if it is commercial practice and the buyer does not give an instruction to the contrary in due time, the seller may contract for carriage on usual terms at the buyer's risk and expense. In either case, the seller may decline to make the contract of carriage and, if it does, shall promptly notify the buyer.

卖方没有义务为买方订立运输合同。但若买方要求，或者如果是商业惯例而买方未适时给予卖方相反指示，则卖方可按照通常条件订立运输合同，费用和风险由买方承担。在任何一种情况下，卖方都可以拒绝订立此合同；如果拒绝，则应立即通知买方。

4) The seller has no obligation to the buyer to make a contract of insurance. However, the seller must provide the buyer, at the buyer's request, risk, and expense (if any), with information that the buyer needs for obtaining insurance.

卖方没有义务为买方订立保险合同。但应买方要求并由其承担风险和费用，卖方必须提供给买方办理保险所需的相关信息。

5) The seller must deliver the goods either by placing them on board the vessel nominated by the buyer at the loading point, if any, indicated by the buyer at the named port of shipment or by procuring the goods so delivered. In either case, the seller must deliver the goods on the agreed date or within the agreed period and in the manner customary at the port. If no specific loading point has been indicated by the buyer, the seller may select the point within the named port of shipment that best

卖方必须将在买方指定的装运港，在买方指定的装运地点，在约定日期或期限内，按照该港习惯方式将货物交至买方指定的船上或取得已交运的货物。若买方没有指定具体交货点，那么卖方可选择指定装运港内最适合其目的的交货点。

suits its purpose.

6) The seller bears all risks of loss of or damage to the goods until they have been delivered.

卖方必须承担货物灭失或损坏的一切风险，直至交货为止。

7) The seller must, at the buyer's risk and expense, give the buyer sufficient notice either that the goods have been delivered or that the vessel has failed to take the goods within the time agreed.

在货物已交付或在约定时间内船舶未能接收货物时，卖方必须给予买方充分通知，由买方承担风险和费用。

8) The seller must provide the buyer, at the seller's expense, with the usual proof that the goods have been delivered in accordance with A4. Unless such proof is a transport document, the seller must provide assistance to the buyer, at the buyer's request, risk and expense, in obtaining a transport document.

卖方必须自担费用向买方提供证明已按照 A4 规定交货的通常单据。如果这些凭证不是运输单据，应买方要求并由其承担风险和费用，卖方必须给予买方协助以取得运输单据。

➢ The buyer's obligations

1) The buyer must pay the price of the goods as provided in the contract of sale.

买方必须按照销售合同规定支付价款。

2) Where applicable, it is up to the buyer to obtain, at his own risk and expense, any import license or other official authorization and carry out all customs formalities for the import of the goods and for their transport through any country.

在需要办理清关手续时，由买方自担风险和费用获得任何进口许可或其他官方授权，并负责办理货物进口和从他国过境的一切海关手续。

3) The buyer must contract, at its own expense for the carriage of the goods from the named port of shipment, except where the contract of carriage is made by the seller.

买方必须自付费用订立自指定装运港运输货物的合同，卖方订立了运输合同时除外。

4) The buyer has no obligation to the seller to make a contract of insurance.

买方没有义务为卖方订立保险合同。

5) The buyer must take delivery of the goods when they have been delivered.

买方必须在卖方按照规定交货时，受领货物。

6) The buyer bears all risks of loss of or damage to the goods from the time they have been delivered.

买方必须承担自按照规定交货之时起货物灭失或损坏的一切风险.

7) The buyer must give the seller sufficient notice of the vessel name, loading point and, where necessary, the selected delivery time within the agreed period.

买方必须就指定船只名称、装运点和必要时约定期限内的指定交货时间给予卖方充分通知。

As the loading of the goods is a continuous process, sometimes it is hard to use the ship's rail as a point to divide responsibilities and costs. To avoid dispute, there are several derived price terms: FOB Liner Terms, FOB Under Tackle, FOB Stowed, FOB Trimmed and FOB Stowed & Trimmed.

由于船方通常多按不负担装卸条件出租船舶，故买卖双方易在装货费由谁负担问题上引起争议。为此，买卖双方订立合同时，应在 FOB 后另列有关装货费由谁负担的具体条件，以明责任，这就导致 FOB 的变形。

常见的 FOB 有下列几种（下述 FOB 后加列各种条件，只是为了明确装货费由谁负担，并不影响风险转移的界限。）:

- FOB 班轮条件（FOB Liner Terms）指装货费按班轮办法处理，即卖方不负担。
- FOB 吊钩下交货（FOB under Tackle）指卖方已将货物交到船舶吊钩所及之处，即卖方不负担装货费用。
- FOB 包括理舱（FOB Stowed）指卖方负拒货物装船和理舱的费用。
- FOB 包括平舱（FOB Trimmed）指卖方负担货物装船和平舱的费用。
- FOB 包括理舱和平舱（FOB Stowed &Trimmed）指卖方负担货物装船、理舱和平舱的费用。按一般惯例：凡 FOB 后未加“理舱”或“平舱”字样，卖方则不负担理舱或平舱的费用。

3.3.2.2 CFR (Cost and Freight) (… named port of destination)

成本加运费（……指定目的港），CFR (Cost and Freight) (… named port of destination)。CFR 术语是指卖方必须负担运至目的港所需的成本和运费，故 CFR 的基本涵义是成本加装运港至目的港的运费。

CFR means that the seller delivers when the goods on board the vessel or procures the goods already so delivered. The seller must pay the costs and freight necessary to bring the goods to the named port of destination but the risk of loss of or damage to the goods, as well as any additional costs due to events occurring after the time of delivery, are transferred from the seller to the buyer. The CFR term requires the seller to clear the goods for export.

该术语仅适用于海运或内河运输。“Cost and Freight” 是指当卖方将货物运至船上或取得已按此送交的货物，即完成交货。当货物已运至船上时，货物灭失或损坏的风险发生转移。

This rule is to be used only for sea or inland waterway transport. “Cost and Freight” means that the seller delivers the goods on board the vessel or procures the goods already so delivered. The risk of loss of or damage to the goods passes when the goods are on board the vessel.

➢ The seller's obligations

卖方义务

1) The seller must provide the goods and the commercial invoice in conformity with the contract of sale and any other evidence of conformity that may be required by the contract.

卖方必须提供符合销售合同规定的货物和商业发票以及按照合同约定必需的有同等作用的其他任何凭证。

2) Where applicable, the seller must obtain, at its own risk and expense, any export licence or other official authorization and carry out all customs formalities necessary for the export of the goods.

在需要办理清关手续时，卖方必须承担风险和费用获得任何出口许可或其他官方授权，办理货物出口所需的一切海关手续。

3) The seller must contract or procure a contract for the carriage of the goods from the agreed point of delivery, if any, at the place of delivery to the named port of destination or, if agreed, any point at that port. The contract of carriage must be made on usual terms at the seller's expense and provide for carriage by the usual route in a vessel of the type normally used for the transport of the type of goods sold.

卖方必须自付费用，按照通常条件订立运输合同，自约定交货地点，经由惯常航线，将货物用通常可供运输合同所指货物类型的海轮运至指定目的港。

4) The seller has no obligation to the buyer to make a contract of insurance. However, the seller must provide the buyer, at the buyer's request, risk, and expense (if any), with information that the buyer needs for obtaining insurance.

卖方没有义务为买方订立保险合同。但应买方要求并由其承担风险和费用，卖方必须提供给买方办理保险所需的相关信息。

5) The seller must deliver the goods either by placing them on board the vessel or by procuring the goods so delivered. In either case, the seller must deliver the goods on the

卖方必须将在约定日期或期限内，按照该港习惯方式将货物运至船上或取得已交运的货物。

agreed date or within the agreed period and in the manner customary at the port.

6) The seller bears all risks of loss of or damage to the goods until they have been delivered, with the exception of loss or damage in the circumstances.

卖方必须承担货物灭失或损坏的一切风险，直至已按照规定交货为止。

7) The seller bears all costs relating to the goods until they have been delivered, other than those payable by the buyer.

除按照规定应由买方支付的费用外，卖方必须支付与货物有关的一切费用，直至已按照规定交货为止。

8) The seller must give the buyer any notice needed in order to allow the buyer to take measures that are normally necessary to enable the buyer to take the goods.

卖方必须给予买方必要的任何通知，以便买方能够为受领货物采取通常必要的措施。

➢ The buyer's obligations

买方义务

1) The buyer must pay the price of the goods as provided in the contract of sale.

买方必须按照销售合同规定支付价款。

2) Where applicable, it is up to the buyer to obtain, at its own risk and expense, any import license or other official authorization and carry out all customs formalities for the import of the goods and for their transport through any country.

在需要办理清关手续时，由买方自担风险和费用获得任何进口许可或其他官方授权，并负责办理货物进口和从他国过境的一切海关手续。

3) The buyer has no obligation to the seller to make a contract of carriage.

买方没有义务为卖方订立运输合同。

4) The buyer has no obligation to the seller to make a contract of insurance. However, the buyer must provide the seller, upon request, with the necessary information for obtaining insurance.

买方没有义务为卖方订立保险合同。但应卖方要求，买方必须提供给卖方办理保险的必要信息。

5) The buyer must take delivery of the goods when they have been delivered and receive them from the carrier at the named port of destination.

买方必须在卖方按照规定交货时受领货物并在指定目的港从承运人处收受货物。

6) The buyer bears all risks of loss of or damage to the goods from the time they have been delivered. If the buyer fails to give notice, then it bears all risks of loss of or damage to the goods from the agreed date or the expiry date of the agreed period for shipment, provided that the goods have been clearly identified as the contract goods.

7) The buyer must, whenever it is entitled to determine the time for shipping the goods and/or the point of receiving the goods within the named port of destination, give the seller sufficient notice thereof.

The difference between CIF and CFR: Under CFR, the seller is not obligated to arrange marine insurance against the risk of loss of, or damage to, the goods in transit. The buyer is obligated to arrange insurance and pay the insurance premium.

Variations of CFR Terms are CFR Liner Terms, CFR Landed, CFR Ex Tackle and CFR EX Ship's Hold.

3.3.2.3 CIF (Cost, Insurance and Freight) (…named port of destination)

CIF means that the seller delivers the goods on board the vessel or procures the goods already so delivered. The risk of loss or damage to the goods passes when the goods are on board the vessel. The seller must contract for and pay the costs and freight necessary to bring the goods to the named port of destination.

Variations of CIF Terms are CIF Liner Terms, CIF Landed, and CIF Ex-ship's hold.

买方必须承担按照规定交货时起货物灭失或损坏的一切风险。如买方未能按照规定给予卖方通知，则买方必须从约定的装运日期或装运期限届满之日起，承担货物灭失或损坏的一切风险，但以该项货物已正式划归合同项下为限。

一旦买方有权决定货物装运时间和/或指定目的港内接收货物的具体地点时，必须给予卖方充分通知。

CFR 术语有以下几种变形（下述 CFR 后面另加附加条件，并不改变交货地点和风险划分的界限）：

→ CFR 班轮（CFR liner Terms）指卸货费按班轮办法处理，即买方不负担卸货费。

→ CFR 卸到岸上（CFR Landed）指由卖方负担卸货费，其中包括驳运费在内。

→ CFR 吊钩下交货（CFR Ex Tackle）指卖方负责将货物从船舱吊起卸到船舶吊钩所及之处（码头上或驳船上）的费用，在船不能靠岸的情况下，租用驳船的费用和货物从驳船卸到岸上的费用，由买方负担。

→ CFR 舱底交货（CFR Ex Ship's Hold）指货物运到目的港后，由买方自行卸舱，并负担货物从舱底卸到码头的费用。

成本加保险费、运费（……指定目的港），CIF (Cost, Insurance and Freight) (…named port of destination)。CIF 术语是指卖方除具有与 CFR 术语相同的义务外，还应为买方办理货运保险。按 CIF 条件成交，虽然货物在运输途中的灭失和损坏的风险由买方负担，但由于货价构成因素中包括保险费，故卖方必须负责签订保险合同，按约定的险别投保货物运输险，并支付保险费和提交保险单。卖方负责保险，具有代办性质，如果事后发生承保范围内的损失，由买方凭保险单直接向保险公司索赔，能否索赔成功，卖方不负责任。

按 CIF 条件成交，虽然由卖方安排装运和办理货运保险，但卖方并不承担保证把货送到目的港的义务。因为，CIF 属于装运港交货的术语，而不是目的港交货的术语，也就是说，CIF 不是"到岸价"。

由于 CIF 的变形同 CFR 的变形雷同，故在此从略。

FOB	负责出口手续	负责运输、运费、进口手续
CFR	办理租船订舱、出口手续，承担运费	负责办理进口手续
CIF	办理租船订舱、投保、出口手续，承担运费	负责办理进口手续

3.3.3 Three Trade Terms Suitable for All Kinds of Transport 适用于所有运输方式的三种贸易术语

The three commonly used trade terms suitable for all kinds of transport are as follows:

3.3.3.1 FCA (Free Carrier) (…named place)

Seller/ Exporter Premises	Export Documents Formalities	Delivered at named place of: Frontier/Terminal/Quay	Loading Port of Shipment	Onboard		Onboard	Discharging Port of Arrival	Delivered at named place destination: Frontier/Terminal/Quay	Import Document Formalities	Buyer/ Importer Premises
SELLER'S RISKS									BUYER'S RISKS	
SELLER'S COSTS									BUYER'S COSTS	

FCA means that the seller fulfills his obligation to deliver when he has handed over the goods, cleared for export, into the charge of the carrier named by the buyer at the named place or point. If no precise point is indicated by the buyer, the seller may choose within the place or range stipulated where the carrier shall take the goods into his charge.

There are some requirements for adopting FCA: the seller must provide export licenses and go through and supply the goods at the prescribed place; the chosen place of delivery has an impact on the obligations of loading and unloading the goods at that place; the risk of loss of or damage to the goods is transferred from the seller to the buyer at the time the goods at the prescribed place.

货交承运人(……指定地点), FCA (Free Carrier) (...named place)。FCA 术语是指卖方在指定地点将货物交给买方指定的承运人。当卖方将货物交给承运人照管，并办理了出口清关手续，即履行了他的交货义务。如果买方未指定确定地点，则卖方可在规定的地区或范围内选择交货地点，将货物交由承运人照管。应当指出，这里所指的承运人，既包括实际履行运输合同的承运人，也包括签订运输合同的运输代理人。按此术语成交，即使运输代理人拒绝接受承运人的责任，卖方也必须按买方指示把货物交给运输代理人。

3.3.3.2 CPT (Carriage Paid To)(...named place of destination)

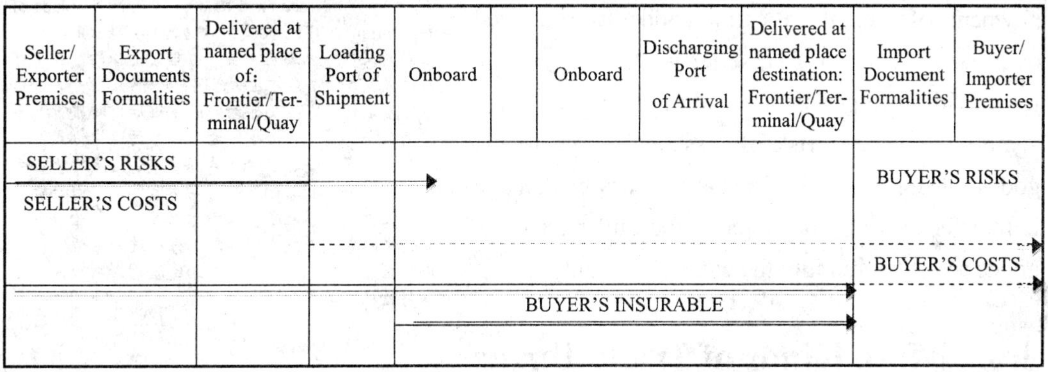

CPT means the seller pays the freight for the carriage of the goods to the named destination. Those destinations could be anywhere in the world, and the risk of loss or damage to the goods, as well as any additional costs due to events occurring after the time the goods have been delivered to the carrier, is transferred from the seller to the buyer when the goods have been delivered into the custody of the carrier. If the buyer does not insure the shipment and if the goods are damaged, you may run the risk of not being paid.

运费付至……(……指定目的地), CPT (Carriage Paid To) (...named place of destination)。CPT 术语是指卖方应支付货物运至指定目的地的运费。这种术语也适用于各种运输方式，其中包括多式联运。按此术语成交，卖方应订立运输合同和支付正常的运费，承担货交第一承运人接管前的一切费用和风险，办理出口清关手续，并提供约定的各项单证；买方则应承担货物在运输途中的灭失或损坏的风险以及货物交由第一承运人接管时起所产生的一切额外费用，在目的地装卸货物，并按合同规定受领单证和支付货款。

3.3.3.3 CIP (Carriage And Insurance Paid to) (…named place of destination)

Seller/ Exporter Premises	Export Documents Formalities	Delivered at named place of: Frontier/Ter-minal/Quay	Loading Port of Shipment	Onboard		Onboard	Dischargin g Port of Arrival	Delivered at named place destination: Frontier/Ter-minal/Quay	Import Document Formalities	Buyer/ Importer Premises
SELLER'S RISKS									BUYER'S RISKS	
SELLER'S COSTS									BUYER'S COSTS	
					BUYER'S INSURABLE					

CIP means that the seller is responsible for the payment of freight to carry goods to a named overseas destination. The seller is also responsible for providing cargo insurance at minimum coverage against the buyer's risk of loss or damage to the goods during transport. The risk of loss or damage is transferred from the seller to the buyer once the goods are delivered into the carrier's custody.

运费、保险费付至（……指定目的地），CIP (Carriage And Insurance Paid to) (…named place of destination)。CIP 术语是指卖方除具有与 CPT 术语相同的义务外，还应为买方办理货运保险。按 CIP 术语成交，卖方签订运输合同，把货物送交承运人，办理货运保险、并提供约定的单证后，即履行了合同的义务。这一术语也可适用于各种运输方式，其中包括多式联运。按 CIP 术语成交，虽然货物在运输途中灭失和损坏的风险由买方负担，但由于货价构成因素包括保险费。故卖方必须签订保险合同，支付保险费，并提交保险单。根据这一术语，卖方应按约定的险别投保。如未约定险别，则卖方只要取得最低限度的保险费即可。

3.4 More Kinds of Trade Terms 其他贸易术语

3.4.1 EXW (Ex Works) (…named place of delivery) 工厂交货

Seller/ Exporter Premises	Export Documents Formalities	Delivered at named place of: Frontier/Ter minal/Quay	Loading Port of Shipment	Onboard		Onboard	Discharging Port of Arrival	Delivered at named place destination: Frontier/Ter minal/Quay	Import Document Formalities	Buyer/ Importer Premises
SELLER'S RISKS									BUYER'S RISKS	
SELLER'S COSTS									BUYER'S COSTS	

EXW means that the seller makes the goods available at its premises. The buyer is responsible for unloading. This term places the maximum obligation on the buyer and minimum obligations on the seller. The Ex Works term is often used when making an initial quotation for the sale of goods without any costs included. EXW means that a seller has the goods ready for collection at his premises (works, factory, warehouse, plant) on the date agreed upon. The buyer pays all transportation costs and also bears the risks for bringing the goods to their final destination. The seller doesn't load the goods on collecting vehicles and doesn't clear them for export. If the seller does load the good, he does so at buyer's risk and cost. If the buyer wishes the seller to be responsible for the loading of the goods on departure and to bear the risk and all costs of such loading, this must be made clear by adding explicit wording to this effect in the contract of sale.

工厂交货（……指定地），EXW (Ex Works) (…named place of delivery)。EXW术语是指卖方在其所在地（即工场、工厂、仓库等）将货物交付买方时，卖方即履行了其交货义务。买方则承担自卖方的所在地将货物运至目的地所需的全部费用和风险。因此，这一术语是卖方承担责任最小的一种。在买方不能直接或间接地办理出口手续的情况下，不宜使用此术语，而应使用 FCA 术语。按此术语成交，除非另有约定，卖方不承担将货物装上买方备妥的运输车辆或办理出口清关手续的责任。

3.4.2 FAS (Free Alongside Ship) (…named port of shipment) 装运港船边交货

Seller/Exporter Premises	Export Documents Formalities	Delivered at named place of: Frontier/Terminal/Quay	Loading Port of Shipment	Onboard		Onboard	Discharging Port of Arrival	Delivered at named place destination: Frontier/Terminal/Quay	Import Document Formalities	Buyer/Importer Premises
SELLER'S RISKS									BUYER'S RISKS	
SELLER'S COSTS									BUYER'S COSTS	

FAS means that the seller must place the goods alongside the ship at the named port. The seller must clear the goods for export. This term is typically used for heavy-lift or bulk cargo.

船边交货（……指定装运港），FAS (Free Alongside Ship) (...named port of shipment)。FAS 术语是指卖方将货物交到指定的装运港船边，卖方即履行了他的交货义务，当卖方履行了船边交货义务后，一切费用和风险即由卖方转给了买方。如果港口吃水浅，船舶不能靠岸，则货物从码头驳运到船边的一切费用和风险，仍应由卖方负担。这一术语，只能适用于海运和内河航运，它要求买方办理出口清关手续，如果买方不能直接地办理出口手续，则不宜使用此术语。

3.4.3 DDP (Delivered Duty Paid) (...named place of destination) 完税后交货

Seller/ Exporter Premises	Export Documents Formalities	Delivered at named place of: Frontier/Terminal/Quay	Loading Port of Shipment	Onboard	Onboard	Discharging Port of Arrival	Delivered at named place destination: Frontier/Terminal/Quay	Import Document Formalities	Buyer/ Importer Premises
SELLER'S RISKS									BUYER'S RISKS
SELLER'S COSTS									BUYER'S COSTS

DDP means that the seller is responsible for delivering the goods to the named place in the country of the buyer, and pays all costs in bringing the goods to the destination including import duties and taxes. The buyer is responsible for unloading. This term is often used in place of the non-Incoterm "Free In Store (FIS)". This term places the maximum obligations on the seller and minimum obligations on the buyer.

完税后交货（……指定目的地），DDP (Delivered Duty Paid) (...named place of destination)。DDP 是指卖方将货物运至进口国指定的目的地，卖方即履行了他的交货义务，按此术语成交，卖方承担的责任最大，即卖方要承担将货物运至进口国最终目的地所产生的一切费用和风险，其中包括关税、捐税及有关交货的其他费用，并需办理进口清关手续。如果双方同意买方办理货物进口清关手续并支付关税，则应使用 DDU 术语为宜。DDP 术语也适用于各种形式的运输。如果卖方不能直接或间接地取得进口许可证，则不要使用这一术语。

3.4.4 DAP (Delivery at Place) (...named place of destination) 指定目的地交货

DAP means that the seller will cover the charges and handle the operations necessary to send the goods to the named place of destination. However, one significant different from the CPT terms is that, DAP requires the seller to bear all risks involved in bring the goods to the named destination. Under DAP, at the time of delivery, the risk and cost related to unloading the goods are for the account of the buyer.

按照 Incoterms 2010 的解释，DAP 的字面意思是“指定目的地交货”。其中，“Place”可以指港口，也可以是陆地的地名。在此情境下，卖方自行负担费用和风险订立运输合同，按惯常路线和方式，在规定日期或期限内，将货物从出口国运到进口国内指定目的地，将货物置于买方支配之下，就算完成交货义务。需要注意的一点是，DAP 合同下，卖方在目的地不需卸货。因此，除了在指定目的地的卸货费用的分担不同外，DAP 和 DAT 的差异并不明显。

3.4.5 DAT (Delivered at Terminal) (...named terminal at port or place of destination) 指定终端交货

The term DAT is one of the two new terms introduced by Incoterms 2010, the other one is DAP. The word "terminal" here is specifically interpreted as the end of a railway line, a bus line, or the centre used by cargo departing for or arriving from. It includes any place, whether covered or not, such as a quay, warehouse, container yard or road, rail or air cargo terminal.

While using DAT, the seller bears all the risks and costs until the goods arrive at the named destination, unloaded from the transporting vehicle at the nominated terminal.

按照 Incoterms 2010 的解释，DAT 是 Delivered At Terminal 的简称，字面意思是“指定终端交货”。其中，“Terminal”可以是目的地的任何地点，如目的地的港口码头、仓库、集装箱堆场或者铁路、公路或航空货运站等，并且卖方需要承担在目的地或目的港港把货物从运输工具上卸下的费用。

在此情境下，卖方自行负担费用和风险订立运输合同，按惯常路线和方式，在规定日期或期限内，将货物从出口国运到进口国内指定目的地或目的港的终端（港口码头、仓库、集装箱堆场或者铁路、公路或航空货运站等），卸货之后，将货物置于买方支配之下，才算完成交货义务。

3.4.6 DAF (Delivered at Frontier) (...named place of delivery) (Unused in Incoterms 2010) 边境交货

根据查证所得的资料，买卖双方仍可在 Incoterms 2010 实施后继续选择使用 Incoterms 2000 的解释，或者如果合同中出现了新版本中没有的术语（如 DAF、DES、DEQ 等）仍将被认为适用早期版本。

Seller/ Exporter Premises	Export Documents Formalities	Delivered at named place of: Frontier/Terminal/Quay	Loading Port of Shipment	Onboard Ship's Rail		Onboard Ship's Rail	Discharging Port of Arrival	Delivered at named place destination: Frontier/Terminal/Quay	Import Document Formalities	Buyer/ Importer Premises
EXAMPLE 1 SELLER'S RISKS					NOT APPLICABLE			EXAMPLE 1 BUYER'S RISKS		
EXAMPLE 1 SELLER'S COSTS					NOT APPLICABLE			EXAMPLE 1 BUYER'S COSTS		
EXAMPLE 2 SELLER'S RISKS								EXAMPLE 2 BUYER'S RISKS		
EXAMPLE 2 SELLER'S COSTS								EXAMPLE 2 BUYER'S COSTS		

DAF can be used when the goods are transported by rail and road. The seller pays for transportation to the named place of delivery at the frontier. The buyer arranges for customs clearance and pays for transportation from the frontier to his factory. The passing of risk occurs at the frontier.

边境交货（……指定地点），DAF (Delivered at Frontier) (...named place of delivery)。DAF 是指卖方将货物运至边境（出口国或进口国边境）指定的地点，并办理了货物出口清关手续后，卖方即履行了他的交货义务。按此术语成交，买卖双方费用和风险的划分，以边境交货地点为界，卖方承担货交买方处置以前的一切费用和风险，买方则承担交货后所发生的一切费用和风险。这一术语，主要适用于铁路或公路运输，也可适用于其他运输方式。

3.4.7 DES (Delivery Ex Ship) (...named port of destination) (Unused in Incoterms 2010) 船上交货

Seller/ Exporter Premises	Export Documents Formalities	Delivered at named place of: Frontier/Terminal/Quay	Loading Port of Shipment	Onboard Ship's Rail		Onboard Ship's Rail	Discharging Port of Arrival	Delivered at named place destination: Frontier/Terminal/Quay	Import Document Formalities	Buyer/ Importer Premises
SELLER'S RISKS								BUYER'S RISKS		
SELLER'S COSTS								BUYER'S COSTS		

Where goods are delivered ex ship, the passing of risk does not occur until the ship has arrived at the named port of destination and the goods made available for unloading to the buyer. The seller pays the same freight and insurance costs as he would under a CIF arrangement. Unlike CFR and CIF terms, the seller has agreed to bear not just cost, but also risk and title up to the arrival of the vessel at the named port. Costs for unloading the goods and any duties, taxes, etc… are for the buyer. A commonly used term in shipping bulk commodities, such as coal, grain, dry chemicals, and where the seller either owns or has chartered, their own vessel.

船上交货（……指定目的港），DES (Delivery Ex Ship) (...named port of destination)。DES 是指卖方将货物运至指定目的港，并在船上交货。按此术语成交，买卖双方责任、费用和风险的划分，以目的港船上办理交接手续为界，卖方承担在目的港船上将货交由买方处置以前的一切费用和风险；买方则承担船上货物交由其处置时起的一切费用和风险，并按合同规定支付货款。

DES 同 CIF 术语存在原则差别，具体表现在下列几个方面：① 交货地点不同，即 CIF 是装运港船上交货，而 DES 是目的港船上交货，② 风险划分不同，即在 CIF 条件下，运输途中的风险由买方负担，而在 DES 条件下，运输途中的风险则由卖方负担。③ 交货方式不同，即 CIF 属象征性交货，而 DES 属实际交货。④ 费用负担不同，即在 CIF 条件下，卖方只负担正常的运费和约定的保险费，而在 DES 条件下，卖方则须负担货物运抵目的港交货前的一切费用，其中包括额外费用。

3.4.8 DEQ (Delivered Ex Quay) (…named port of delivery) (Unused in Incoterms 2010) 码头交货

Seller/ Exporter Premises	Export Documents Formalities	Delivered at named place of: Frontier/Ter-minal/Quay	Loading Port of Shipment	Onboard Ship's Rail		Onboard Ship's Rail	Discharging Port of Arrival	Delivered at named place destination: Frontier/Ter-minal/Quay	Import Document Formalities	Buyer/ Importer Premises
SELLER'S RISKS								BUYER'S RISKS		
SELLER'S COSTS								BUYER'S COSTS		

This is similar to DES, but the passing of risk does not occur until the goods have been unloaded at the port of destination.

码头交货（……指定目的港），DEQ (Delivered Ex Quay) (...named port of delivery)。DEQ 术语是指卖方在指定的目的港码头向买方交货并办理了进口清关手续，即履行了他的交货义务。按此术语成交，卖方应承担将货运至目的港码头所产生的一切费用和风险，其中包括关税、捐税及因交货而发生的其他各项费用，如果双方同意买方办理货物进口清关手续并支付关税，则应使用“关税未付”一词，而不是“关税已付”。DEQ 术语只能适用于海运和内河航运。

3.4.9 DDU (Delivered Duty Unpaid) (…named place of destination) (Unused in Incoterms 2010) 未完税交货

Seller/ Exporter Premises	Export Documents Formalities	Delivered at named place of: Frontier/Terminal/Quay	Loading Port of Shipment	Onboard Ship's Rail		Onboard Ship's Rail	Discharging Port of Arrival	Delivered at named place destination: Frontier/Terminal/Quay	Import Document Formalities	Buyer/ Importer Premises
SELLER'S RISKS									BUYER'S RISKS	
SELLER'S COSTS									BUYER'S COST'S	

DDU means that the seller delivers the goods to the buyer to the named place of destination in the contract of sale. The goods are not cleared for import or unloaded from any form of transport at the place of destination. The buyer is responsible for the costs and risks for the unloading, duty and any subsequent delivery beyond the place of destination. However, if the buyer wishes the seller to bear cost and risks associated with the import clearance, duty, unloading and subsequent delivery beyond the place of destination, then this all needs to be explicitly agreed upon in the contract of sale.

未完税交货（……指定目的地），DDU (Delivered Duty Unpaid) (…named place of destination)。DDU 术语是指卖方将货物运至进口国的指定目的地，卖方即履行了他的交货义务。按此术语成交，卖方应承担将货物运至指定目的地所产生的各项费用和风险，但不包括关税、捐税及进口时应缴纳的官费。买方则应承担因其未能及时办理货物进口清关手续而引起的额外费用和风险。如果双方同意卖方办理海关手续并承担由此引起的风险，应予以明文规定。这一术语，适用于各种形式的运输。采用此术语时，对办理进口清关手续困难和费时的国家，卖方在清关前承担交货义务可能有风险，因此，对那些办理货物进口清关手续困难的国家，卖方不宜使用 DDU 术语。

3.5 Choosing the Proper Trade Terms 选择恰当的贸易术语

The main objective of the Incoterms is to give the two trading parties a guideline of the obligations they need to fulfill. In an actual transaction, which term to choose is eventually determined by the traders' degree of acceptance of cost, obligation and risk. It is very important to consider all the possible aspects while choosing the Incoterms. Traders should not accept any term which requires a performance beyond his ability.

Other criteria for choosing terms may include:

- Competitive position on the transport market
- Pricing purpose
- Exporting and importing possibility
- Ability of risk control
- Availability of transport

Notes

1. Warsaw-Oxford Rules (W.O.Rules) 1932
《华沙—牛津公约》
2. Revised American Foreign Trade Definitions 1941
《1941 美国对外贸易定义修订本》
3. International Rules For the Interpretation of Trade Terms 2010
《国际贸易术语解释通则 2010》
4. FOB (Free on Board) (…named port of shipment)
卖方必须在指定装运港于合同规定装运期内将货物交至买方指定船上，并承担货物装船后的一切费用和货物丢失和损坏风险。
5. CIF (Cost Insurance and Freight) (…named port of destination)
卖方须在合同规定的装运期于装运港将货物装至运往指定目的港的船上，负担货物装船后的一切费用和风险，并负责办理货运保险、支付保费，以及负责租船订舱，支付从发运港至目的港的正常运费。
6. CFR (Cost and Freight) (… named port of destination)
卖方须在合同规定的装运期内在装运港将货物装至运往目的港的船上，负担货越船舷为止的一切费用和风险，并负责租船订舱并支付至目的港的正常运费。
7. FCA (Free Carrier) (…named place)
卖方负责办理货物的出口手续，在指定地点将货物交给买方指定的承运人，即作为履行交货，卖方应承担承运人掌管货物前的一切费用和风险。

8. CPT (Carriage Paid To)(…named place of destination)
卖方支付货物运至指定目的地的运费，在约定地点，在规定日期或期限，将货物交给第一承运人，负责办理出口手续，并承担货物交给第一承运人之前的一切费用和风险。可适用于各种运输方式。

9. CIP (Carriage And Insurance Paid to) (…named place of destination)
卖方除了承担在 CPT 术语下同样的义务外，还须对货物在运输途中的买方风险取得货物保险，订立保险合同，支付保费。

Exercise

1. Translate the following into Chinese or English.

FOB	FCA	CFR
CPT	EXW	DES
CFR	DAF	DDP
DAP		

CFR 班轮条件	CFR 舱底交货
投保	多式联运
内陆水运	

2. Multiple Choices. Make the best choice to fill in the blank of each sentence.

1) There are altogether ______ terms defined by the Incoterms 2010.
A. 6 B. 9 C. 11 D. 13

2) Among all the Incoterms ______ imposes the minimum obligation and cost to the seller.
A. EXW B. DDP C. CIF D. DAP

3) Among all the Incoterms ______ imposes the minimum obligation and cost to the buyer.
A. DDP B. FOB C. EXW D. CIF

4) According to the Incoterms 2010, under FCA the risk of goods will be transferred from the seller to the buyer ______.
A. when the goods are delivered to the named place in the exporting country.
B. when the goods are loaded on the vehicle of a carrier.

C. when the goods are given to the nominated carrier.

D. when the goods are placed at the disposal of the buyer.

5) FOB and CFR share one thing that ________.

A. the seller will be responsible for the unloading at the port of destination.

B. risk is transferred when the goods are loaded on board the vessel.

C. they can be used in any mode of transport.

D. None of above.

6) Under ________ term, it is especially important for the seller to provide shipment notice to the buyer.

A. CIF B. FAS C. CFR D. FOB

7) According to the Incoterms 2010, under CIF if the goods get loose from the hook and fall into the sea during the loading stage, ________ should hold liable for the loss.

A. the seller B. the buyer

C. the carrier D. both the buyer and the seller

3. Match each of the items on the left with its Chinese equivalent on the right.

a. EXW (Ex Works)	1. 船边交货
b. FAS (Free Alongside Ship)	2. 运费付至
c. FCA (Free Carrier)	3. 目的港船上交货
d. FOB (Free On Board)	4. 未完税交货
e. CFR (Cost and Freight)	5. 工厂交货
f. CIF (Cost, Insurance and Freight)	6. 货交承运人
g. CPT (Carriage Paid To)	7. 运费、保险费付至
h. CIP (Carriage and Insurance Paid To)	8. 装运港船上交货
i. DAF (Delivered At Frontier)	9. 成本加运费
j. DES (Delivered Ex Ship)	10. 目的港码头交货
k. DEQ (Delivered Ex Quay)	11. 完税后交货
l. DDU (Delivered Duty Unpaid)	12. 边境交货
m. DDP (Delivered Duty Paid)	13. 成本、保险费加运费

4. Decide whether the following statements are true (T) or false (F).

1) Since under CFR the risk will be transferred when the goods loaded on board the vessel, the seller will not hold any responsibility if the buyer finds the goods not in

conformity with the contracted specifications.

2) If the sales contract contains provisions contrasting to the definition of the Incoterms used, as far as the provisions are legally recognized by relevant lawsuit and regulations, they will be valid.

3) Suppose you are importer, you will select hard currency to go through your business.

4) FCA and CPT have one thing in common that the seller delivers when the goods are handed over to the first carrier nominated by the buyer.

5) Warsaw-Oxford Rules clearly explain the thirteen kinds of trade terms incurrent use.

6) Under CIF term，the seller is responsible for marine insurance，but under CFR term，it is borne by buyer, so on the former occasion the seller take responsible for the risk about loss and damage during transit, and on the latter occasion the buyer is responsible for it.

7) According to the Incoterms 2010, under DAP the buyer is not responsible for unloading the goods from the arriving vehicle at the place of destination.

8) All the trade terms on D group is arrival price.

5. Translate the following sentences into English with the words or phrases given.

1) As the risks and obligations involved on CIF terms, __________(请参考《国际贸易术语解释通则》2010 年版)。(refer to)

2) __________ (关于贵方 6 月 5 日交到的货), we are pleased to inform you that we have today remitted USD15,000 by a promissory note issued by us payable not later than 15 days after its issuance. (in reference to; consignment)

3) As our business is concluded on the basis of CFR, _________ (按照 Incoterms 的规定，你方必须将货物装上船)。(in accordance with)

4) Thank you for your order, which we wish to execute at once, _________(但是我们做生意的宗旨，不论新旧客户一律交现金)。(on cash payment)

5) _________ (由于市场价格经常变动，要保持价格一星期有效是不可能的)。Therefore, they are subject to change without notice and without engagement. (keep the prices open)

6) _________(价格有变动，不另行通知). Please confirm when placing your order and refer to the catalogue Model Number and specifications concerning design and capacity. (subject to)

7) However, in view of your long patronage, we propose _________ (双方各让一步，并

给你方 10%的折扣)。We trust to have you appreciation of our doing so. (meet halfway).

8) We are pleased to _________ (接到贵方 7 月 15 日报价，样品号 1302 衬衫 300 打，到纽约运费、保险费在内价，每打 35 美元) for immediate shipment. (offer)

9) Thank you for your cable of June 5. Please let us know by return of cable _________ (下列货物在 Liverpoop 船上交货 FOB 的最低价格)。(lowest FOB)

10) _________ (因为这是大订单，希望你方照表列价格打 5%的特别折扣)。If our request is agreeable, we will be most anxious to place an order with you.

6. Case Analysis

1) A Chinese import and export company concluded a Sales Contract with a Holland firm on August 5, 2000, selling a batch of certain commodity. The contract was based on CIF Rotterdam at USD 2,500 per metric ton. The Chinese company delivered the goods in compliance with the contract and obtained a clean-on-board Bill of Lading. During transportation, however, 100 metric tons of the goods got lost because of rough sea. Upon arrival of the goods, the price of the contracted goods went down quickly. The buyer refused to take delivery of the goods and effect payment and claimed damages from the seller. How would you deal with this case?

2) A Chinese trading company W concluded a transaction in steel with a US company on the basis of FOB China Port. Company W immediately resold the steel to Company H in Libya on the terms of CFR Liberia. The L/C from W required the price terms to be FOB China Port and the goods to be directly delivered to Liberia. The L/C also required "Freight Prepaid" to be indicated on Bill of Lading. Why did Company W perform so? What should we do about it?

Chapter 4

Delivery of Commodity

货物的交付

Delivery, in the sense of business transaction, denotes the transportation and arrival of the commodity at a designed destination. By shipment it generally means the loading of commodity on board a carrier. Therefore, delivery can never be accomplished without the process of shipment. In international trade, especially during the transportation, commodity is exposed to many unexpected risks that may cause serious loss. In order to avoid such kind of loss, parties of the contract choose transportation insurance as well as forwarding agency. This chapter deals with the delivery issues, including methods of international transportation, types of international transportation insurance, characteristic of forwarding agency and customs system.

货物的交付，简称交货（Delivery），是指卖方自愿将其对货物的占有权转移给买方的行为。

☞ **Learning Objectives:**

After learning this chapter, you are expected to:

→ Distinguish different kinds of cargo transportation;

- → Describe different types of transportation insurance;
- → Remember basic concepts about transportation insurance.

4.1 Transportation of Commodity in International Trade 国际贸易货物的运输

Transportation is an essential facility for the exploitation or development of economic resource on a national or international scale. It allows articles or materials to be conveyed from areas of low utility to areas of high utility and thus minimums costs. It also makes possible specialization in economic development whether it be mining, farming or manufacturing, according to the comparative advantage theory provided by David Ricardo. The commonly used methods of cargo transportation are ocean transport, rail transport, road transport, air transport, postal transport, container transport and international multimodal transportation.

比较优势理论（Comparative advantage theory），由英国经济学家大卫·李嘉图提出，其核心观点是国际贸易的基础是生产技术的相对差别（而非绝对差别），以及由此产生的相对成本的差别。

运输方式的种类很多，其中包括海洋运输、铁路运输、公路运输、航空运输、邮政运输、江河运输、管道运输和联合运输等，具体应由买卖双方在磋商交易时约定。

4.1.1 Ocean Transport 海洋运输

Ocean transport, also called ocean shipping or maritime transport, is the most widely used form of transportation in international trade. For most counties involved in international trade, it is generally regarded as a cheap method of transportation for large quantities of commodities over long distances, due to its low freight cost and conditions and large capacity. However, it may be slow (compared with air), vulnerable to bad weather and inefficient in punctuality. There are two

海洋运输（Ocean transport），是国际贸易中最主要的运输方式。海洋运输不受道路和轨道的限制，通过能力很大，万吨以上、甚至数十万吨的巨轮都可以在海洋中航行，由于海洋运输的运量很大，而运输成本较低，所以许多国家、特别是沿海国家的进出口货物，大部分都采用海洋运输。

但是，海洋运输也有一定的缺点，如易受自然条件限制和季节性影响（如暴风巨浪、港口冰封），航行速度较慢，风险较大等。因此，对于不宜经受长期运输的货物以及需用急切和易受气候条件影响的货物，一般不宜采用海洋运输方式。

main types of ocean transport: liner transport and charter transport, of which the former is more commonly used in international transportation.

4.1.1.1 Liner Transport

A liner is a large commercial ship, especially one that carries passengers on a regular schedule. The liner vessel operates on a scheduled service between a group of ports. Liner transport, also called liner shipping, offering cargo space or passenger accommodation to all shipper and passengers who require them.

所谓班轮（Liner），即指在预先固定的航线上，按照规定的时间和停靠港口航行的船舶。班轮运输（Liner Transport，简称 Liner）也叫定期船运输，它是在一定航线上，在一定的停靠港口，定期开航的船舶运输。班轮运输通常是在固走的航线和港口往返运载货物，按照预先规定的时间表航行，并且由船方负责装卸，其运费按相对固定费率收取，所以对回际贸易货物的运输提供了很大的便利。

The features of liner transport can be summarized as: a fixed freight rate, fixed sailing schedule, fixed route and fixed calling ports.

班轮运输具有“四固定”的特点，即是固定航线、固定港口、固定船期和相对固定的费率。这是班轮运输的最基本特征。

➢ Types of liner transport

Basically, liner transport can be divided into two types: conference liner transport and non-conference liner transport.

Conference liner transport service is provided by shipping conferences which is an association formed by a number of shipping companies of different nationalities. The incentive of conference is that it provides stable freight rate and regular service.

正规班轮运输（Conference liner transport）是以固定的船舶,按照以运行周期为依据编制的船期表靠离港日期组织运行，即定期定港班轮运输。

Non-conference liner transport service, however, is provided by shipping companies that do not belong to any shipping conference. Non-conference liners may or may not have regular sailing schedules between ports. Moreover, the freight rates are determined independently among carriers. Overall, the non-conference liner transports are flexible but they sometimes face the problem of insufficient cargo supply.

非正规班轮运输（Non-conference liner transport）是不定期、不定港、不定船的定线班轮运输，除固定的几个港口外，其余港口视货源情况而定是否停靠，事先不能编制一定期间的船期表。

➢ The freight of liner transport

Freight is the charge for transporting something by common carrier. Generally, the freight of liner transport

运费（transportation expenses，freight）是指支付货运或全部或部分使用船只、火车、飞机或其他类似运输手段的费用。

service consists of two main parts: one is the basic freight rate; the other one is the surcharges.

The basic freight rate is charged for carriage of goods from the port of shipment to the destination.

In practice, the calculation rules of basic freight rate are listed as follows:

1) Weight ton (W)

For items marked with “W” in the tariff, the freight is calculated on the basis of weight ton (WT). Conventionally, one weight ton equals to one metric ton (1,000kg), or one long ton (1,016kg) or one short ton (907.18kg), depending on the measurement system adopted by the shipping company.

2) Measurement ton(M)

For items marked with “W” in the tariff, the freight is calculated on the basis of measurement ton (MT). It is mainly applicable to light cargo of which the weight per cubic meter is less than one metric ton. Conventionally, weight ton and measurement ton are named as freight ton as a basic unit to calculate freight.

3) Weight ton or measurement ton (W/M)

For items marked with “W/M” in the tariff, the freight is calculated on the basis of comparison, one has to follow the larger one between the weight ton and measurement ton. When making a notion that 1 WT is equal to 1 MT.

4) Ad valorem freight (Ad Val)

For items marked with “Ad Val” in the tariff, the freight is calculated on the basis of the value or price of the cargo. It is suitable for high value goods such as valuable artworks, precious metal and sophisticated machines.

基本运费（basic freight rate），货物从装运港到卸货港的基本费用，又分传统的件杂货运费率和集装箱包箱费率。在同一票货或同一提单下出现混装情况时，按“就高不就低”原则计费。

基础费用的计算标准主要有以下几种：

1）货物毛重，即以重量吨（Weight ton）为计算单位收取费用。

2）货物体积，即以尺码吨（Measurement ton）为计算单位收取费用。

3）货物重量或尺码从高收费，即在重量吨和尺码吨中选择较高者收费。

4）货物价格，也称从价运费，一般以有关货物的 FOB 总价值的一定百分比收费。

5) W/M or Ad Val

For items marked with "W/M or Ad Val" in the tariff, the freight is calculated on the basis of the highest one among weight ton, measurement ton and value of cargo.

5）货物重量、尺码或价值中选择最高者收费。

6) Open rate (Open)

For items marked with "Open" in the tariff, the freight is calculated on the basis of temporary or special agreement entered into between carrier and consignor. It is always used for bulk primary cargo of low value.

6）临时议定计价（Open rate），即由货主和船公司临时协商议定。

7) Freight per head (Unit)

For items marked with "Unit" in the tariff, the freight is calculated on the basis of the number of the cargo. Obviously, it is suitable for transporting animals.

7）将每件货物作为一个计费单位收费。

The surcharges are charges in addition to basic freight rate. Main surcharges include: Alteration for excess of liability, Deviation Surcharge, Bunker Adjustment Factor, Port Congestion Surcharge, Heavy Lift Additional, Transshipment Surcharge, Optimal Additional, Over-Length Surcharge, Direct Additional and Port Surcharge.

附加费用（Surcharge）是基本运费外的收费。附加费名目繁多，常见的有：超重附加费、超长附加费、转船附加费、直航附加费、洗舱费、选港附加费、港口附加费、港口拥挤附加费、燃油附加费、货币贬值附加费等等。

➢ The total freight can be calculated according to the following formula:

Total freight = Basic freight rate × Total quantity of cargo × (1+Surcharges rate)

货物运输费用（Freight），简称运费，由基础运费和附加费用构成。

班轮总运费计算公式：

班轮运费=基本运费率×总货运量×(1+附加费率)

4.1.1.2 Charter Transport

Charter transport is another mode of ocean transport. It is a tramp transport service, which means that it has no regular sailing schedule and routes. A tramp picks up cargo only when it is hired by the ship operator. Generally, charter transport is most commonly

租船运输（Charter Transport）是指租船人向船东租赁船舶用于运输货物的业务。租船运输没有预定的船期表，船舶航线和停靠港口不固定。船舶的航线、运输货物种类、航行时间、运费或租金由船货双方在租船合同中议定。适用于大宗货物

used for bulk cargo such as coal, oil and ore as a result of its low freight rate.

如粮食、油料、矿物、化工等运输。

➢ Types of charter transport

In the international transport industry, charter vessels are conventionally divided into three types: voyage charter, time charter and bare boat charter.

在国际运输业务中，租船方式主要有定程租船（Voyage Charter）、定期租船（Time Charter）和光船租船（Bare Boat Charter）三种方式。

Voyage charter, also called trip charter, is the hire of a ship for the carriage of cargos from one specified port to another, or for a round trip. The ship owner is not only responsible for the carriage of cargo including all necessary charges and fees, but also responsible for the management of the whole ship and all crews.

定程租船（Voyage Charter），又称程租船或航次租船，即指按航程（包括单程、来回程和连续单航次）租赁船舶。船舶所有人提供船只，在指定港口间进行一个或数个航次，承运指定货物的租船运输。

Time charter is the hire of a ship for a period of time. It is similar to the voyage charter in terms of the crewing and operating of the ship. However, the ship owner of time charter is only responsible for the management of the ship, the carriage of cargo and the costs incurred therefrom are the obligations of the charterer.

定期租船（Time Charter）是指船舶所有人将船舶出租给承租人，供其使用一定时期的租船运输。承租人可将定期租船作为班轮或定程租船使用。一般期租船在各自航次中所产生的燃料费、港口费、装卸费、垫舱物料费等项费用，均由租船人负担。

Bare boat charter (BBC), or demise charter, is mainly used when there is an unexpected or sudden increase of export cargos to be transported. It is less popular than voyage charter and time charter. Bare boat charter means the hire of the vessel only, and the charterer crews and operates the ship in the charting period.

光船租船（Bare Boat Charter）是指船舶所有人将船舶（空船）租给承租人使用一段时间，而不提供船员和船舶的营运。

➢ Division of loading and unloading cost

There are four methods adopted to divide the cost of loading and unloading:

1) Free In (F.I.)

F.I. indicates that the loading charges are for the account of the charterer/seller.

2) Free out (F.O.)

F.O. indicates that the unloading charges are for the

account of the charterer/receiver.

3) Free in and out (F.I.O.)

F.I.O. indicates that the charterer of a vessel is responsible for the cost of loading and unloading goods from the vessel.

4) Liner terms (Berth Terms)

Berth terms indicate that the carrier is responsible for the cost of loading and unloading of the cargos.

4.1.2 Land Transportation 陆上运输

Land transportation, literally, is used to transport cargo on land. There two main kinds of land transportation: road transport and rail transport.

4.1.2.1 Road Transport

The road vehicle is a low capacity but very versatile unit of transport which is most flexible in its operations. Since the early 1970s, the international road haulier has become increasingly dominant in the UK/Continental trade with some services extending to Asia and the Middle East.

公路运输（Road Transport）是利用汽车在公路上运送客货的运输方式。

One of its most significant advantages is the road vehicle distributive ability. Overall it can offer a door-to-door service without intermediate handling. Moreover, it is very flexible in operation which is particularly useful when circumstances demand a change in routing through road works, a blockage or disrupted shipping services. Therefore, road transport is ideal for carrying general merchandise and selective bulk cargos in small quantities.

公路运输可实现“门到门”直达运输。并且由于公路运输网一般比铁路、水路网的密度要大十几倍，分布面也广，因此公路运输车辆可以“无处不到、无时不有”。公路运输在时间方面的机动性也比较大，车辆可随时调度、装运，各环节之间的衔接时间较短。尤其是公路运输对客、货运量的多少具有很强的适应性。

However, road transport is limited in capacity and vulnerable to high risk of pilferage and damage in transit. Besides, the operation cost of road transport is relatively higher. All of those prevent it from more

然而，公路运输载货有限，运输风险较大，运输成本也高。这些制约了公路运输在国际运输中的广泛使用。

widely used in international transportation.

4.1.2.2 Rail Transport

Rail transport means transporting cargos from a dispatching station to a destination station. The growth of railways as an international link contributes the spread of rail transport. Most of the features of rail transport are quite different from that of road transport.

在国际贸易货物运输中，铁路运输（Railway Transportation）占着相当重要的地位，特别是在内陆国家之间的贸易，铁路运输的作用更为显著。

First of all, rail transport is a major mode of transportation in capacity, only second to ocean transport. Moreover, it is less prone to be interrupted by bad weather conditions. Besides, rail transport is capable of achieving relatively high speed and is most economical especially if it provides the complete trainload for a shipper on a regular basis.

铁路运输具有许多特点，例如铁路火车运行速度较快，载运量较大，不易受气候条件的影响，能终年正常运行，而且在运输当中遭受的风险较小，所以铁路运输具有高度的连续性。

Also, it must be stressed that the rail transport is confined to railroad and therefore less flexible.

4.1.3 Air Transport 航空运输

Air transportation, or air freight, is one of the youngest modes of transportation and undoubtedly continues to make a major contribution to the exploitation of world resources. It simplifies documentation system and provides quick and reliable transits, thus lowering the risks of damage/pilferage, storage and capital tie-up. It is also ideal for palletized consignments and a wide variety of consumer-type cargos.

航空运输（Air Transport）是一种现代化的运输方式，它不受地面条件的限制，航行便利，运输速度很快，航行时间很短，货物中途破损率小。因此，某些急需物资、易损货物和贵重商品适于用航空运输。

航空运输的运费，就其绝对值而言，一般比海洋运输和铁路运输高，但有些商品利用航空运输，其运费反而可以降低。这是因为一方面航空运输计收费的方法不同于其他运输方式，另一方面，采用航空运输还有助于减少包装费、装卸搬运费、仓储费、保险费和利息开支等项附属费用。

However, there are disadvantages of air transportation as well: limited capacity, very high operating expenses as well as initial costs and vulnerability to disruption by the weather.

There are four mainly types of air freight services:

1) Scheduled airlines

Scheduled airlines are operated on a regular service,

over a fixed airline and between fixed airports. Regular schedule departures, specified routes with fixed base ports at fixed freight rates are the characteristics of scheduled airlines. Therefore, they are suitable for conveying fresh, seasonal and perishable goods.

班机运输（Scheduled Airlines），是指客、货班机定时、定点、定线的运输，它适用于载运数量较小的货物。

2) Chartered carriers

Charter carriers are the hire of the entire of partial space of an aircraft by a shipper or several shippers to deliver goods. They are usually adopted for carrying cargos of large quantities or carrying cargos of different shippers to the same destination.

包机运输（Chartered carriers），是指包租整架飞机运输货物而言，它适用于载运数量较大、有急需或有特殊要求的货物。

3) Consolidated consignment

Consolidated consignment means that the air freight agent/forwarder usually assembles several individual shipments arriving at the same destination into one consignment and dispatches them on one air waybill. Many shippers prefer this kind of shipment since the freight rate is 7%—10% lower than that of a scheduled airline published by IATA (i.e. International Air Transport Association).

集中托运（Consolidated consignment）是指航空货运公司把若干单独发运的货物组成一整批货物，用一份总运单整批发运到预定目的地，由航空货运公司在那里的代理人收货、报关、分拨后交给实际收货人。

4) Air express

In international trade practice, air express is regarded as the fastest and safest mode to carry goods from one place to another place. However, its freight rate is much higher than that of the other types of air transport.

航空急件传送（Air express），也称为桌到桌运输（Desk to Desk Service），是目前国际运输中最快捷的运输方式。它是由一个专门经营此项业务的机构与航空公司密切合作，设专人用最快的速度在货主、机场、收件人之间传送急件。

The growth of the international air freight market has been spectacular in recent years, and the trend towards developing larger capacity air freight will continue to meet such demand and facilitate optimum performance and operation. Moreover, the air freight operator tends to formulate a global approach to the market using high tech means, involving the most advantage satellite and computer links available.

4.1.4 Container Transport 集装箱运输

集装箱运输（Container Transport）是一种新型的现代运输方式。集装箱运输是以集装箱作为运输单位进行货物运输的一种现代化运输方式。集装箱运输可适用于海洋运输、铁路运输、公路运输、航空运输等。

Containerization is a method of distributing merchandise in a unitized form thereby permitting an inter-model transports system to be evolved providing a possible combination of ocean, rail, road and canal transport. It is an important element of the logistics revolution that changed freight handling in the 20th century. With the fast development of containerization, container transport, therefore, are wildly used in delivery of commodity.

The growth of containerization will continue throughout the next decades, emerging from three sectors:

1) The transfer from the bulk cargo diversion, particularly the reefer, dry bulk and fruit carriers;
2) Organically as the benefits of containerization through multi-modalism and logistic focus accelerate trade development;
3) The outsourcing/relocation of industrial production from high labor cost, highly regulated developed economies in European and North American to lower cost, less regulated developing economies in the Far East and China/India.

The containerization process of recent years is resulting in increased carrying capacity being deployed by the largest liner operator. Meanwhile, the growth of containerization is further stimulated by the accelerating expansion of the integration of containerized shipping movement with either air freight or a rail land-bridge.

Undoubtedly, long-term containerization will be

virtually the only method of general merchandise distribution in the major deep-sea trades, and already some 90 percent of such trades are containerized. Moreover, to transport cargo by container transport, the carriers must stow large quantity of cargo into standard-sized and reusable vans at the manufacturer's plant inland, or at Container yard (CY) or the container freight station (CFS), and then ship them in unit loads to its destination. During transit, containers are loaded and unloaded by mechanical devices. From the moment a container is lacked and sealed, the cargo inside is kept intact until it reaches the final destination.

➢ Features of containerization

集装箱运输的特征：

The main feathers of containerization can be summarized as follows:

1) Low risk of cargo damage and pilferage enables more favorable cargo premiums to be obtained compared with break-bulk cargo shipments and individual air freight consignments;

1）提高了货运速度，加快了运输工具、货物及资金的周转。

2) Less packing fees for containerized consignments. In some cases, especially with specialized ISO (International Standard Organization) containers such as refrigerated ones or tanks (liquid or powder), packing is required. This leads to substantial cost savings and raising service quality;

2）节省货物包装费用，减少货物运杂费支出。

3) The elimination of intermediate handling coupled with the other inherent advantages of containerized shipments tends to permit the cargo to arrive in a better condition thereby enhancing the quality of service;

3）加速船舶周转，降低营运成本。

4) Faster transits, coupled with more reliable maritime schedules and ultimately increased service frequency,

4）提高了货运速度，加快了运输工具、货物及资金的周转。

produce savings in warehouse accommodation needs, lessen the risk of obsolescent stock and speed up capital turnover;

5) It can be handled quickly and easily by standardized equipment and can thus save labors and loading and unloading charges.

5）提高装卸效率，扩大港口吞吐能力，节省人力及装卸费。

➢ Types of container and container transport service

There are many kinds of container to serve various needs of cargo transportation. Containers can be divided into dry freight container (formally called general purpose container), refrigerated container, tanker container (used for liquid cargo in bulk) and car container (used for carrying cars).

A brief description of container types is given below:

1) Dry freight container

The dry freight container, formally called general purpose container, is designed for all types of general merchandise and, with suitable modification, for the carriage of bulk cargos both solid and liquid.

普通集装箱，又称干货集装箱（Dry freight container），以装运件杂货为主，通常用来装运文化用品、日用百货、医药、纺织品、工艺品、化工制品、五金交电、电子机械、仪器及机器零件等。这种集装箱使用范围极广，占集装箱总数的 70%～80%，常用的有 20 英尺和 40 英尺两种，其结构特点是常为封闭式，一般在一端或侧面设有箱门。

2) Insulated container

The Insulated container protects against heat loss or gain and is used in conjunction with a blown-air refrigeration system to convey perishable or other cargo which needs to be carried under temperature control.

保温集装箱（insulated container）箱内有隔热层，箱顶又有能调节角度的进出风口，可利用外界空气和风向来调节箱内温度，紧闭时能在一定时间内不受外界气温影响。适宜装运对温度及湿度敏感的货物。

3) Fruit container

The fruit container has been developed to carry fresh deciduous and citrus fruit, the internal dimensions being slightly larger than the standard insulated container to accommodate the pacing of standard fruit pallets and cases.

4) Refrigerated container

The refrigerated container is designed to operate independently of a blown-air refrigerated system and is fitted with its own refrigeration units which require an electrical power supply for operation. Each container is capable of being set at its own individual temperature.

冷藏集装箱（Refrigerated Container），是指具有一定隔热性能，能保持一定低温，适用于各类食品冷藏储运输而进行特殊设计的集装箱。

Basically, the majority of containers used are built to ISO specification thereby permitting their ease of ubiquitous use on an international scale. The basic container most commonly built of steel or aluminum modal sizes are 2.45m (8ft)×2.45m (8ft)×12.20m (40ft), 2.60m (8.6ft)×2.45m (8ft)×12.20m (40ft) and 2.45m (8ft)×2.45m (8ft)×6.10m (20ft).

Container transport provides diversified services as well. Responding to the capacity needed, container transport offers both FCL and LCL services. If the cargo is of a container load, FCL service shall be adopted while if the cargo is of small quantity, FCL is not suitable as freight for FCL is calculated based on container capacity and the origin and destination of the cargo, not on the quantity of the cargo involved. In such cases, LCL service is preferred as it enables the shipper to have his cargo shipped at reasonable freight rate. In terms of cargo in small quantity, total freight under LCL is much less than that under FCL because LCL allows the carrier to ship the cargo at lower cost by consolidating them with consignments of different shippers, which are to be delivered to the same destination.

4.1.5 International Multi-modal Transport 国际多式联运

International multi-modal transport, also called international combined transport, means the carriage of

国际多式联运（International Multi-modal Transport）是在集装箱运输的基础

cargo by at least two modes of transportation on the basis of a multi-modal transport contract from the place of sellers in one country to the place of buyers in another country. It is a brand new mode of transportation in the transport industry following the development of containerization of international transportation, and has become more and more popular in the competitive market.

上产生和发展起来的综合性连贯运输方式，一般是以集装箱为媒介，把海陆空各种传统的单一运输方式有机结合起来，组成一种国际间的连贯运输。

A strong feature of the practice of international multi-model transport is that only one multi-modal transport operator takes the responsibility for taking the cargo from the consigner and delivering them to the consignee. So, only one contract and one fright rate are required for the whole process. This leads to great improvements in the operating efficiency, lowering the operating cost and cutting down the time of cargo delivery. All of these advantages make it no doubt that international multi-modal transport will contribute significantly to a changing international trade pattern.

4.1.6 Other Means of Transportation 其他运输方式

Besides the above main means of international transportation, there are also other means of transportation adopted in the industry.

4.1.6.1 Canals and Inland Waterway Transport

Canals and inland waterway throughout the world are developing at a time of intermodal development driven by a logistics environment. In many countries, especially Europe, increased road congestion and the need introduction of tolls on major highways, coupled with the need for a cleaner environment, is encouraging the pro-canal and inland waterway political lobby. The growth of containerization is also making a contribution

内河运输（Inland Water Transportation）是指使用船舶通过国际内江湖河川等天然或人工水道，运送货物和旅客的一种运输方式。它是水上运输的一个组成部分，是内陆腹地和沿海地区的纽带，也是边疆地区与邻国边境河流的连接线，在现代化的运输中起着重要的辅助作用。

with its ease of intermodal transfer.

Inland waterway barge distribution acting as port feeder services operates in many developing and less developed countries. Such services are long established and examples are found in the markets of Africa, the subcontinent and the Far East. Meanwhile, the developed economies of the world, particularly Europe, are now putting more emphasis and investment on providing a transport infrastructure in which inland waterway plays a more significant role in their economic development.

Overall, it remains a low-cost form of distribution for volume cargos often of low value with modern transshipment facilities and high economic utilization of modern tonnage. The development of containerization with inland hub distribution centres, as found in Duisburg, is an example of intermodal transport logistically driven networks.

4.1.6.2 Pipeline Transport

The basic advantage of a pipeline is the low cost of distribution with virtually no labor content transport in the distribution network. Although costs of installing the pipeline system may be moderately high, the distribution costs are relatively low. Another basic advantage is the 24-hour availability of the pipeline and its low maintenance. Conversely, the pipeline has a fixed capacity which inhibits market growth unless a further pipeline is installed. It has many advantages from an environmental point of view with virtually no noises or fumes. Little disruption is caused to the environment during installation compared with road or rail development. Moreover, it permits more than one type of product to be distributed.

管道运输 (Pipeline Transport) 是用管道作为运输工具的一种长距离输送液体和气体物资的输方式，是一种专门由生产地向市场输送石油、煤和化学产品的运输方式，是统一运输网中干线运输的特殊组成部分。管道运输石油产品比水运费用高，但仍然比铁路运输便宜。大部分管道都是被其所有者用来运输自有产品。

4.1.6.3 Palletization

Palletization is a growth market in container shipment involving multi-modalism. It is the process of placing or anchoring the consignment to a pallet or base made of wood or metal, and is a very common technique in air freight where the pallet accompanies the consignment throughout the transit from the factory premises to the retailer. A shrink wrapping technique is frequently used. It may be a stillage involving base plates; the box pallets where one side can be dropped; or the skeleton pallet for lightweight cargos.

托盘运输（Palletization）也是一种比较先进的运输方式。目前世界上许多国家，特别是在一些还没有条件采取集装箱运输的地方，都在大力推广托盘化运输。因为托盘化不需大量投资，普通库场、码头都可使用。一般船舶只要甲板、货仓平整，能允许铲车作业，即能承运托盘化货物。

4.1.7 Transport Documents 运输单据

An important part of international trade practice is a good comprehension of the various documents involved in processing the trade consignment. Moreover, the need to understand the role of these documents and their limitations is likewise important.

4.1.7.1 Ocean Bill of Landing

A bill of landing (abbreviated generally as B/L) is a receipt for goods shipped on board a vessel, signed by the person (or his or her agent) who contracts to carry them and stating the conditions in which the goods were delivered to (and received by) the ship. It is not the actual contract, which is inferred from the action of the shipper or ship owner in delivering or receiving the commodities, but forms excellent evidence of the terms of the contract. It is a document of title to the goods which is the subject of the contract between the buyer (importer) and seller (exporter). It is the most important commercial document in international trade, and is used to control delivery of goods transported by sea.

提单（Bill of Lading 简称 B/L）是货物承运人（或其代理人）在收到货物后签发给托运人的一种证件，它体现了承运人和托运人之间的相互关系。

提单的性质与作用主要表现在以下三个方面：

1. 它是承运人（或其代理人）签发给托运人的货物收据（Receipt for the goods）证实已按提单记载的事项收到货物，承运人应凭提单所列内容向收货人交货。

2. 它是代表货物所有权的凭证。

3. 它是承运人和托运人双方同意的运输契约的证明。

The bill of landing starts its life (in most cases) containing or evidencing the contract of carriage between the carrier and the shipper, under which the carrier and the shipper promises that the goods will be carried from the port of landing and safely delivered at the port of discharge. During the voyage, the ownership of the goods will be normally transferred from the initial seller to the ultimate receiver who will take delivery of the goods from the ship. There may in exceptional cases be 100 or more buyers who (or whose banks) will pay for the goods and then receive payment from the next buyer in the chain. During this process the goods are, of course, not in the possession of any of the parties. They are, or should be, safely on board the ship, steadily crossing the ocean. Neither the buyer of an unascertained portion of a bulk nor an indorsee after discharge has rights against the carrier.

Basically, the B/L indicates that the goods have been loaded on board or have been shipped on a named vessel, and it will be signed or authenticated by the carrier or the master, or the agent on behalf of the carrier or the master.

➢ Types of B/L

海运提单的类型

The bill of landing can be divided into various types according to different standards.

1) Shipped B/L and received B/L

Based on whether the goods have been loaded on board the carrying vessel, B/L can be divided into shipped (also called on board) B/L and received B/L (also called received for shipment B/L).

→ Shipped B/L confirms the goods are actually on board the vessel. It is the most satisfactory type of receipt and the shipper prefers such a bill as

已装船提单（Shipped B/L）是指货物装船后，由承运人签发给托运人的提单，它必须载明装货船名和装船日期。

there is no doubt about the goods being on board and, in consequence, disputes on this point will not arise with the banks or consignee, thereby facilitating the earliest financial settlement of the export sale.

装船日期经常以签发提单的日期来证明。由于已装船提单对收货人按时收货有保障，因此，在买卖合同中一般都规定卖方须提供已装船提单。

→ Received B/L arises where the word 'shipped' does not appear on the bill of landing. It merely confirms that the goods have been handed over to the ship-owner and are in his or her custody. Such a bill does not show the name of the carrying vessel and the date of shipment, therefore, the date of arrival of the goods is difficult to anticipate. Generally, the received B/L is usually not acceptable to buyers and banks.

备运提单（Received B/L）又称收讫待运提单，是承运人在收到托运货物等待装船期间，向托运人签发的提单。这种提单有利于船方争揽货载。由于这种提单没有肯定的装货日期，而且往往不注明装运船只的名称，即使注明也多系拟装船名，将来货物能否装出，以及能否凭单提到货物，都很难预料，加之，在有些国家还可能发生根本未收到货物就出具备运提单的欺诈行为，因此，进口商一般都不愿接受这种提单。

2) Direct B/L, transhipment B/L and through B/L

According to the means of transportation involved in transit, we can divide bill of landing into three types: direct B/L, transhipment B/L and through B/L.

→ A direct B/L means that the cargoes are transported from the port of landing direct to the port of destination without involving transhipment.

直达提单（Direct B/L）是指承运人对自装运港直接运到目的港的货物所签发给托运人的提单。

→ A transhipment B/L means that the cargoes need to be transshipped at an intermediate port from one vessel to another before reaching the final destination.

转船提单（Transhipment B/L）是指在装运港装货的船舶，不直接驶往目的港。而在中途其他港口换船，转运至目的地，由第一程承运人在装运港签发运往最后目的港的提单。

→ Besides, the on-carriage may be either by a second vessel or by a different form of transport. That induces the use of through B/L, which enables a through rate to be quoted and is growing in popularity with the development of containerization.

联运提单（Through B/L）是由第一承运人或其代理人在货物起运地签发运往货物最终目的地的提单，并收取全程运费，货物到达转运港后，由前一承运人或其代理人代为将货物交给下一段航程的承运人或其代理人，继续运往目的地。联运提单用于海陆联运或海河联运或海海联运。

3) Clean B/L and unclean B/L

Based on the condition of cargoes, bill of landing can be divided into two types: clean B/L and unclean B/L.

→ A clean B/L states that the cargoes have been shipped in apparent good order and condition. By issuing the clean B/L, the ship-owner admits his or her full liability of the cargo described in the bill under the law and his or her contract. This type is much favored by banks for financial settlement purpose.

→ An unclean B/L, also named foul B/L or dirty B/L, contains unfavorable notation about the apparent condition of the cargoes. It is usually unacceptable to the buyer and banks.

清洁提单是指交运货物的外表状况良好（In Apparent Good Order and Condition），承运人未加有关货损或包装不良之类批注的提单。在买卖合同中，一般都明确规定卖方提供的已装船提单必须是清洁提单。卖方提交了清洁提单，才能取得货款。

不清洁提单（Unclean B/L，Foul B/L，Dirty B/L）是指承运人加注了这类表明货物外表状况不良或存在缺陷的批语的提单。

4) Long form B/L and short form B/L

According to the complexity or simplicity of the bill content, bill of landing can be divided into two types: long form B/L and short form B/L.

→ A long form B/L is more detailed with shipping contract clause printed on the back of the page.

→ Meanwhile, a short form B/L, also called blank back B/L, is an abbreviated type of B/L, smaller and not containing the long list of detailed clauses that generally appear on bill of landing.

全式提单（Long Form B/L）是指通常应用的带有背面条款的提单。这种提单除其正面必要的项目外，在其背面还列有各项有关装运的条款，以表明承运人和托运人的权利与义务。

略式提单（Short Form B/L）是指内容简略而不带背面条款的提单。这种提单仅保留其正面的必要项目。

5) Straight B/L, bearer B/L and order B/L

Based on the address of the consignee, bill of landing can be divided into three types: straight B/L, bearer B/L and order B/L.

→ A straight B/L indicates that the shipper will deliver the goods to the consignee. It is often used when payment for the goods has been made in advance.

记名提单（Straight B/L）是指发给指定的收货人的提单，在提单中的收货人栏内，具体填明收货人的名称。这种提单只能是指定的收货人提货，不能转让，因而又称为“不可转让提单”。

→ A bearer B/L, also called open B/L or blank B/L, means that the bill in which the name of a definite consignee is not mentioned and left blank of open. A bearer B/L can be transferred without endorsement.

→ An order B/L is made out in such way that the goods are consigned or destined to the order of a named person instead of a definite consignee. As it is a negotiation, a shipper's order B/L can be bought, sold or traded while cargoes are in transit and is commonly used for letter of credit transaction. The buyer usually needs the original or copy as a proof of ownership to take possession of the cargoes.

不记名提单（Bearer B/L）又称空名提单，即指在提单收货人栏内不填写收货人或指示人的名称而留空，提单持有人可不作任何背书，就能凭提单转让货物所有权或提取货物，承运人只凭提单交货。

指示提单（Order B/L）是指在提单的收货人栏内只填写："凭指定书"（To order）或"凭某人指定"（To order of...）字样的一种提单。这种提单可以背书转让。背书的方法有两种：单纯签字盖章的，称空白背书；除背书人签字盖章以外，还列有被背书人的名称的，称记名背书。提单经背书后可转让给其他第三者，因而又称为"可转让的提单"。

6) Other types of bill of landing

→ Stale B/L is presented to the consignee or the buyer or his bank after the goods are due at the port of destination.

过期提单（Stale B/L）是指货物装船后，卖方向当地银行提交装船提单时，银行按正常邮程预计收货人不能在船抵目的港之前收到的提单。

→ On deck B/L indicates that the goods are stowed and shipped on deck. It applies to cargoes like livestock, plant, dangerous cargo or awkwardly-shaped cargoes that cannot fit into the ship's holds.

舱面提单（On Deck B/L）是指承运人对装于船舶甲板上的货物所签发给托运人的提单，故又称甲板货提单。

→ Ante-dated B/L means that when the actual shipment date is later than that stipulated in the letter-of-credit, the carrier sometimes, at the shipper's request, issues a bill of landing with a date of signature that suits the requirement so as to avoid non-acceptance by the bank.

倒签提单(Ante-dated B/L)，是指承运人应托运人的要求在货物装船后，提单签发的日期早于实际装船完毕日期的提单。

→ Advanced B/L is issued before actual loading of the cargoes is completed or even before the commencement of the actual loading operation. The difference between advanced B/L and

预借提单（Advanced B/L），是指货物尚未装船或尚未装船完毕的情况下，信用证规定的结汇期（即信用证的有效期）即将届满，托运人为了能及时结汇，而要求承运人或其代理人提前签发的已

ante-dated B/L is that an advanced B/L is issued before actual loading is finished while an ante-dated B/L is issued after it.

装船清洁提单，即托运人为了能及时结汇而从承运人那里借用的已装船清洁提单。

4.1.7.2 Consignment Note (for land)

Consignment note are adopted for both rail transport and road transport. The consignment note for rail transport is also named rail waybill, which serves as the contract of carriage between the railway and consignor, evidencing the receipt of the goods and the date of acceptance for the carriage by the carrier. The consignment note will be delivered with the goods from the departure station to the consignee at the destination against payment of the amounts by the consignee. Different from bill of landing, it isn't a document of title and isn't negotiable.

托运单（Booking Note, B/N）俗称下货纸，是托运人根据贸易合同和信用证条款内容填制的，向承运人或其代理办理货物托运的单证。承运人根据托运单内容，并结合船舶的航线、挂靠港、船期和舱位等条件考虑，认为合适后，即接受托运。

Likewise, road consignment note evidences the place and the date of taking over carriage of the goods and the place designed for delivery.

The consignment note is made out in three copies that signed by sender and carrier. In addition, only the first one is original kept by the seller, the second copy accompanies the consignment which is finally delivered to the consignee at the destination and the third copy usually goes to the carrier.

4.1.7.3 Air Waybill

Air waybill, also called air consignment note, is the consignment note used for the carriage of goods by air. It is not a document of title or a transferable or negotiable instrument. The air waybill is basically a receipt for the goods for dispatch and is prima facie evidence of the conditions of carriage. Overall, there are usually three originals and twelve copies of each air waybill.

空运提单(Air Waybill)是指承运货物的航空承运人（航空公司）或其代理人，在收到承运货物并接受托运人空运要求后，签发给托运人的货物收执。空运提单不是代表货物所有权的凭证，不能通过背书进行转让，也不以交出提单作为提货的条件。

4.1.7.4 Multi-modal Transportation Document

Multi-modal transportation document, also called combined transportation document, evidences the contract of the carriage of the goods by at least two means of transport. It is issued by a multi-modal transportation operator under a multi-modal transportation contract. Multi-modal transportation document is similar to through B/L but is boarder than that. Moreover, multi-modal transportation document can be made out either negotiable or non-negotiable.

多式联运单据（Multimodal Transport Document or Combined Transport Documents，简称 MTD 或 CTD）是指证明国际多式联运合同成立及证明多式联运经营人接管货物，并负责按照多式联运合同条款支付货物的单据。

4.1.8 Shipment Clause in Contract 合同中的装运条款

In a sales contract, the shipment clause usually include: time of shipment, quantity of shipment, port of shipment and port of destination, partial shipments, transshipment and shipping advice.

4.1.8.1 Time of Shipment

Time of shipment is an important element of the shipment clause in the sales contract. Obviously, if the time of shipment does not conform to that stipulated in the contract, the buyer may ask for a claim or even cancel the contract. It must be stressed that time of shipment is indifferent from time of delivery for all shipment contracts, but completely different from time of delivery for all arrival contracts.

When deciding on the time of shipment, there are many issues need to be concerned:

1) The time of shipment stipulated in contract should be sufficient in terms of availability in goods, shipping space and payment. That is, we should try to have a clear mind about the sailing route and the ports. Also, we are expected to understand the

features of the goods to be carried. Moreover, we should make sure that the expiry date of the L/C should be about fifteen days later than the shipping date to convenience the seller to prepare documents.

2) The time of shipment should be stipulated in a clear and explicit way. However, we must try to know the market condition and the sale season of the goods. That is, some customary terms must be adopted to give the definite time or period of time and to fix the time of shipment to the time of the L/C.

4.1.8.2 Port of Shipment and Port of Destination

Port of shipment is the port where the goods are shipped and depart from, while port of destination is the port where the goods are ultimately discharged. The port of shipment is usually decided by the seller and the port of destination is decided jointly by the seller and the buyer.

装运港（Port of Shipment），一般是指将货物装上运载工具的港口。

目的港（Port of Destination），是指货物运载工具的航程终点和最终卸货的港口。在国际贸易实践中，目的港通常是由买方提出并经卖方同意后确定的。

When determining the port of shipment and the port of destination, the following should be considered:

1) The stipulation of the port of destination should be definite and specific.
2) Problems about port facilities, regulations, specific transportation conditions, charges and possible sanction should be taken into consideration.
3) The shipment port should be close to the origin of the goods.
4) Name of the country and the place should be put in front of the name of the port to avoid the possibility of different ports having the same name.

4.1.8.3 Partial Shipment and Transshipment

To facilitate delivery, clause about the issue of partial shipment and transshipment must also be carefully stipulated in the contract. According to UCP 600, when

转船（Transshipment）指在远洋运输中，货物装船后允许在中途港换装其他船舶转运至目的港。按照《跟单信用证统一惯例》的规定，如果信用证未明确

the contract or L/C does not clearly stipulate the partial shipment or transshipment is prohibited, transshipment or partial shipment are allowed. Generally, partial shipment and transshipment are popular to sellers, as they put the sellers in a more flexible position to perform the contract.

规定禁止转船，则视为可以转船。

Partial shipment means that the commodities under a contract are to be shipped in more than one lot. Meanwhile, transshipment means unloading and reloading from one vessel to another during the course of ocean carriage from the port of loading to the port of discharge stipulated.

分批装运（Partial shipment）是一个合同项下的货物先后分若干期或若干次装运。在国际贸易中，凡数量较大，或受货源、运输条件、市场销售或资金的条件所限，有必要分期分批装运、到货者，均应在买卖合同中规定分批装运条款。如为减少提货手续，节省费用，在进口业务中要求国外出口人一次装运货物的，则应在进口合同中规定不准分批装运（partial shipment，not allowed）条款。

4.2 International Transportation Insurance 国际运输保险

In international trade, it's most important to have insurance cover against loss or damage that may occur during shipment. The export sales contract with the buyer must clearly state who is responsible for arranging the insurance at all stages from the time the commodities leave the exporter's premises until the buyer takes possession.

One of the basic principles of this type of insurance is that the cause of loss or damage must be an external calamity which was unforeseeable and on which the parties could exert no influence. Loss or damage caused by the insured's own fault or negligence cannot be covered.

Consequently, the transport insurance contract never provides cover for loss arising as a result of inherent defects or spoilage of the commodities.

4.2.1 Basic Concepts of Cargo Insurance 货物保险的基本概念

4.2.1.1 Parties Involved in Cargo Insurance

The two basic parties involved in a cargo insurance are insurer and insured. However, in some cases, there may be an insurance broker in between. Meanwhile, once damages occur, the party suffers will lodge a claim against the insurance policy. This party is called claimant.

- Insurer. It is the party to the insurance contract who promises to indemnify losses or provides service, which always indicates the insurance company or the individuals who run an insurance firm. In China, the People's Insurance Company of China (PICC) has made great contributions to the prevention of Chinese exports/imports from perils and dangers.

保险人（Insurer），又称“承保人”，是指与投保人订立保险合同，并承担赔偿或者给付保险金责任的保险公司。

中国人民人寿保险股份有限公司（People's Insurance Company of China, PICC）

- Insured. It refers to the one who buys insurance from the insurer or the insurance firm. Basically, the insured may be the buyer under FOB contract, or the seller under CIF contract, or the insurance company that may have no insurable stake such as the carrying vessel.

被保险人（Insured），是指其财产或人身受保险合同保障，享有保险金请求权的人。

- Insurance broker. It is the middleman in insurance business. The broker has the advantage of being familiar not only with the technicalities of marine insurance but also has an unbiased view over the coverage and premium rates offered by all insurance companies. For big companies, it is usually worth using the service of the insurance broker.

保险经纪人（Insurance Brokers），是指代表被保险人在保险市场上选择保险人或保险人组合，同保险方洽谈保险合同条款并代办保险手续以及提供相关服务的中间人。

- Claimant（索偿人）. Whenever an actual loss occurs, the insured can get fair, efficient and rapid adjustment of his claim. While insurance may be arranged by the exporter, the importer is the rightful owner consequently; claims are usually made by the importer, after discovering a loss.

4.2.1.2 Fundamental Principles of Cargo Insurance

货物保险遵循的基本原则

The basic principles of cargo insurance are insurable interest, utmost good faith, indemnity and proximate cause.

➢ Insurable interest

Insurable interest refers to the legal right to enter into an insurance contract. A person will have an insurable interest in a marine advantage (any ship goods or other movables exposed to maritime perils) if the event insured against could cause that person a financial loss.

保险利益原则（Insurable Interest Principle），又称"可保利益"或"可保权益"原则。所谓保险利益是指投保人或被保险人对其所保标的具有法律所承认的权益或利害关系。即在保险事故发生时，可能遭受的损失或失去的利益。

It is important to classify between the subject matter insured and insurable interest. Insurable interest is the financial interest of a person in the subject matter insured. Therefore, the insurable interest of the cargo owner is not the commodities—the subject matter insured—but his financial interest in such commodities and, accordingly, he should insure to the extent of that interest.

The most common forms of insurable interest in cargo insurance are as follows:

→ Ownership of the goods. The cargo owner has an insurable interest in the goods since he will benefit by their safe arrival or be prejudiced by loss of or damage thereto. Ownership often involves two parties—the seller and the buyer, or consignee and consignor. The insurance requirements of these parties will depend on the terms of the contract of sale.

→ Charges of insurance (premium). The assured

has an insurable interest in the premium paid in respect of any insurance he may affect. The sum insured reflects the cost of the goods plus the cost of insurance.

→ Freight. Freight is the cost of transporting the commodities from the consignor's premises to the consignee's premises and is either pre-paid or payable at destination. The sum insured reflects the cost of the commodities plus the cost of insurance plus the cost of transportation.

➢ Utmost good faith

Utmost good faith must be observed by both the assured and insurer in the formation of a contract of cargo insurance. If either party fails to observe the utmost good faith, the other party may avoid the contract.

In fact, it would not be practical or, indeed, possible for insurers to check the accuracy or completeness of information submitted to them in respect of a risk to be insured. The have to rely on the other party—the proposer or the broker acting on his behalf—observing the principle of utmost good faith which means a full disclosure of all material circumstances relating to the risk before the contract is concluded. A material circumstance is one which would influence a prudent insurer as to the desirability of the risk. Where there is a non-disclosure of a material circumstance, the insurer may avoid the contract. The insurer may also avoid the contract if the broker is guilty of misrepresenting the risk during the placing negotiations.

➢ Indemnity

The principle of indemnity provides that after indemnity the insured may not be in a better, or worse,

最大诚信原则(Utmost Good Faith),其含义可表述为：保险合同当事人订立合同及合同有效期内，应依法向对方提供足以影响对方做出订约与履约决定的全部实质性重要事实，同时绝对信守合同订立地约定与承诺。否则，受到损害的一方，按民事立法规定可以此为由宣布合同无效，或解除合同，或不履行合同约定的义务或责任，甚至对因此受到的损害还可以要求对方予以赔偿。

position than they were in before the loss. In the event of loss of or damage to the subject matter insured resulting from an insured peril, he is placed in the same position that he enjoyed immediately before the loss occurred.

While replacement is the means of effecting indemnity in some types of insurance, it would not be practical for marine insurers to replace ships and cargos. The manner of indemnity is, therefore, a cash settlement.

➢ Proximate cause

The proximate cause principle is employed in the judgment of causation between accidents and losses. It refers to the major and/or effective reason that has caused the accident. That is to say, the proximate cause is not necessarily the first cause or the last cause, but the dominant cause. Therefore, the insurer shall only be responsible for the loss which has a direct link to the risks covered.

4.2.1.3 Cargo Insurance Claim

Most insurance companies' policies require that immediate notice be given to the closest branch or agency in the event of damage giving rise to a claim under a policy on goods. When notified of the damage, the company's agent proceeds to appoint a suitable surveyor to inspect the goods and to report on the nature and extent of the damage. A common practice is for a report or certificate of loss incorporating the surveyor's findings to be issued to the consignees, the latter paying the fee. This certificate of loss is included with the claim papers and, if the loss is recoverable under the insurance cover, the fee is refunded to the claimants.

The presentation of claims is by negotiation on documents supporting the insured's case. It is very difficult to state with any degree of legal precision

损失补偿原则（The Principle of Indemnity），是指保险合同生效后，如果发生保险合同责任范围内的损失，被保险人有权按照合同的约定，获得全面、充分的赔偿；保险赔偿是弥补被保险人由于保险标的遭受损失而失去的经济利益，被保险人不能因保险赔偿而获得额外的利益。

近因原则（Proximate Cause Principle），是指保险人对于承保范围的保险事故作为直接的、最接近的原因所引起的损失，承担保险责任，而对于承保范围以外的原因造成的损失，不负赔偿责任。

exactly on whom the onus of proof falls in every case, but generally speaking, the insured must be able to prove a loss by a peril against which he was insured.

4.2.2 Marine Transportation Insurance 海上运输保险

Marine insurance is defined in the Marine Insurance Act 1906:"a contract of marine insurance is a contract whereby the insurer undertakes to indemnify the assured in a manner and to the extent thereby agreed, against marine losses, that is to say, the losses incidental to marine adventure." Hence this includes cargo insurance involving the maritime conveyance of merchandise from one country to another.

英国《1906年海上保险法》第1条：海上保险合同是一种保险人按照约定的方式和范围对于海上冒险有关的海上灭失，向被保险人承担赔偿责任的合同。

4.2.2.1 Marine Risks

Marine risks indicate the dangers existing during the course of the ocean transportation. There are mainly two types of risks covered by marine insurance: perils of the sea and fortuitous accidents.

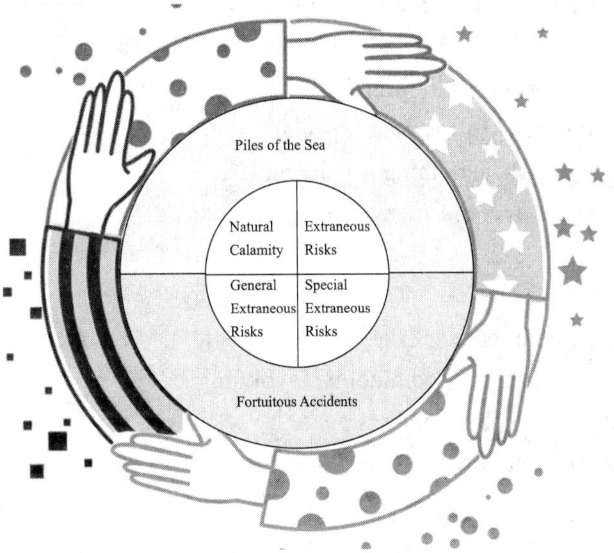

Perils of the sea include both natural calamity and extraneous risks. Natural calamity refers to natural disaster such as vile weather, tsunami, earthquake, volcanic eruption, storm and so on. Fortuitous accidents, also called unexpected accidents, are accidents due to haphazard causes such as fire, explosion, vessel standing, grounding, sinking, missing and so on.

海上风险（Perils of the Sea），在保险界又称为海难，是指包括海上发生的自然灾害和意外事故所带来的风险，但它并不包括海上的一切风险。

Extraneous risks, or external risks, include general extraneous risks and special extraneous risks. General extraneous risks are risks due to theft, rain, leakage, shortage, breakage, dampness, mildewing, heating, taint of odor, hooking, resting and so on. Special extraneous risks are caused by military factors, political factors and government regulation such as war, striking, confiscation and so on.

附加险（Additional Risks or Extraneous Risks），是指不能单独投保，只能附加于主险投保的保险险种。

4.2.2.2 Marine Losses

Marine insurance defines its losses in terms of the nature of the loss or damage, the extent of the loss or damage and the conditions under which it happens. Generally, losses caused during the transit of commodities can be classified into total losses and partial losses. In addition, in the practice of cargo insurance, loss is referred to as the special term "average", which actually has nothing to do with its normal meaning. That is, average in marine insurance simply means loss.

海上损失（Marine Loss），是指被保险货物在海洋运输中由于发生海上风险所造成的损坏或灭失，又称为海损（Average）。

➢ Total losses

Total losses refer to the losses of the entire value of the subject matter to the insured, commonly involving the maximum amount for which a policy is liable.

全部损失（Total Loss），简称全损，是指整批或不可分割的一批保险货物全部灭失或可视同全部灭失的损害。

Based on the situations of the losses, total losses can be further divided into actual total losses and constructive total losses. Actual total losses mean that

实际全损（Actual Total Loss），是指被保险货物（保险标的物）全部灭失或指货物毁损后不能复原或完全丧失原有

the complete loss of the insured cargo in value, and the insured can get indemnity against the total loss of the insured value of cargo. Constructive total losses occur when the actual loss of the insured goods is unavoidable, or when the ship or the consignment has to be abandoned because the cost of salvage or recovery will exceed the value of the ship and the consignment on arrival. In case of constructive total losses, most insurance policies provide for the payment of a total loss up to the insured amount.

用途，已不具有任何使用价值；或指货物以无法挽回地全部被海盗劫走等。

推定全损（Constructive Total Loss），是指被保险货物受损后，完全灭失已不可避免或修复、恢复受损货物的费用将超过货值；或被保险货物遭受严重损失后，继续运抵目的地的运费将超过残损货物的价值。

➢ Partial losses

Different from total losses, partial losses means a partial damage to or the total loss of part of the insured cargo. Basically, it can be divided into general average and particular average.

部分损失（Partial Loss），是指被保险货物的一部分毁损或灭失。

General average (GA) is the partial loss resulting from a deliberate act of the ship's master, such as throwing overboard all or part of the cargo to save the ship. In this case, all beneficial parties will share the loss of the specific consignor. Particular average is the partial loss suffered by the party whose consignment is partially lost or damaged. When the loss or damage occurs, no cargo of other parties has to be sacrificed to save the voyage.

共同海损（General Average），是指载货船舶在航行途中遇到威胁船货共同安全的自然灾害和意外事故，船长为了维护船货的共同安全或使航程得以继续完成，有意识地、合理地采取措施而造成的特殊损失或支出的额外费用。

单独海损（Particular Average），是指货物由于遭受承保范围内的风险所造成非属共同海损的部分损失，它是针对共同海损而言的。

Moreover, the following criteria determine that the partial loss is a general average:

1. The danger that threats the common safety of cargo and/or vessel shall be materially existent and is not foreseen;
2. The measures taken by the master shall be aimed or remove the common danger of both vessel and cargo and shall be undertaken deliberately and reasonably for common safety;

3. The sacrifice shall be specialized and not caused by perils directly and the expense incurred shall be additional expense which is not within the operation budget;
4. The actions of the ship's master shall be successful in saving the voyage.

4.2.2.3 Expenses Incurred

Losses sustained by the insured because of the risks come from not only the loss of the goods or the damage done to the goods, but also from the expenses the insured sustained in rescuing the goods in danger. Therefore, marine cargo insurance should also cover the expenses incurred to avoid or rescue the loss or damage of the insured cargo. There are mainly two kinds of expenses: one is sue and labor expense, the other is salvage charges.

Sue and labor expenses are extraordinary expenditures made in time of peril to avert or minimize any loss of or damage to the cargo insured. Different from general average, sue and labor expenses are not something carried out for the benefit of a common interest, but for the singular benefit of the goods insured. As the expenses incurred for suing and laboring are recoverable, it is the responsibility of the insured to keep his insured loss at a minimum level.

施救费用（Sue and Labor Expenses），是指保险标的在遭遇保险责任范围内的风险事故时，被保险人或其代理人、雇佣人员等为了避免或减少损失，采取各种抢救或防护措施而产生的费用。

Salvage charges mean charges recoverable by salvor independently of contract. Such expenses, where properly and effectively incurred, can be recovered as particular changes or as a general average loss, according to the circumstances under which there were incurred.

救助费用（Salvage Charge），指保险标的遭遇保险责任范围内的灾害事故时，由保险人和被保险人以外的第三者采取救助行动而支付的费用。

4.2.2.4 Coverage under C.I.C.

中国保险条款涵盖的险别

In China, the most commonly adopted terms in

cargo insurance is C.I.C. (China Insurance Clause). Under C.I.C., there are three kinds of basic insurance coverage: F.P.A., W.P.A. and All Risks. Besides, there are two other kinds of additional insurance coverage: general additional risks and special additional risks.

- Basic marine insurance coverage

  The risks under basic marine insurance coverage refer to those that can be covered independently without being attached to any other particularly coverage.

  F.P.A. (Free from Particular Average) is a limited form of cargo insurance cover under which no partial loss or damage is recoverable. It only provides coverage for total losses and general average emerging from the actual "marine perils" like vessel sinking, stranding or grounding.

  W.P.A. (With Particular Average) covers wider than F.P.A. W.P.A. provides extensive cover against all losses or damages due to marine perils throughout the duration of the policy, including partial losses or damages which may be attributed to natural calamities like bad weather.

  All risks mean that the insurer is responsible for all total or partial losses of or damages to the goods insured either arising from sea perils or general external causes. It is the most comprehensive basic coverage of the three. However, it doesn't cover losses, expenses or damages caused by inherent voice, nature of the cargo insured or special external risks of war, strike and so on.

- Additional risk

  The additional risk shall be made complementarily with the insurance companies according to the

平安险（Free from Particular Average，简称F.P.A.），原来的含义是只保全损，即承保自然灾害和意外事故造成货物的全部损失。自然灾害系指恶劣气候、雷电、海啸、地震、洪水等。后来又加上了运输工具遭受搁浅、触礁、沉没、互撞、与流冰或其他物体碰撞以及失火、爆炸造成货物的部分损失。

水渍险（With Average/With Particular Average，简称WA/WPA），又称"单独海损险"，英文原意是指单独海损负责赔偿，海洋运输货物保险的主要险别之一。这里的"海损"是自然灾害及意外事故，导致货物被水淹没，引起货物的损失。

一切险（All Risks），是海洋运输货物保险的主要险别之一，其负责的范围很广泛。它除了承保"平安险"和"水渍险"的各项责任外，还负责承保货物在运输途中由于外来原因所致全部或部分损失。外来原因通常所致的损失有：偷窃、提货不着、淡水、雨淋、短量、混杂、沾污、渗漏、碰损、破碎、串味、受潮受热、钩损、包装破裂、锈损等。

附加险（Additional Risks/Extraneous Risks），是指不能单独投保，只能附加于

actual situations, while the basic insurance coverage can be taken out independently. That is to say, any additional risk should go with one of the three types of basic insurance coverage mentioned before.

主险投保的保险险种，主险因失效、解约或满期等原因效力终止或中止时，附加险效力也随之终止或中止。

General additional coverage covers the general external risks that we introduced previously. Totally, there are 11 types of risks that are covered under the general additional coverage: TPND (Theft, Pilferage and Non-delivery), Fresh Water Rain Damage, Risk of Shortage, Risk of Intermixture and Contamination, Risk of Clash and Breakage, Risk of Odor, Risk of Rust, Heating and Sweating Risk, Hook Damage, Breakage of Packing Damage etc.

一般附加险（General Additional Risk），承保一般外来原因引起的货物损失，亦称"普通附加险"，它们包括在一切险之中。若投保了一切险，就无须另行加保。若投保了平安险或水渍险，则由被保险人根据货物特性和运输条件选择一种或几种附加险，经与保险人协议加保。

Similarly, special additional coverage covers the special extraneous risks. There are 8 types of special additional risks: War Risk, SRCC (Strike, Riots and Commotions), Failure to Delivery Risk, Import Duty Risk, On Deck Risk, Rejection Risk, Aflatoxin Risk, Fire Risk Extension Clause etc.

特殊附加险（Special Additional Risk）是以导致货损的某些政府行为风险作为承保对象的，它不包括在一切险范围，不论被保险人投任何基本险，要想获取保险人对政府行为等政治风险的保险保障，必须与保险人特别约定，经保险人特别同意。否则，保险人对此不承担保险责任。特殊附加险只能在投保"平安险"、"水渍险"和"一切险"的基础上加保。

4.2.3 Other Types of Transportation Insurance 其他类型的运输保险

As there is a high volume of business covered by other means of transportation, it is essential to learn other types of transportation insurance including insurance of overland, air and postal.

According to the Overland Transportation Cargo Insurance Clause, insurance coverage for overland transportation can be divided into two kinds: overland transportation risks（陆运险）, similar to W.P.A., and overland transportation all risks（陆运一切险）, similar to marine all risks.

According to the Air transportation Cargo Insurance Clause, insurance coverage for air transportation can also be divided into two kinds: air transportation risks（航空运输险）, similar to W.P.A., and air transportation all risks（航空运输一切险）, similar to marine all risks.

According to Parcel Post Insurance Clause, insurance coverage for postal transportation can also be divided into two kinds: parcel post risks（邮包险）, similar to W.P.A., and parcel post all risks(邮包一切险), similar to marine all risks. Moreover, some additional risks may also be added if required.

4.2.4 Insurance Clause in Contract 合同中的保险条款

条款内容主要包括：
保险相关方、保险利益、险别等。

Insurance clause is one of the most important parts of international sales contract. Usually, insurance clauses will specify the following: which party is to effect insurance; how much the insured amount is; the type of insurance coverage and so on.

In an FCA, FOB, CFR or CPT contract, the insurance clause may simply be stipulated as "Insurance to be covered by the buyer". However, in a CIF or CIP contract, the insurance clause should stipulate the name of the party who shall arrange for insurance, the insurance amount, the risks covered and the name of the insurance clause applied, which includes the date on which the clause is to be attached.

It must be stressed that insurance clause should be made in a clear and definite way and ambiguous clauses should be avoided.

4.3 Forwarding Agency in International Trade 国际贸易中的货物运输代理业务

4.3.1 Concept and Function of Forwarder 代理人的概念和作用

A freight forwarder is a private service company licensed to support shippers and the movement of their goods. These specialists in international physical distribution act as agents for the exporter (shipper) in moving cargo to an overseas destination. Generally, the forwarding agent arranges the transportation of the goods and is an intermediary, acting on behalf of the shipper.

货运代理人（Freight Forwarder），安排他人货物海上货物运输的一方当事人，所收取的费用按运费的某一百分比加上开支计算。

有时货运代理人作为托运人的主承揽人（principal contractor）并承担公共承运人（common carrier）的责任；而有时货运代理人仅作为托运人的代理人，仅负有合理小心和能力的义务（reasonable care and skill）。

4.3.2 Characteristic of Forwarding Agency 代理人的特征

One of the forwarding agent's specializations is consolidation or joint cargo: he contracts cargo space at discounted wholesale rates from his carriers, and contracts it out to his customer at lower discounts or at the normal cargo rate.

A consolidated service is generally provided between the forwarding agent's warehouse or terminal, for example in Rotterdam, and his correspondent's facility's at the destination, for example in Singapore.

Delivery to the forwarding agent's facility and collection from the correspondent's facility may or may not be arranged separately. If not, the forwarding agent can provide door to door transport, under a single document.

Moreover, the term NVOCC or non-vessel- operating common carrier is sometimes used for indicating a consolidator.

4.4 Customs Service for Merchandise Export and Import 进出口货物的报关

The customs service involvement in the entry process can be characterized by five steps:

- Check and verify

  For this step, customs officers check the entry documents and verify evidence of a bond. Of course, on arrival of the goods at the port of entry, the owner or agent is responsible to immediately make arrangements for the shipment and storage of the goods. Those goods that are not claimed are stored in a general warehouse. Storage is billed to the owner when the goods are retrieved, or sold at auction.

检查与核实

检查进口文件和核实合约，货物存放在海关监管的综合仓库中直至交予收货人或被拍卖。

- Examine

  This step, which is the customs officer's examination to determine the value of the goods and their suitability for entering has five substeps:

  - ✓ Valuation of the goods for customs purposes and their dutiable status.

检验

1. 关税应税价值

✓ Checking the proper marking of the goods with the country of origin.

✓ Determining whether the shipment contains prohibited items.

✓ Determining whether the goods are correctly invoiced.

✓ Taking inventory to determine whether there are excesses or shortages of the invoiced quantities.

➢ Validate

The validation step consists of checking the classification of the goods and appraising them to ensure correct valuation.

➢ Authorize entry

After the classification and valuation, and after other required import information has been reviewed for correctness, proper appraisement, and agreement of the submitted data, the merchandise may be authorized for actual import.

➢ Liquidation

If the goods are accepted without changes, they are liquidated "as entered". This step is finalized in the traditional way of posting a notice on the public bulletin board at the customs house. The bulletin board is now a computer printout.

2. 原产地

3. 是否有违禁物

4. 发票的正确性

5. 是否有溢短装

验证分类与准确价值

批准进入

清算

Notes

1. Delivery

交货，是指卖方自愿将其对货物的占有权转移给买方的行为。

2. Liner
   班轮，即指在预先固定的航线上，按照规定的时间和停靠港口航行的船舶。
3. Transportation expenses/Freight
   运费，是指支付货运或全部或部分使用船只、火车、飞机或其他类似运输手段的费用。
4. Basic freight rate
   基本运费，货物从装运港到卸货港的基本费用，又分传统的件杂货运费率和集装箱包箱费率。
5. Charter Transport
   租船运输，是指租船人向船东租赁船舶用于运输货物的业务。
6. Scheduled airlines
   班机运输，是指客、货班机定时、定点、定线的运输，它适用于载运数量较小的货物。
7. Chartered carriers
   包机运输，是指包租整架飞机运输货物而言，它适用于载运数量较大、有急需或有特殊要求的货物。
8. Consolidated consignment
   集中托运，是指航空货运公司把若干单独发运的货物组成一整批货物，用一份总运单整批发运到预定目的地，由航空货运公司在那里的代理人收货、报关、分拨后交给实际收货人。
9. Container Transport
   集装箱运输，是以集装箱作为运输单位进行货物运输的一种现代化运输方式。
10. International Multi-modal Transport
    国际多式联运，是在集装箱运输的基础上产生和发展起来的综合性连贯运输方式，一般是以集装箱为媒介，把海陆空各种传统的单一运输方式有机结合起来，组成一种国际间的连贯运输。
11. Inland water transportation
    内河运输，是指使用船舶通过国际内江湖河川等天然或人工水道，运送货物和旅客的一种运输方式。
12. Pipeline transport
    管道运输，是用管道作为运输工具的一种长距离输送液体和气体物资的输方式，是一种专门由生产地向市场输送石油、煤和化学产品的运输方式，是统一运输网中干线运输的特殊组成部分。

13. Bill of Lading
提单（简称B/L），是货物承运人（或其代理人）在收到货物后签发给托运人的一种证件
14. Booking Note
托运单（简称B/N），俗称下货纸，是托运人根据贸易合同和信用证条款内容填制的，向承运人或其代理办理货物托运的单证。
15. Air waybill
空运提单，是指承运货物的航空承运人（航空公司）或其代理人，在收到承运货物并接受托运人空运要求后，签发给托运人的货物收据。
16. Multimodal Transport Document
多式联运单据（简称MTD），是指证明国际多式联运合同成立及证明多式联运经营人接管货物，并负责按照多式联运合同条款支付货物的单据。
17. Transshipment
转船，是指在远洋运输中，货物装船后允许在中途港换装其他船舶转运至目的港。
18. Insurable interest principle
保险利益原则，又称“可保利益”或“可保权益”原则。所谓保险利益是指投保人或被保险人对其所保标的具有法律所承认的权益或利害关系。即在保险事故发生时，可能遭受的损失或失去的利益。
19. Utmost good faith
最大诚信原则，即保险合同当事人订立合同及合同有效期内，应依法向对方提供足以影响对方做出订约与履约决定的全部实质性重要事实，同时绝对信守合同订立的约定与承诺。
20. The principle of indemnity
损失补偿原则，是指保险合同生效后，如果发生保险合同责任范围内的损失，被保险人有权按照合同的约定，获得全面、充分的赔偿。
21. Proximate cause principle
近因原则，是指保险人对于承保范围的保险事故作为直接的、最接近的原因所引起的损失，承担保险责任，而对于承保范围以外的原因造成的损失，不负赔偿责任。
22. Perils of the Sea
海上风险，在保险界又称为海难，是指包括海上发生的自然灾害和意外事故所带来的风险，但它并不包括海上的一切风险。
23. Extraneous risks
附加险，是指不能单独投保，只能附加于主险投保的保险险种。

24. Sue and Labor Expenses
施救费用，是指保险标的在遭遇保险责任范围内的风险事故时，被保险人或其代理人、雇用人员等为了避免或减少损失，采取各种抢救或防护措施而产生的费用。
25. Salvage Charge
救助费用，指保险标的遭遇保险责任范围内的灾害事故时，由保险人和被保险人以外的第三者采取救助行动而支付的费用。
26. Freight forwarder
货运代理人，安排他人货物进行海上货物运输的一方当事人，所收取的费用按运费的某一百分比加上开支计算。

Exercise

1. Translate the following into Chinese or English.

Liner transport
Bill of lading
Perils of sea
All risk
Insured amount
光船租船
定程租船
估损费用
freight
surcharge
voyage charter
particular average
additional risks coverage
定期租船
意外事故

2. Decide whether the following statements are true (T) or false (F).

1) Sometimes when the buyer cannot determine a specific port of discharge, he may require two or three ports to be written on the contract for option.
2) When there are optional ports in the contract, the goods may be unloaded at any one of the ports at the shipping company's disposal.
3) When importing on FOB terms, we can generally stipulate the port of discharge.
4) An order bill of lading may be negotiable after being endorsed.
5) A bill of lading is a transport contract in which the shipping company promises to transport the goods received to the destination.
6) A letter of indemnity is issued by the seller to the buyer to certify that the goods

delivered are in good condition.

7) According to the UCP 500, a bill of lading which is issued subject to a Charter Party must be accepted unless the Credit stipulates otherwise.

8) When you transport your goods by a Time Charter, you have to pay for loading and unloading fees.

9) When the ship owner speeds up his ship and arrives at the destination at an earlier date than is stipulated, he can obtain dispatch money from the shipper.

10) When the charterer fails to load or unload the goods within the stipulated period of time, he has to pay demurrage to the ship owner.

3. Multiple Choices. Make the best choice to fill in the blank of each sentence.

1) In the import and export business, ________ can be made out to negotiation document.

A. a rail waybill　　B. a parcel post receipt
C. an ocean B/L　　D. an air waybill

2) A bill of lading is ________ when item date of shipment is indicated earlier than the actual time of shipment.

A. straight B/L　　B. confirmed B/L
C. stale B/L　　D. ante-deted B/L

3) The bill of lading presented to the consignee or buyer or his bank after the stipulated expiry date of presentation or after the goods are due at the port of destination is a ________.

A. straight B/L　　B. confirmed B/L
C. stale B/L　　D. ante-dated B/L

4) A (n) ________ B/L refers to one that is made out to a designated consignee.

A. order　　B. bearer　　C. straight　　D. specific order

4. Translate the following senteces into Chinese or English.

1) Advantages of containerization include less handling of cargo, more protection against pilferage, less exposure to the elements, and reduced cost of shipping.

2) Liner companies usually publish their sailing schedule in newspapers or distribute it among the consignors.

3) War clause is an insurance clause included in policies to cover against losses as a result of war.

4) If the damage or losses done to the goods are caused by the perils covered by the insurer, the consignor should send the documents to the insurer for claim settlement.
5) 清洁运输单据系指有明确宣称货物及/或包装情况有缺陷的条款或批注的运输单据。
6) 如托运人在提单中故意谎报货物的性质或价值，则承运人或船公司在任何情况下，对货物或与货物有关的灭失或损坏概不负责任。
7) 货物按照装在舱内的条款投保，但实际上装在舱面上，受到损失后保险公司不负责赔偿。
8) 在商业信用风险或政治风险中，当投保人不能取得货款或不能取得全部货款时，承保人负责赔偿。
9) 有关保险的索赔条件应尽快提交保险公司或其代理商以便他们有足够时间去向造成过错的有关方面进行追偿。

5. **Case Analysis**

1) A ship started on its voyage after loading, but in the course of the journey a fire broke out during transit in Hold A, which had been loaded with stationary and tea. The captain ordered his crew to pour water on the fire. It was found out, after the fire was extinguished, that part of the stationery had been burned; the remainder and all the tea had been soaked through. Then, what were the natures of the respective losses? What risk would you have covered if you had wanted to be compensated for the losses?
2) 某载货船舶在航行途中突然触礁，致使部分货物遭到损失，船体个别部位的船板产生裂缝，急需补漏。为了船、货的共同安全，船长决定修船，为此，将部分货物卸到岸上并存仓，卸货过程中部分货物受损。经统计这次事件造成的损失有：

   ① 部分货物因船触礁而损失；

   ② 卸货费用、存仓费用及货物损失。

   从上述各项损失的性质来看，它们各属于什么海损?

Chapter 5

Payment of Commodity

货款的支付

In international trade, how and when an exporter receives payment for the goods he sends abroad are problems that he should most concern. Payment in domestic trade is a fairly simple matter. It can be made either in advance or within a reasonably short period after delivery. However, these problems are magnified many times in international trade. Much time is lost in correspondence, dispatch and delivery.

☞ **Learning Objectives:**

After learning this chapter, you are expect to:

→ Distinguish different of payment;

→ Compare characteristics of different payment methods;

→ Outline determining factors when selecting methods of payment;

→ Identify payment clause in contract;

→ Establish a basic framework about financing and risk prevention.

5.1 Instrument of Payment 结算工具

In international trade, the most frequently used means of payment include currencies and bills. The former is used for account, settlement and payment; the latter for settlement and payment. In practice, sellers of goods, in general, almost never insist on their rights to demand cash for payment, but readily take certain bills, such as bill of exchange(draft), promissory note and check for substitutes, among which draft are widely used.

5.1.1 Bill of Exchange 汇票

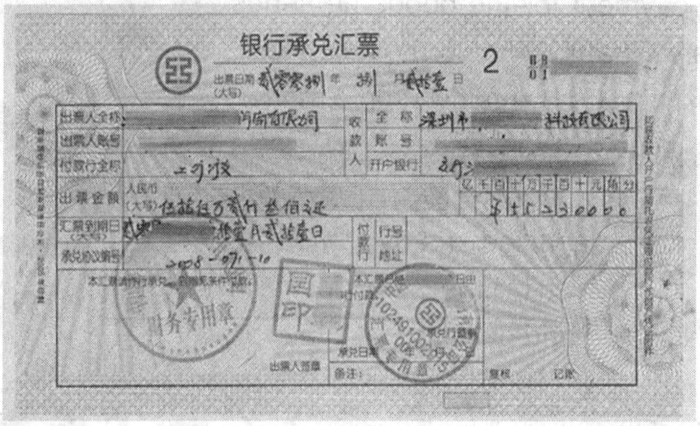

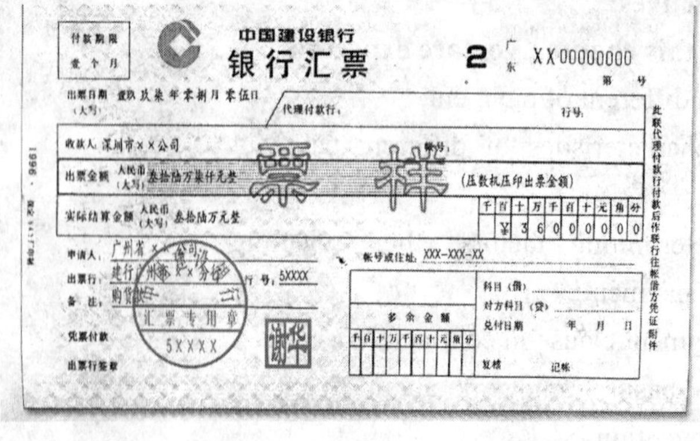

A bill of exchange, also called draft, is defined as "an unconditional order in writing, addressed by one person to another, signed by the person giving it, requiring the person to whom it is addressed to pay on demand, or at a fixed or determinable future time, a sum certain in money, to, or to the order of a specified person, or to bearer". The operation process of draft includes: drawing, presentation, acceptance, payment, endorsement, dishonor and recourse. Drafts are negotiable instrument and may be sold.

汇票（Bill of Exchange/Postal Order/Draft）是由出票人签发的，要求付款人在见票时或在一定期限内，向收款人或持票人无条件支付一定款项的票据。汇票是国际结算中使用最广泛的一种信用工具。

5.1.1.1 Parties Involved in Bill of Exchange

汇票相关方

Generally, a bill of exchange involves three parties:

- Drawer. The person who writes the order and gives directions to the person to make a specific payment of money. He is usually the exporter or his banker in import and export trade; usually, he is also a creditor of the drawee.
- Drawee. The person to whom the order is addressed and who is to pay the money. He is usually the importer or the appointed bank under a letter of credit in import and export trade. In addition, when a time bill has been accepted by the drawee, he becomes an acceptor who is the same person as the drawee. The drawer and the acceptor must be different persons.
- Payee. One who receives a payment, through cash, check, money order and promissory note.

出票人（Drawer）是开立票据并将其交付给他人的法人、其它组织或者个人。出票人对收款人及正当持票人承担票据在提示付款或承兑时必须付款或者承兑的保证责任。

付款人（Drawee），或称受票人，是指出票人或者出票人在汇票上记载的委托其支付票据金额的人。付款人并非因出票人的支付委托即成为当然的票据债务人，而是必须经其承兑，才能成为票据债务人。付款人一经承兑后，即成承兑人，是汇票的主债务人。

受款人（Payee），又称汇票的抬头，受领汇票所规定金额的人，进出口业务中可以是：出口人、卖方、指定的银行或正当持票人。

5.1.1.2 Classification of Bill of Exchange

汇票的种类

Based on different criteria, the bill of exchange can be classified into different types:

- According to different drawee, the bills of exchange can be classified into commercial bill and banker's bill. If the drawer is a commercial concern,

商业汇票（Commercial Bill of Exchange / Commercial Draft），是出票人签发的，委托付款人在指定日期无条件支付确定的金额给收款人或者持票人的票据。在银行开立存款账户的法人以及其他组织之间，必须具有真实的交易关系或债权债

the bill is called a commercial bill. It is often used in foreign trade finance. If the drawer is a bank, the bill is called a banker's bill. It is mainly used in remittance.

务关系，才能使用商业汇票。它适用于同城或异地结算。商业汇票分为商业承兑汇票和银行承兑汇票。

银行汇票（banker's bill），是汇款人将款项存入当地出票银行，由出票银行签发的,由其在见票时，按照实际结算金额无条件支付给持票人或收款人的票据。适用于先收款后发货或钱货两清的商品交易。单位和个人各种款项结算都可以使用银行汇票。银行汇票可以用于转账，填明“现金”字样的银行汇票还可以用于支取现金。银行汇票的付款期限一般为出票日起一个月内，超过付款期限提示不付款的，持票人应当在票据权利时效内作出说明，并提供本人身份证或单位证明，持银行汇票和解讫通知书向出票银行请求付款。

➢ In the transfer of the bill of exchange, if the bill of exchange is accompanied by shipping documents, it is a documentary bill, if not, it is a clean bill. In international trade, mostly it is the documentary bill that is used, occasionally the clean bill is used to collect payment in small or sundry charges，such as commission, interest, sample fee and cash in advance, etc.

光票（Clean Bill）是指不附带商业单据的汇票（如货运等相关单据），而在国外付款的外币票据。银行汇票多是光票。光票的流通全凭出票人、付款人或背书人的信用。在国际结算中，一般仅限于贸易从属费用、货款尾数、佣金等费用的支付。光票一般用于偿债、赠予、接济、留学支出等。由于光票签章不一定能鉴定，必须寄送国外代收银行才可收到票款，因此目前许多银行外汇部门皆有办理光票托收（clean collection）业务，即受顾客委托，将汇票、支票、本票或付款收据等财务单证，寄往国外付款地代收银行并带为向付款人收取票款。程序上，通常托收银行会将相关票据汇至国外代收银行兑现成外币，再将外币兑换为本国币汇回委托人的账户，并收取手续费。

跟单汇票（Documentary bill），又称信用汇票、押汇汇票,是需要附带提单、仓单、保险单、装箱单、商业发票等单据,才能进行付款的汇票。商业汇票多为跟单汇票，在国际贸易中经常使用。

➢ According to the time when the bill falls due, bills of exchange may be divided into sight (or demand) bill or a time (or usance) bill. A sight bill demands immediate payment by the drawee at the sight of the bill. In case of a time bill, the drawee is required to accept it first and pay it at a fixed or determinable future time, in other words, it requires acceptance before payment.

即期汇票（sight bill，demand bill），即见票即付的汇票。包括载明即期付款、见票即付或提示付款以及未载明付款日的汇票。逾期后再经承兑或背书的汇票，对该种承兑人或背书人而言，应视为即期汇票。即期汇票是指以提示日为到期日，持票人持票到银行或其他委托付款人处，后者见票必须付款的一种汇票，这种汇票的持票人可以随时行使自己的票据权利，在此之前无须提前通知付款人准备履行义务。

- In time or usance commercial bill, when the drawer is a commercial firm and the drawee is another commercial firm, the bill after acceptance by the commercial firm or the drawee is called a commercial acceptance bill; when the drawer is a commercial firm or bank and the drawee is a bank, the bill after acceptance by the bank or the drawee is called a banker's acceptance bill.

5.1.1.3 Use Bill of Exchange in Foreign Trade

A bill of exchange (draft) is an order to pay. It is made out by an exporter and presented to an importer, usually through a bank. It may be payable immediately on presentation (a sight or demand draft), or so many days after presentation (a time draft). In the latter case, the drawee writes "Accepted" across it and signs his name. The exporter can then get immediate payment by discounting the draft and supplying a letter of hypothecation. If a time draft is not honored at maturity, it will be noted and protested by a Notary Public, and represented the drawee. Such a draft, and the corresponding payment terms, "Documents against Acceptance", obviously involve risk to the exporter or his bank.

- To draw

  To draw is to fill up by the drawer the particulars in a bill of exchange the date of drawing, the name of the drawee, the time and amount of the payment, etc. The draft is signed by the drawer and then sent to the payee.

  There are three kinds of ways to fill up the payee:

  → Restrictive payee, such as pay…Co. only, pay … Co. not transferable;

  → To order, such as pay … Co. or Order or Pay

远期汇票（time bill, usance bill），是指在出票一定期限后或特定日期付款。在远期汇票中，记载一定的日期为到期日，于到期日付款的，为定期汇票；记载于出票日后一定期间付款的，为计期汇票；记载于见票后一定期间付款的，为注期汇票；将票面金额划为几份，并分别指定到期日的，为分期付款汇票。远期汇票不是见票即付，持票人不能随时请求付款。

商业承兑汇票（Commercial Acceptance Bill），是由银行以外的付款人承兑的票据。商业承兑汇票可以由付款人签发并承兑，也可以由收款人签发交由付款人承兑。商业承兑汇票的出票人，为在银行开立存款账户的法人以及其他组织，与付款人具有真实的委托付款关系，具有支付汇票金额可靠的资金来源。

银行承兑汇票（Banker's Acceptance Bill）是由在承兑银行开立存款账户的存款人出票，向开户银行申请并经银行审查同意承兑的，保证在指定日期无条件支付确定的金额给收款人或持票人的票据。对出票人签发的商业汇票进行承兑是银行基于对出票人资信的认可而给予的信用支持。

出票

出票人在汇票上填写出票日期、付款人、付款时间和付款金额，出票人签字后交给收款人。

to the Order of ... Co. This type requires endorsement when transferable.

→ To bearer, such as pay bearer. This type requires no endorsement.

➢ Presentation

The act of taking the bill to the drawee and demanding that he make the payment or accept the bill is known as presentation. For a sight bill, payment should be made at the same time when the presentation is made, and for a time bill, the drawee is required to accept the bill when the bill is presented to him.

提示

持票人将汇票交给付款人要求其承兑或付款。即期汇票在持票人提示汇票时付款人立即付款，而远期汇票付款人承兑后在汇票到期日付款。

➢ Acceptance

The formal act whereby the drawee adopts the bill as his own obligation is known as acceptance. Acceptance is the written signification by the drawee of his assent to the order of the drawer. This is accomplished in the regular manner by writing the word "Acceptance", with the date and the signature of the drawee, across the face of the bill. When the bill is accepted by the drawee, he is then known as an acceptor.

➢ Payment

Under a sight bill, the drawee is required to make the payment when the bill is presented to him while for a time bill, the drawee is required to accept the bill when the bill is presented to him and make the payment at the maturity of the bill. When paid, the bill is retained by the payer while the receipt is made and signed by the holder of the bill.

➢ Endorsement

The bill of exchange is negotiable and transferable as the payee on most bills is to "to the order of...".

背书

背书（Endorsement），是指收款人以转让票据权利为目的的在汇票上签章并作必

Negotiation and transfer is effected with endorsement. If the payee on the bill is to "to the bearer", then negotiation and transfer is done with mere delivery of the bill. Endorsement is done when the payee has signed his name on the back of the bill with or without additional words conveying instructions or qualifying liability.

要的记载所作的一种附属票据行为。原票据持有人转让票据时必须在票据背面签名，由于背书人拿到了票据中的款项，因此一旦票据发生违约，票据的最终持有人拥有对背书人的追索权，背书人承担第二付款人责任。

Generally speaking, there are three main endorsements, namely special, blank, and restrictive.

- → Restrictive Endorsement. The endorser may write clearly on the upper part of the signature on the back of the bill the endorsee with restrictive conditions. A restrictive endorsement is one which limits the bill for further negotiation, such as "Pay … only" or "Pay … non-transfer". Once the bill is restrictively endorsed, it cannot be transferred any more.

限定性背书（Restrictive Endorsement），又称限制性背书，规定汇票只交付一次，受让人只能自行使用汇票而无再次转让的权利。有些背书人写明持票人只能把汇票存在银行，而不能做它用。

- → Demonstrative Endorsement. A demonstrative endorsement is one which specifies the person to whom, or to whose order, the bill is to be payable, such as "Pay … or to order of".

指示性背书（Demonstrative Endorsement），又称"特别背书"或"记名背书"，指背书人在票据背面签名外，还写明被背书人名称或其指定人。

- → Blank Endorsement. A blank endorsement, or endorsement in blank, is one which specifies no payee. The effect of a blank endorsement is to make the bill payable to bearer and to make delivery and without additional endorsement. The bearer or holder of a bill so endorsed may sometimes require, however, to place his endorsement upon it at the time of making a further negotiation.

空白背书（Blank Endorsement），又称无记名背书、略式背书、不完全背书，是指不记载被背书人名称而仅由背书人签章的背书。国外的票据实践中，存在空白背书的情况。

5.1.2 Promissory Note and Check 本票与支票

5.1.2.1 Promissory Note

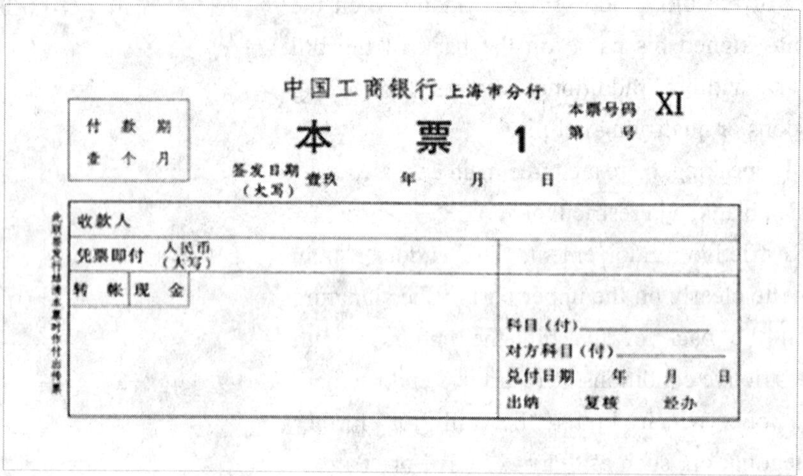

中国工商银行 上海市分行

付款期 壹个月

本票 1

本票号码 XI 第 号

签发日期（大写） 壹玖 年 月 日

收款人

凭票即付 人民币（大写）

转帐 现金

科目（付）

对方科目（付）

兑付日期 年 月 日

出纳 复核 经办

A promissory note is an unconditional promise in writing made by one person to another signed by the maker, engaging to pay, on demand or at a fixed or determinable future time, a sum certain in money, or to the order, of a specified person or to bearer.

The main difference between a promissory note and a draft lies in that there are three parties, namely drawer, drawee and payee involved in a draft but only two, drawer and payee in a promissory note. The party of promissory note is the drawer himself.

Promissory notes can be made by commercial firms, called commercial promissory notes, or bankers, called bank promissory notes. Commercial promissory notes can be sight promissory notes or time promissory notes, while bank promissory notes can only be sight. In international trade, most promissory notes are drawn by bankers which are mostly not negotiable.

本票（Promissory Note）是一个人向另一个人签发的，保证即期或定期或在可以确定的将来的时间，对某人或其指定人或持票人支付一定金额的无条件书面承诺。中国票据法第 73 条规定本票的定义是：本票是由出票人签发的，承诺自己在见票时无条件支付确定的金额给收款人或持票人的票据。第 2 款还规定，本法所指的本票是指银行本票，不包括商业本票，更不包括个人本票。

5.1.2.2 Check

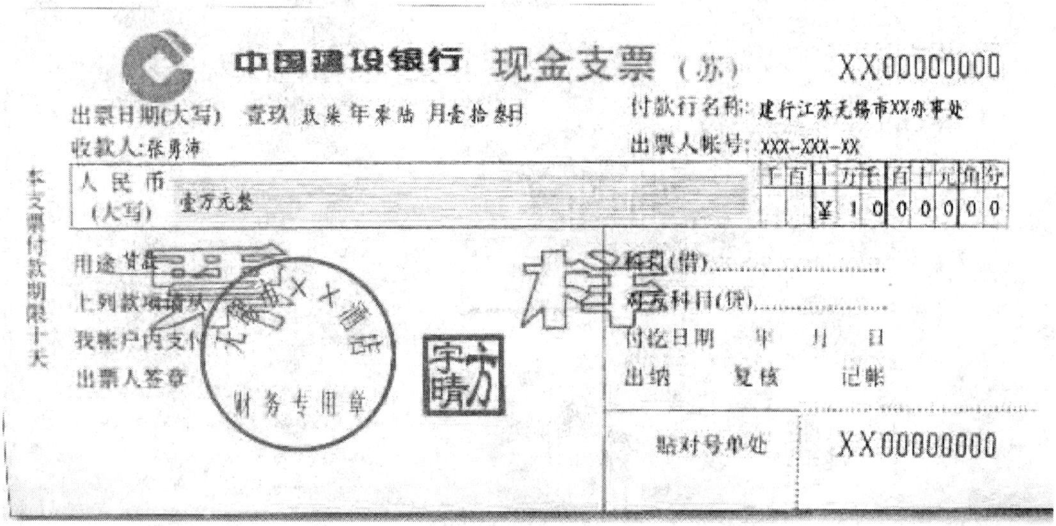

A check is an unconditional order in writing drawn on a banker signed by the drawer, requiring the banker to pay on demand a sum certain in money to or to the order of a specified person or to bearer.

The payer of a check is the drawer of the check. A check drawn on a bank overseas could be readily negotiated by the exporter if the exporter's bank were prepared to negotiate it for him, then he would receive payment right away but at the cost of the discount. Failing to do this the exporter would have to ask his bank to collect the check for him and this would be both time-consuming and relatively expensive.

支票（Check）是指发票人签发的委托银行等金融机构于见票时支付一定金额给收款人或其他指定人的一种票据。

5.2 Remittance and Collection 汇付与托收

5.2.1 Remittance 汇付

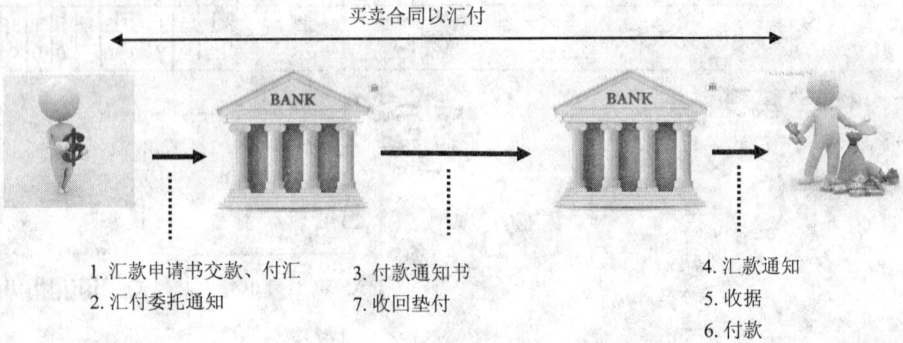

Remittances are playing an increasingly important role in many economies, contributing to economic growth and to the livelihoods of less prosperous people (though generally not the poorest of the poor). According to World Bank estimates, remittances totaled US$414 billion in 2009, of which US$316 billion went to developing countries that involved 192 million migrant workers.

汇付（Remittance），也称为汇款，是付款方通过银行，使用一定的结算工具（票据），将款项交收款方的结算方式。汇款主要是用于贸易中的货款、预付款、佣金等方面，是支付货款最简便的方式。

5.2.2 Collection 托收

Collection means that the exporter asks his bank to arrange for the acceptance or payment of the bill overseas, and the bank will carry his task through it's own branch office abroad or a correspondent bank.

➢ Parties involved in collection:
  → The remitting bank
  → The collecting bank
  → The payer or importer

托收（Collection），是出口商（债权人）为向国外进口商（债务人）收取货款，开具汇票委托出口地银行通过其在进口地银行的联行或代理行向进口商收款的结算方式。其基本做法是出口方先行发货，然后备妥包括运输单据（通常是海运提单）在内的货运单据并开出汇票，把全套跟单汇票交出口地银行（托收行），委托其通过进口地的分行或代理行（代收行）向进口方收取货款。

    - → Presenting bank
- Kinds of collection:
    - → Collection on clean bill. It means that the exporter collects the purchase price against the draft only, without any shipping documents attached thereto. This method is usually used in collecting balance under L/C, advance, commission and costs of samples.
    - → Collection on documentary bill

光票托收（Collection on clean bill），是指出口商仅开具汇票而不附带货运单据的托收。主要用于货款的尾数、样品费用、佣金、带垫费用、贸易从属费用、索赔以及非贸易的款项。

跟单托收（Collection on documentary bill），是指在卖方（出口商）所开具汇票以外，附有货运单据的托收。跟单托收又可进一步分为承兑交单（D/A）和付款交单（D/P）。

5.3 Letter of Credit（L/C）信用证

The most commonly used method of payment in the financial business of international trade is the letter of credit which is a reliable and safe method of payment, facilitating trade between unknown parties and giving protection to both sellers and buyers.

5.3.1 Concept of L/C 信用证的概念

The letter of credit is the guarantee that the issuing bank gives to the beneficiary, if the beneficiary carries out contract according to the L/C, the issuing bank shall pay.

信用证（Letter of Credit，L/C），是指开证银行应申请人的要求并按其指示向第三方开立的载有一定金额的，在一定的期限内凭符合规定的单据付款的书面保证文件。信用证是国际贸易中最主要，最常用的支付方式。

5.3.2 Characteristics of L/C 信用证的特征

The characteristics of the letter of credit can be summarized as:

- It is a kind of bank credit.
- It is a self-sufficient document.
- It is a document deal.

5.3.3 Types of L/C 信用证的类型

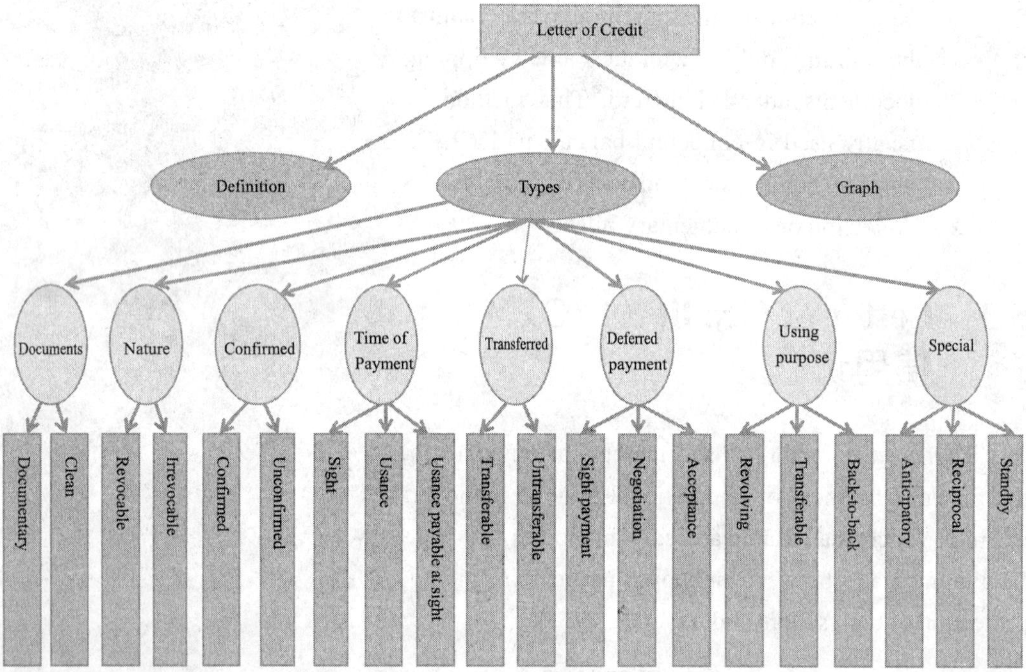

Based on different criteria, L/C can be classified into different types:

1. According to whether the draft is accompanied with the shipping documents, L/C is divided into two kinds: documentary L/C and clean L/C. A documentary L/C means that the bill of exchange should be accompanied with shipping documents. A clean L/C means that the bill of exchange isn't accompanied with shipping documents.

2. According to the responsibilities that the issuing bank bears, L/C is classified into revocable L/C and irrevocable L/C. Revocable L/C means that the opening bank may amend or revoke the credit before

跟单信用证（Documentary L/C），有时也称为"银行家的商业信用证(banker's commercial credits)"及"银行商业信用证(commercial letters of credit)"，为国际货物买卖的卖方提供担保，确保他能够在货物装运后获得付款，即使买方无法付款或买方的票据被拒收（dishonored）。

光票信用证（Clean Credit）是凭不随附货运单据的光票（Clean Draft）付款的信用证。贸易结算中的预支信用证和非贸易结算中的旅行信用证都属光票信用证。

可撤销信用证（Revocable L/C）是指开证行对其所开出的、在有效期内可以不经过受益人和其他当事人同意，也可在不必事先通知受益人的情况下，有

negotiation, acceptance or payment without agreement of the beneficiary. Once the L/C is opened, without the agreement of the beneficiary, the opening bank can't amend or revoke the L/C within its validity. That is called an irrevocable L/C. As long as the beneficiary provides the documents in accordance with the stipulation in the L/C, the opening bank shall perform its duty of payment.

3. According to whether the bank confirms, L/C is classified into Confirmed L/C and Unconfirmed L/C.

Confirmed L/C means a second guarantee is added to the document by another bank, which is called Confirmed Bank. While Unconfirmed L/C means the Issuing Bank bears the guarantee alone.

4. According to the time of payment, L/C is divided into Sight L/C and Deferred L/C.

Sight Credit means payment is due upon presentation of all documents request in the L/C within the required timeframe. A Deferred L/C is used to provide assurance that payment will be made after a certain period of time.

权随时作出修改或撤销的信用证。凡使用这种信用证，也应在该证上注明“可撤销”(Revocable)的字样，或载有开证行有权随时修改或撤销的文句。

不可撤销信用证（Irrevocable L/C）是指开证行一经开出、在有效期内未经受益人或议付行等有关当事人同意，不得随意修改或撤销的信用证；只要受益人按该证规定提供 有关单据，开证行（或其指定的银行）保证付清货款。凡使用这种信用证，必须在该证上注明“不可撤销”(Irrevocable)的字样，并载有开证行保证付款的文句。按《跟单信用证统一惯例》（第400号出版物）第7条C款的规定，“如无该项表示，信用证应视为可撤销的。”

保兑信用证系指开证银行开出的信用证经另一定银行加以保兑，保证兑付受益人所开具的汇票，称保兑信用证（Confirmed L/C）。凡在信用证上载文，愿意承担保兑者称保兑银行（Confirming Bank），保兑银行通常是由通知银行担任。

不保兑信用证（Unconfirmed L/C）是指开证银行开出的信用证没有经另一家银行保兑。即便开证行要求另一家银行加保，如果该银行不愿意在信用证上加具保兑，则被通知的信用证仍然只是一份未加保的不可撤销信用证。当开证银行资信好和成交金额不大时，一般使用这种不保兑的信用证。不保兑信用证的特点是：只有开证行一重确定的付款责任。

即期信用证（Sight Credit）是指开证行或付款行收到符合信用证条款的跟单汇票或装运单据后，立即履行付款义务的信用证。即期信用证是受益人根据信用证的规定，可凭即期跟单汇票或仅凭单据收取货款的信用证。其特点是受益人收汇安全迅速。

延期付款信用证（Deferred L/C）是远期信用证的一种，亦称无汇票远期信用证。延期付款信用证的功能与远期信用证的功能相同，只是在期限上不同而已。有的国家和地区颁布的票据法规定，凡超过六个月期限的承兑汇票，或超过一年以上的远期汇票，不得在市场上贴现。同时对远期汇票的期限不得超过180天，在这种情况下为了解决远期至一年以上或数年时间后的支付方式，在国际贸易的实践中，延期付款信用证就应运而生，而且被广泛予以运用。

5. According to whether the L/C can be transferred, it is classified into Transferable L/C and Non-transferable L/C.

A Transferable L/C means that the beneficiary can assign part or whole of the L/C amount to a third party called Second Beneficiary. While the Non-transferable L/C can not be transferred.

可转让信用证（Transferable L/C），指经出口商请求，进口商同意，由开证银行开立可转让信用证，并载明授权受益人（即原信用证受益人）有权将信用证所列金额的全部或部分转让给出口商以外的第三者，即第二受益人（Second Beneficiary）有权使用转让后的权力。这种转让称一次转让，但第二受益人不得再作转让。第二受益人称受让人（Transferee）承担交货的职责，但原信用证受益人（即第一受益人）仍对契约所列的诸条款承担责任。

不可转让信用证（Non-transferable L/C）是指受益人不能将信用证的权利转让给他人的信用证。凡可转让信用证，必须注明“可转让”（Transferable）字样，如未注明，则被视为不可转让信用证。

6. According to the way of payment, L/C is divided into Sight Payment Credit, Acceptance L/C, Negotiation L/C and Deferred Payment L/C.

1) Acceptance L/C. This kind of L/C is accepted by the bank. When the beneficiary presents the time draft to the bank, the bank will accept it and pay the price on the due date.

承兑信用证(Acceptance L/C)，是指信用证指定的付款行在收到信用证规定的远期汇票和单据，审单无误后，先在该远期汇票上履行承兑手续，等到该远期汇票到期，付款行才进行付款的信用证。由于这种信用证规定的远期汇票是由银行承兑的，所以，也称为“银行承兑信用证”(Banker's Acceptance Credit)。因此，这种信用证业务，除了要遵循有关信用证的国际惯例外，还要遵守有关国家的票据法的各项规定。即采用此种信用证时，指定银行应承兑信托受益人向其开具的远期汇票，并于汇票到期日履行付款义务。

2) Negotiation L/C. The opening bank invites other banks to buy draft and /or documents. This kind of L/C allows the beneficiary to negotiate the purchase price from an indicated bank or any bank.

议付信用证（Negotiation L/C）是指开证行承诺延伸至第三当事人，即议付行，其拥有议付或购买受益人提交信用证规定的汇票/单据权利行为的信用证。如果信用证不限制某银行议付，可由受益人（出口商）选择任何愿意议付的银行，提交汇票、单据给所选银行请求议付的信用证称为自由议付信用证，反之为限制性议付信用证。我国出口业务中，大多使用议付信用证，也有少量使用付款信用证和保兑信用证的。

5.3.4 Use of L/C 信用证的使用

Attention should be paid to the following when using letter of credit:

➢ Checking and Amending of the Letter of Credit

Once the letter of credit is opened, the opening bank will send the credit either directly to the seller or to the notifying bank. Upon arrival of the credit, the seller should check the credit immediately. If the credit contains unacceptable requirements, it should be amended at once.

仔细检查和修改

信用证一旦开立，开证行将马上寄给出口商或通知行。收到信用证时，出口商应马上检查，若有无法接受之处应马上拒绝，最好通过传真要求修改。

5.4 Bank Guarantee and Standby Letter of Credit 银行保证书及备用信用证

5.4.1 Bank Guarantee 银行保证书

A Bank Guarantee is a guarantee from a lending institution ensuring that the liabilities of a debtor will be met. In other words, if the debtor fails to settle a debt, the bank will cover it. A bank guarantee enables the customer (debtor) to acquire goods, buy equipment, or draw down loans, and thereby expand business activity.

A bank guarantee is a pledge on the part of a bank to make someone's debt good in the event that he or she cannot pay it. Bank guarantees are essentially like agreements to stand as a consigner on a transaction; in the event that the original party cannot follow through, the bank can be called upon to provide the payment. Many banks offer bank guarantees as a service to their customers for the purpose of facilitating large business

银行保函（Bank Guarantee）是由银行开立的承担付款责任的一种担保凭证，银行根据保函的规定承担绝对付款责任。银行保函大多属于"见索即付"(无条件保函)，是不可撤销的文件。银行保函的当事人有委托人（要求银行开立保证书的一方）、受益人（收到保证书并凭以向银行索偿的一方）、担保人（保函的开立人）。

operations and deals, and this particular banking tool is primarily used by big customers such as corporations and governments.

From the perspective of a seller in such transactions, a bank guarantee is a letter of surety. It means that if the buyer takes possession and fails to pay, the seller can still recover the payment, from the buyer's bank. Bank guarantees may be used in situations where large amounts of financing are needed and it is not possible to obtain a loan from one location, for example, when the World Bank provides a bank guarantee for a development project, and for deals on a smaller scale.

在开立了银行保函的情况下，若买方收货却无法支付，则卖方可以从买方银行处得到这笔付款。

In a direct guarantee, a bank directly guarantees someone, usually for a set amount and within a set period of time. The guarantee may also be generated for a specific transaction. Indirect guarantees are issued by one bank on behalf of another's customer, for example, when a foreign bank stands surety for someone by arrangement through that person's domestic and primary bank.

5.4.2 Standby Letter of Credit 备用信用证

Standby Letter of Credit, also known as a "non-performing letter of credit", is a guarantee of payment issued by a bank on behalf of a client and is used as "payment of last resort" when the client fails to fulfill a contractual commitment with another party. Standby letters of credit are created as a sign of good faith in business transactions, and are proof of a buyer's credit quality and repayment abilities. The bank issuing this kind of L/C will perform brief underwriting duties to ensure the credit quality of the client seeking the letter of client, and then send a notification to the bank of the

备用信用证（Standby Letter of Credit）是开证人（一般是银行）应支付人的请求开给受益人，保证在受益人出示特定单据或文件，开证人在单证相符的条件下必须付给受益人一笔规定的款项或承兑汇票的一种书面凭证。

clint requesting the letter of credit (typically a seller or creditor).

A standby letter of credit will typically be in force for about one year, allowing for enough time for payment to be made through standard contractual guidelines.

Standby letters of credit are often used in international trade transactions, such as the purchase of goods from another country. The seller will ask for a standby letter of credit, which can be cashed on demand if the buyer fails to make payment by the date specified in the contract. The cost to obtain a standby letter of credit is typically 1-8% of the face amount annually, but the letter can be canceled as soon as the terms of the contract have been met by the purchaser or borrower.

Notes

1. Bill of Exchange（Draft）
   汇票，是由出票人签发的，要求付款人在见票时或在一定期限内，向收款人或持票人无条件支付一定款项的票据。
2. Commercial Bill of Exchange
   商业汇票，是出票人签发的，委托付款人在指定日期无条件支付确定的金额给收款人或者持票人的票据。
3. Banker's bill
   银行汇票，是汇款人将款项存入当地出票银行，由出票银行签发的，由其在见票时，按照实际结算金额无条件支付给持票人或收款人的票据。
4. Clean Bill
   光票，是指不附带商业单据的汇票（如货运等相关单据），而在国外付款的外币票据。
5. Documentary bill
   跟单汇票，又称信用汇票、押汇汇票，是需要附带提单、仓单、保险单、装箱单、商业发票等单据才能进行付款的汇票。

6. Endorsement

背书，是指收款人以转让票据权利为目的在汇票上签章并作必要的记载所作的一种附属票据行为。

7. Promissory Note

本票，是一个人向另一个人签发的，保证即期或定期或在可以确定的将来的时间，对某人或其指定人或持票人支付一定金额的无条件书面承诺。

8. Check

支票，是指发票人签发的委托银行等金融机构于见票时支付一定金额给收款人或其他指定人的一种票据。

9. Remittance

汇付，也称为汇款，是付款方通过银行，使用一定的结算工具（票据），将款项交收款方的结算方式。

10. Collection

托收，是出口商（债权人）为向国外进口商（债务人）收取货款，开具汇票委托出口地银行通过其在进口地银行的联行或代理行向进口商收款的结算方式。

11. Letter of Credit

信用证（简称L/C），是指开证银行应申请人的要求并按其指示向第三方开立的载有一定金额的，在一定的期限内凭符合规定的单据付款的书面保证文件。

12. Irrevocable L/C

不可撤销信用证，是指信用证一经开出，在有效期内未经受益人或议付行等有关当事人同意，不得随意修改或撤销的信用证。

13. Unconfirmed L/C

不保兑信用证，是指开证银行开出的信用证没有经另一家银行保兑。即便开证行要求另一家银行加保，如果该银行不愿意在信用证上加具保兑，则被通知的信用证仍然只是一份未加保的不可撤销信用证。

14. Acceptance L/C

承兑信用证，是指信用证指定的付款行在收到信用证规定的远期汇票和单据，审单无误后，先在该远期汇票上履行承兑手续，等到该远期汇票到期，付款行才进行付款的信用证。

15. Negotiation L/C

议付信用证，是指开证行承诺延伸至第三当事人，即议付行，其拥有议付或购买受益人提交信用证规定的汇票/单据权利行为的信用证。

16. Bank Guarantee

    银行保函，是由银行开立的承担付款责任的一种担保凭证，银行根据保函的规定承担绝对付款责任。

17. Standby Letter of Credit

    备用信用证，是开证人（一般是银行）应支付人的请求开给受益人，保证在受益人出示特定单据或文件，开证人在单证相符的条件下必须付给受益人一笔规定的款项或承兑汇票的一种书面凭证。

Exercise

1. Translate the following into Chinese or English.

Confirmed L/C	Transferable L/C
Check	Bill of exchange
Remittance	Collection
Bank guarantee	
支付结算	交付运单
远期信用证	信用状况
信用证有效期	

2. Translate the following sentences into Chinese or English.

1) All other bank charges, except establishing bank charges, are for account of the beneficiary.
2) Signed commercial invoice in 5 copies indicating this L/C No. and contract No. and shipping mark.
3) This credit is not operative only after having obtained the import license and in any case only after our telex advice to you.
4) 我希望你们能在收到我方信用证后马上发货。
5) 信用证应该保持在装船后 15 日内有效。
6) 如果采用信用证支付，我们能给予你们一些折扣。
7) 在跟单托收中，银行起中介作用，把汇款人的单据转给代收银行，并从代收银行接收款项。
8) 结算时，出口商应向议付银行提交信用证所需要的各种单据。

3. **Case Analysis**

The ABC Company exported a consignment of silk. As the shipping marks in the relevant L/C were not clear, the person in charge thought that the L/C did not stipulate the shipping marks. He, then, made the shipping marks himself. As a result, discrepancies occurred between the made shipping marks and those stated in the L/C. The buyer, therefore, refused to pay for the documents. However, after negotiation, the buyer agreed to pay only when the ABC Company had reduced the original prices by 10 percent. What can we learn from this case?

Chapter 6

Precaution and Settlement of Disputes

争议的预防与处理

In international trade, disputes often arise when one party thinks that the other fails to carry out the duties stipulated in the contract wholly or partially, which may lead to claim, arbitration and legal actions.

☞ **Learning Objectives:**

After learning this chapter, you are expected to:

→ Understand the concepts and importance of inspection;

→ Identify the conditions for disputes and settlement of claims;

→ Remember the concepts and procedure of arbitration;

→ Stipulate arbitration clause in contract;

→ Understand concepts and application of force majeure.

6.1 Inspection of Commodity 商品的检验

6.1.1 Foundation of Inspection 检验的根据

The inspection is the physical examination of a property or commodity to confirm that it meets the standards of the contract.

In international trade, most of sellers and buyers are far away from each other. They cannot make delivery face-to-face, which is quite different from the domestic trade, so the damage due to the long distance transportation is hard to avoid.

In order to verify the reasons for the damages and clarify the respective responsibilities of the parties involved, an usual practice has come into being, that is to say, the qualified third party who has no conflict of interest with the concerning parties is authorized to inspect the quality, quantity, weight, packing of the goods etc., and issue the relevant certificate as the evidence for the delivery of goods, and the settlement of payment and claims. Commodity inspection has become an indispensable part in international trade, which is the extension of the qualified clause of contract and the warranty of it as well.

商品检验（Commodity Inspection）是指在国际货物买卖中,对卖方交付给买方货物地质量、数量和包装等项目进行检验,以确定合同的标的物是否符合买卖合同规定。

商检已成为国际贸易中不可缺少的环节。

6.1.2 Timing, Location and Buyer's Right of Inspection 检验的时间、地点及买方的权利

➢ Time and location of inspection

The time and location of inspection means that

检验的时间、地点是指在何时、何地行使对货物的检验权。

when and where to make inspection in import country or export country, and at the port/place of shipment, or at the port/place of destination.

➢ Buyer's right of inspection

According to "Sale of Goods Act, 1893" (revised in 1979), the buyer who has not made inspection on the goods cannot be assumed to accept the goods. He is not deprived of the right of refusing the goods until he is granted reasonable opportunity to inspect.

英国《1893年货物买卖法》(1979年修订本)规定：凡是事先未经过检验的货物，都不能认为是买方已经接受了货物，因而他没有丧失拒收货物的权利，直至有合理的机会检验货物为止。

According to "United Nations Convention on Contract for the International Sale of goods", the buyers shall implement the inspection or have others to do it in the shortest practical time. The inspection can be put off to the time when the goods arrive at the destination in case of the involvement of the transportation.

《联合国国际货物销售合同公约》规定，买方必须在按实际情况可行的最短时间内检验货物或由他人检验货物。如果合同涉及到运输，检验可推迟到货物到达目的地后进行。

There is a common principle in the above-mentioned law and convention: the buyer shall be granted the inspection right before accepting the goods unless there is another agreement between the buyers and the sellers.

上述有关法律和公约都体现了一个共同的原则：除非双方另有约定，买方在接受货物之前应享有对货物进行检验的权利。

6.1.3 Inspection Institution and Inspection Certification 检验机构及检验证书

6.1.3.1 Inspection Institution

Inspection certificates are issued only when they are proved to be up to certain standards. Generally, the types of Inspection institutions are classified as following:

➢ Official inspection institutions or government organs

→ The State General Administration for Quality Supervision and Inspection and Quarantine (AQSIQ)

国家质量监督检验检疫总局

→ China Animal and Plant Quarantine Office in

动植物检疫所

charge of the quarantine of all imported and exported animals and plants and their by-products

→ China Register of Shipping in charge of the inspection of imported ships and ships equipment
船籍登记

→ China State Bureau of Metrology in charge of the inspection on measuring instruments
国家计量局

➢ Semi-official inspection institutions

→ Underwriter's Laboratories (UL) Inc. inspects chemicals, electrical appliances, heaters, water-proof equipment.
美国担保人实验室

➢ Non-official inspection institutions

→ Lloyd's Surveyor
英国劳埃氏公证行

→ Societe General de Surveillance S. A., SGS
瑞士日内瓦通用鉴定公司

In China, General Administration of Quality Supervision, Inspection and Qurantine of the People's Republic of China. is the competent authority that supervises the work of inspection of the whole nation. The main duties of the inspection bureau are as follows:

➢ Making legal inspection

➢ Supervision and administration

➢ Authentic attesting business

6.1.3.2 Inspection Certificate
检验证书

After the commodities are inspected and proved up to the standards recognized by the inspection authorities, the inspection authorities will issue inspection certificates. The common types of inspections certificates may include:

→ Inspection Certificate of Quality
质量检验证书

→ Inspection Certificate of Weight
重量检验证书

→ Inspection Certificate of Quantity
数量检验证书

→ Veterinary Certificate
兽医检验证书

- → Sanitary Inspection Certificate 卫生检验证书
- → Inspection Certificate of Disinfection 消毒检验证书
- → Inspection Certificate on Damaged Cargo 验残检验证书
- → Certificate of Origin 原产地证书
- → Inspection Certificate of Value 价值检验证书
- → Inspection Certificate on Tank/Hold 验船/验舱证书
- → Certificate of Temperature 温度检验证书

Functions of Inspection Certificate are as followed:

1) guarantee the imported goods as to their quality, quantity, specifications, etc.;
2) serve as the basis upon which solution can be reached should disputes arise between the buyer and the seller after the goods reach the port of destination;
3) serve as the basis upon which it is possible to ascertain whether the goods shipped by the exporter conform to the stipulations of the contract;
4) serve as the basis upon which the importer can lodge his claims against the seller;
5) can be used by the importer for the Customs declaration and clearance;
6) make it imperative for the exporter to remain trustworthy and abide by the contract.

6.1.4 Inspection Clauses in the Contract 合同中的检验条款

The inspection clauses are provision in a supply contract under which the customer has the right to test or inspect all goods upon delivery (or during manufacture) to detect defects in materials, workmanship, or other conditions that may not be in conformity with the customer's (or the standard) specifications.

The inspection clauses cover the following:

- Inspection time and place
- Inspection authority
- Inspection certificate
- Inspection methods, contents and standards
- Re-inspection

检验的时间、地点
检验机构
检验证书
检验方法、内容、标准
复验

6.2 Claim 索赔

6.2.1 Concept of Claim 索赔的概念

Claim means that in international trade, one party breaks the contract and causes losses to the other party directly or indirectly, the party suffering the losses may ask for compensation for the losses. In some contract, the two parties often stipulate clauses on settlement of claim as well as inspection and claim clauses.

索赔（Claim），是指国际贸易业务的一方违反合同的规定，直接或间接地给另一方造成损害，受损方向违约方提出损害赔偿要求。

Settlement of claim means that the party breaking the contract declares that he will accept and handle the claim.

6.2.2 Claim Clause in Contract 合同中的索赔条款

The sellers may settle the claim upon the agreement of the buyers in the following ways:

- Agree to the rejection of the goods and refund to the buyers the value of the rejected goods in the same currency as contracted herein, and bear all direct losses and expenses incurred from the rejection, including interest, banking charges, freight, insurance premium, inspection charges, storage charges and all other necessary expenses required for the custody and protection of the rejected goods.

- Devaluate the goods according to the degree of inferiority, extent of damage and amount of losses suffered by the buyers.
- Replace the defective goods with new ones which conform to the specification, quality and performance as stipulated in the contract, and bear all expenses incurred and direct losses sustained by the buyers. The sellers shall, at the same time, guarantee the quality of the replaced goods for a further agreed period.

6.3 Arbitration 仲裁

Arbitration means that the two parties, before or after the disputes arise, reach a written agreement that they will submit the disputes which cannot be settled through amicable negotiations to the third party for arbitration.

仲裁（Arbitration），是指纠纷当事人在自愿基础上达成协议，将纠纷提交非司法机构的第三者审理，由第三者作出对争议各方均有约束力的裁决的一种解决纠纷的制度和方式。仲裁在性质上是兼具契约性、自治性、民间性和准司法性的一种争议解决方式。

Normally a board of arbitration consists of three arbitrators. Firstly, the plaintiff and the defendant choose one arbitrator respectively. Then, the two arbitrators chosen by the plaintiff and defendant choose a third arbitrator.

When performing the arbitration, the general procedures are: applying for arbitration, forming arbitration tribunal, hearing of an arbitration case, issuing an award, setting aside an award and enforcing an award.

→ Applying for arbitration

申请仲裁

When applying for arbitration, the claimant must submit to the Secretariat of the Arbitration Commission an arbitration agreement, an application for arbitration in writing, and the facts and evidence on which his claim is based. At the same time, he also shall pay an arbitration fee in advance to the Arbitration Commission. The application for arbitration shall include such information as the name and address of the claimant and those of the claimee, the arbitration agreement relied upon by the claimant, the facts of the case and the main points of dispute, and the claimant's claim and the facts and evidence on which his claim is based.

→ Forming arbitration tribunal

After receipt of the notice of arbitration, an arbitration tribunal should be formed. There are normally two types of arbitration tribunal: sole-arbitrator tribunal composed of one arbitrator and collegiate tribunal with three arbitrators. An arbitrator (or arbiter) is the impartial third party chosen by a higher or neutral body, or by the two parties in dispute to deal with a claim.

→ Hearing of an arbitration case

After an arbitration tribunal is formed, it is time to arrange the hearing of an arbitration case. However, if an oral hearing is needed, before hearing, the arbitration tribunal shall fix the date of the oral hearing after consultation with the Secretariat of the Arbitration Commission, and then communicate to the parties 30 days (for foreign economic cases and maritime cases) or 15 days (for domestic economic cases) before the date of the hearing

组成仲裁庭

仲裁庭（Arbitral Tribunal），是指由当事人选定或者仲裁委员会主任指定的仲裁员组成的，对当事人申请仲裁案件依仲裁程序进行审理并作出裁决的组织形式。按照《仲裁法》的规定，仲裁委员会受理仲裁案件后，应按程序组成仲裁庭对案件进行审理和裁决。因此，仲裁庭是行使仲裁权的主体。

仲裁听证

so that the parties concerned may have sufficient time to make necessary arrangements. However, at the request of the parties or with their consent, oral hearings may be omitted if the arbitration tribunal also deems that oral hearings are unnecessary. In this case, the arbitration tribunal may examine the case and make an award on the basis of documents only.

→ Issuing an award

As conclusion of the hearing, an award will be issued. For international arbitration cases, the time limit of the issuing of such award is within 9 months from the date on which the arbitration tribunal is formed. In case of oral hearing, the arbitration tribunal shall make an award within 30 days from the date of the oral hearing. The date on which the arbitral award is made is the date on which the arbitral award is final and the award comes into effect. The arbitration award is final and binding upon both parties. Neither party may bring a suit before a law court or make a request to any other organization to revise the arbitral award.

作出裁决

仲裁裁决（Arbitration award），是指仲裁庭对当事人之间所争议的事项进行审理后所作出的终局权威性判定。仲裁裁决的作出，标志着当事人之间纠纷的最终解决。

→ Setting aside an award

取消裁决

Although the arbitration award is final and binding upon both parties, if one party deems that there are matters not in conformity with the statutory procedure in the award, after receipt of the arbitral award, he can apply for setting aside the arbitral award. For example, the parties have neither included an arbitration clause in their contract nor subsequently concluded a written arbitration agreement or the formation of an arbitrator or arbitration tribunal is not in conformity with arbitration rules.

→ Enforcing an award

执行裁决

If no award is set aside, the parties must execute the arbitral award within the time limit specified. In case one party fails to execute the arbitral award, the other party may apply to the competent court for enforcement. If the residence or the properties of the losing party is located within the territory of China, the other party may apply to the Intermediate People's Court for enforcement of the award; if the residence of the losing party or the property of the losing party is located outside China, the other party may apply to the competent court in that country for enforcement. Whenever one party applies for enforcement to the competent court, he shall submit a written application for enforcement together with the arbitration agreement and the original copy of arbitral award.

The functions of arbitration agreement are as followed:

- Arbitration agreement is the basis for settlement of disputes, and is binding upon both parties.
- It is the warranty for arbitration authorities and arbitrators to obtain the jurisdiction.
- The arbitration agreement eliminates the jurisdiction of the court over the relative case. In case an arbitration agreement is reached, the interested parties can't appeal to the court anymore.

6.4 Force Majeure 不可抗力

6.4.1 Concept of Force Majeure 不可抗力的概念

Force majeure means that the frustration of the contract by the party in question results from natural or social forces including flood, earthquake, typhoon, fire, war and government decrees of prohibition beyond the control of man. This party shall be free from liability for performance, or be given an option of prolonging the performance of the contract owing to the above-mentioned event or series of events.

不可抗力（Force Majeure），又称人力不可抗拒，它是指在货物买卖合同签订以后，不是由于订约者任何一方当事人的过失或疏忽，而是由于发生了当事人既不能预见，又无法事先采取预防措施的意外事故，以一致不能履行或不能如期履行合同，遭受意外事故的一方可以免除履行合同的责任或延期履行合同。

6.4.2 Force Majeure Clause in Contract 合同中的不可抗力条款

In order to clarify what the term of force majeure covers under a particular contract, different ways have been adopted.

- Stipulate the Force Majeure clause in a general way
- Stipulate the Force Majeure clause in a way to list the contents
- Stipulate the Force Majeure clause in a way to colligation

Notes

1. Commodity Inspection
   商品检验，是指在国际货物买卖中，对卖方交付给买方货物地质量、数量和包装等项目进行检验,以确定合同的标的物是否符合买卖合同规定。

2. Claim
索赔，是指国际贸易业务的一方违反合同的规定，直接或间接地给另一方造成损害，受损方向违约方提出损害赔偿要求。
3. Arbitration
仲裁，是指纠纷当事人在自愿基础上达成协议，将纠纷提交非司法机构的第三者审理，由第三者作出对争议各方均有约束力的裁决的一种解决纠纷的制度和方式。
4. Force Majeure
不可抗力，又称人力不可抗拒，它是指在货物买卖合同签订以后，不是由于订约者任何一方当事人的过失或疏忽，而是由于发生了当事人既不能预见，又无法事先采取预防措施的意外事故，以致不能履行或不能如期履行合同，遭受意外事故的一方可以免除履行合同的责任或延期履行合同。

Exercise

1. Translate the following into Chinese or English.

Inspection
Inspection certificate
Force majeure
Litigation
仲裁条款
提出仲裁申请
Claim
Breach of contract
Arbitration
Penalty clause
索赔
听证

2. Decide whether the following statements are true (T) or false(F).

1) According to the CISG, once the offerer stipulates the validity on the offer, the offerer can still cancel the offer.
2) Offer and acceptance are two indispensable links for reaching an agreement and concluding a contract.
3) During the negotiation, the offer is made by seller and acceptance is made by buyer.
4) In international trade, effective establishment of a contract must be subject to 5 steps: Inquiry, Offer, Counter-offer, Acceptance and Signing.
5) Enquiry, offer and acceptance is indispensable part of a negotiation.
6) If the offeror makes no constrained meaning in the offer, then it does not constitute an

offer, but invites the other party to offer.

7) An advertisement on paper is an effective offer.
8) If an offer remarks "irrevocable", it means the offerer has no right to withdraw the offer.
9) Same to the offer, acceptance also can be cancel.
10) Convention provides that an offer is in effect when it reaches the offeree.

3. Translate the following sentences into Chinese or English.

1) The sellers shall not be held responsible for late delivery or non-delivery of the goods owing to the generally recognized force majeure causes.
2) The arbitral award is final and binding upon both parties.
3) Any dispute arising out of or in connection with the contract shall be finally settled by arbitration without recourse to courts.
4) The certificate should indicate that inspection had been carried out just before loading.
5) We regret to inform you that there were fifteen cartons damaged when your goods reached here and it was apparently caused by your bad packing.
6) 我们希望能够将仲裁的地点定在进口国。
7) 这是由伦敦一家非常有名的公证行提供的检验报告。
8) 对于运输途中产生的任何损失我们不承担赔偿责任。
9) 因货号有误，让你方收到错货。对此我们深表歉意，并且接受你方索赔。

4. Case Analysis

1）我方某公司从国外进口一批手套，合同上规定每箱 60 双，共 100 箱。货物运抵大连海关后，经检验发现外商擅自改为每箱 50 双，共计 120 箱。请问我方若据此提出拒收和索赔是否合理？
2）某公司向国外出口一批仪器，合同规定由买方提供唛头，但截至买方提供时间届满为止，仍未见其通知设计情况，而该公司货已备好。请问该公司应如何处理此事？

Chapter 7

Procedure of International Trade

国际贸易程序

Generally speaking, from the beginning to the end of a transaction, the whole operation undergoes four stages. This chapter is about the procedure of international trade.

Learning Objectives

After learning this chapter, you are expected to:

→ Outline the procedure of international trade;

→ Understand the principles and methods of negotiation;

→ Remember basic concepts of signing and implementation of contract;

→ State principles and settlement of breach of contract.

7.1 Arrangements before Trade 交易前的准备

Any exporter who wants to sell his products in a foreign country or countries must first conduct a lot of

出口商在销售前需进行市场调研，了解国外市场的产品需求及供货方式等。

market research. Market research is a process of conducting research into a specific market for a particular product. Export market research, in particular, is a study of a given market abroad to determine the needs of that market and the methods by which the products can be supplied. The exporter needs to know which foreign companies are likely to use his products or might be interested in marketing and distributing the products in their country.

After finding the right market, the next step involved is to find the potential partners. There are various channels through which one can make contacts with the potential foreign partners: trade fairs, wholesalers, direct mails, direct sales, etc. Moreover, there are also other sources available for international traders to find the potential business partners, for example, consulting firms, local chamber of commerce, ICC (International Chamber of Commerce), and publications such as *Economist*, *Financial Times*, etc.

市场定位后，需寻找潜在合作伙伴，可通过：贸易交流会、零售商、直邮、直销等方式联系潜在合作伙伴。此外，还可通过咨询公司或出版商寻找。

In order to ensure your rights and benefits, you need to know more information about potential partners, such as their credit reference from local bank or correspondent bank, major customers, business and so on.

为了保证自身权益，需了解潜在合作伙伴的其他信息。如，通过银行及客户等了解其信用水平。

In addition, when the right customer has been determined, you will have to make sure whether the products you intend to transact are within some certain controls. If so, you must deal with them before negotiation.

此外，确定目标客户后，应确保产品在控制范围内。

7.2 Negotiation 磋商

Contract negotiations are about ensuring that the two parties set out in a clear and an enforceable manner the elements that have been agreed. Once a contract is signed, further negotiations are not permitted.

7.2.1 Concept of Negotiation 谈判的概念

Negotiation is a dialogue between two or more people or parties, intended to reach an understanding, resolve point of difference, or gain advantage in outcome of dialogue, to produce an agreement upon courses of action, to bargain for individual or collective advantage, to craft outcomes to satisfy various interests of two people/parties involved in negotiation process. Negotiation is a process where each party involved in negotiating tries to gain an advantage for themselves by the end of the process. Negotiation is intended to aim at compromise.

在国际货物买卖中，交易双方就买卖商品的有关条件进行协商以期达成交易的过程，称为交易磋商（Negotiation），通常又称作贸易谈判。

Negotiation occurs in business, non-profit organizations, and governments, legal proceedings, among nations and in personal situations such as marriage, divorce, parenting, and everyday life. The study of the subject is called negotiation theory. Professional negotiators are often specialized, such as union negotiators, leverage buyout negotiators, peace negotiators, hostage negotiators, or may work under other titles, such as diplomats, legislators or brokers.

谈判无处不在，企业、非盈利组织、政府、司法程序、国家间及个人情形下都需要谈判。该学科被称为谈判理论。职业谈判家是非常专业的。

7.2.2 Procedures of Negotiation 谈判程序

○Inquiry
↓
○Offer
↓
○Counter-offer
↓
○Acceptance
↓
○Conclusion of Contract

询盘
↓
发盘
↓
还盘
↓
接受
↓
达成合同

7.2.2.1 Inquiry

An inquiry is a request for business information, such as price lists, catalogue, samples, and details about the goods or trade terms. It can be made by either the importer or the exporter. On receiving the enquiry, it is a regular practice that the exporter should reply to it without delay.

询盘（enquiry）也叫询价，是指交易的一方准备购买或出售某种商品，向对方询问买卖该商品的有关交易条件。

The seller and the buyer both can make an inquiry. Usually, the inquiry made by the buyer is also called bid, and the inquiry made by the seller is also called selling inquiry.

询盘的内容可涉及：价格、规格、品质、数量、包装、装运以及索取样品等，而多数只是询问价格。所以，业务上常把询盘称作询价。

Inquiry will not bind upon both parties, but usually when you receive an inquiry, you should reply it as soon as possible.

7.2.2.2 Offer

➢ The meaning of an offer

An offer is a proposal made by sellers to buyers in order to enter into a contract. In other words, it refers to trading terms put forward by offerers to offerees, on which the offerees are willing to conclude business with the offerers. There are two kinds of offers: firm offer and non-firm offer.

发盘（Offer），也称报盘、发价、报价。法律上称之为"要约"。发盘可以是应对方询盘的要求发出，也可以是在没有询盘的情况下，直接向对方发出。发盘一般是由卖方发出的，但也可以由买方发出，业务称其为"递盘"。

The party who makes an offer is called an offerer, in the case of the seller, the offer is called a selling offer, while in the case of the buyer, and it is called a buying offer.

➢ The basic conditions of an offer:

→ **The offer shall be made to one or more specific persons.**

发盘应向一个或一个以上特定的人提出。

The offer shall be the definite representation in which the offerer expresses that he shall conclude transaction on the terms and conditions stipulated therein.

→ **Contents of the offer shall be sufficiently definite, i.e., trade terms of the offer shall be complete, clear and final.**

发盘内容必须十分确定，发盘的贸易条件应完全、明晰，一个清晰完整的发盘应包括三个基本要素：名称、数量和价格。在我国，一个完整的发盘应包括：质量、数量、包装、价格、运输条件和付款条件。

The "Convention" stipulates that a sufficiently definite offer should include three basic elements: name, quantity and price. In our foreign trade practice, a complete offer shall include the quality, quantity, packing, price, terms of delivery of the goods and terms of payment.

→ **The offer shall indicate the intention of the offerer to be bound in case of acceptance.**

发盘应表明经受盘人接受，发盘人即受约束的意思。

This intention may be indicated by terms as "firm" offer, "offer with engagement", etc. If the offer has a restrictive condition, i.e., "subject to our final confirmation", then it's a non-firm offer regarded as an invitation for offer.

- Time of Validity or Duration of Offer

发盘的有效期

→ Stipulate the term of validity clearly.

The term of validity is not an indispensable condition of an offer:

- Stipulate the latest date for acceptance.
- Stipulate a period of time for acceptance.

→ If an offer doesn't clearly stipulate the time of validity, it will be valid within a reasonable time. An oral offer, unless otherwise agreed, must be accepted immediately unless the circumstances indicate otherwise.

- 明确规定有效期
- 若未明确规定有效期，发盘将在一个合理时间内有效。口头发盘，除发盘人发盘时另有声明外，受盘人只能当场表示接受。

- Time that an offer becomes effective. Different views of the time that a written form offer becomes effective: Dispatch Theory and Arrival Theory. Both "convention" and our "contract law" adopt arrival theory.

发票生效的时间

书面形式作出的发盘，《联合国国际货物销售公约》及我国《合同法》认为发盘送达受盘人时生效。

- Withdrawal or revocation of an offer.

发盘的撤回与撤销

A. Withdrawal. The British laws and the American laws have different explanations to withdrawal.

B. Revocation. As to whether an offer can be revoked or not, different laws have different explanations.

A. 撤回。英国法与美国法有不同解释。

B. 撤销。不同法律有不同解释。

- Termination of an offer

In the following cases, an offer is terminated: The time validity stipulated in the offer becomes due; the offeree rejects or makes a counter offer; the oferer revokes the offer before acceptance.

发盘效力的终止

如下情形，发盘效力终止：

有效期到了

受盘人拒绝或还盘

发盘人在受盘人接受前撤回

7.2.2.3 Counter-offer

A reply to an offer which purports to be an acceptance but contains additions, limitations or other modifications is a rejection of the offer and constitutes a counter offer.

- A reply to an offer which alters the terms of the offer materially constitutes a counter-offer.
- An acceptance with restrictive conditions is another form of counter-offer, such as "subject to our final confirmation".
- If the offeree accepts the original offer after he made a counter-offer, the contract is invalid.

还盘（Counter Offer），是指受盘人不同意发盘中的交易条件而提出修改或变更的意见。在法律上叫反要约。还盘实际上是受盘人以发盘人的地位发出的一个新盘。原发盘人成为新盘的受盘人

7.2.2.4 Acceptance

Acceptance means that the offeree agrees with the trade terms of the offer unconditionally within the validity period of the offer, and is willing to conclude the contract with the offerer based on these terms. The contract is established once the offer is accepted. The both parties concerned shall perform the obligation stipulated in the contract and own the relevant rights.

接受（Acceptance），是指受盘人在发盘的有效期内，无条件地同意发盘中提出的各项交易条件，愿意按这些条件和对方达成交易的一种表示。

Negotiation of contract

国际货物买卖合同的订立

国际贸易的程序（**Procedure of International Trade**）

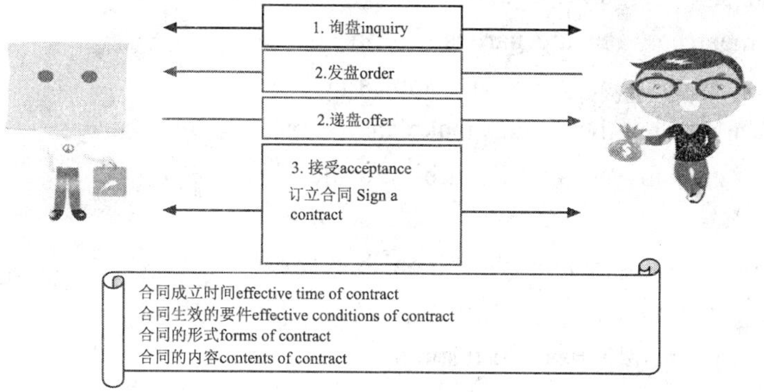

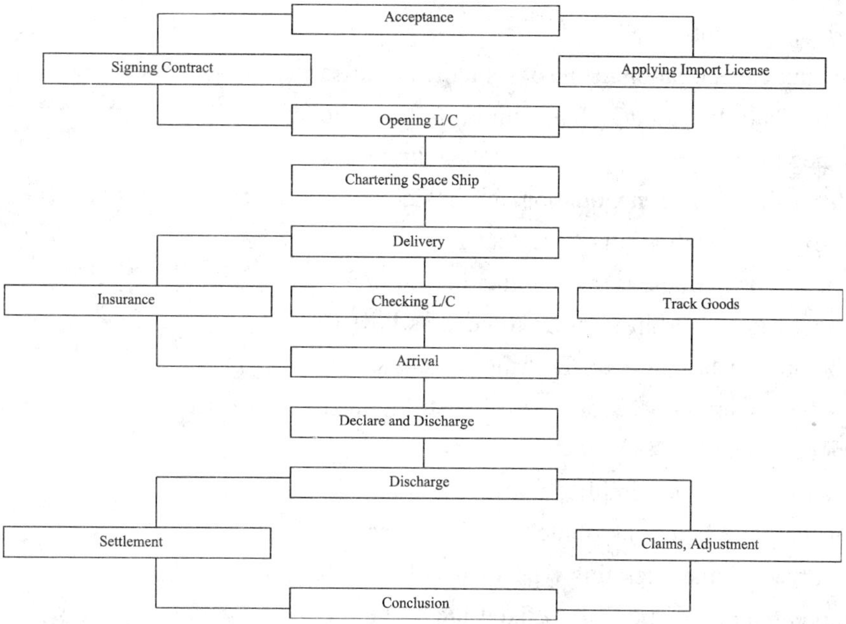

7.2.3 Negotiation Strategies 谈判策略

Negotiation can take a wide variety of forms, from a trained negotiator acting on behalf of a particular organization or position in a formal setting, to an informal negotiation between friends. Negotiation can be contrasted with mediation, where a neutral third party

从受过训练的谈判家代表其组织谈判到朋友间非正式谈判，谈判有多种形式。调解与谈判相比，需第三方在中间倾听和调解。仲裁与谈判相比，更像司法程序。

listens to each side's arguments and attempts to help draft an agreement between the parties. It can also be compared with arbitration, which resembles a legal proceeding. In arbitration, both sides make an argument as to the merits of their case and the arbitrator decides the outcome.

Negotiation theorists generally distinguish between two types of negotiation. Different theorists use different labels for the two general types and distinguish them in different ways.

谈判学家将谈判分为两类。

➢ Distributive negotiation

Distributive negotiation is also sometimes called positional or hard-bargaining negotiation. It tends to approach negotiation on the model of haggling in a market. In a distributive negotiation, each side often adopts an extreme position, knowing that it will not be accepted, and then employs a combination of guile, bluffing, and brinksmanship in order to cede as little as possible before reaching a deal. Distributive bargainers conceive of negotiation as a process of distributing a fixed amount of value.

分配谈判（Distributive Negotiation），是在零和条件下进行的谈判，即以谈判的一方获得收益而另一方付出代价为前提，这是一种非赢即输的谈判。在进行分配谈判时，谈判方的战术主要是试图使对手同意自己的具体目标点或尽可能接近它。这种谈判的过程是申诉各自的目标是公正的，并试图激发对手感情用事使他觉得应对你慷慨，从而达到目标。

The term distributive implies that there is a finite amount of the thing being distributed or divided among people involved. Sometimes this type of negotiation is referred to as the distribution of a "fixed pie." There is only so much to go around, but the proportion to be distributed is variable. Distributive negotiation is also sometimes called win-lose because of the assumption that one person's gain results in another person's loss. A distributive negotiation often involves people who have never had a previous interactive relationship, nor are they likely to do so again in the near future. Simple everyday examples would be buying a car or a house.

➤ Integrative negotiation

Integrative negotiation is also sometimes called interest-based or principled negotiation. It is a set of techniques that attempts to improve the quality and likelihood of negotiated agreement by providing an alternative to traditional distributive negotiation techniques. While distributive negotiation assumes there is a fixed amount of value (a "fixed pie") to be divided between the parties, integrative negotiation often attempts to create value in the course of the negotiation ("expand the pie"). It focuses on the underlying interests of the parties rather than their arbitrary starting positions, approaches negotiation as a shared problem rather than a personalized battle, and insists upon adherence to objective, principled criteria as the basis for agreement.

The word integrative implies some cooperation. Integrative negotiation often involves a higher degree of trust and the forming of a relationship. It can also involve creative problem-solving that aims to achieve mutual gains. It is also sometimes called win-win negotiation.

整合式谈判（Integrative Negotiation），又称双赢模式，其目的是为了寻找更好的和解方案，并能建立双赢、共赢的局面，也是一种彼此互利的方式。

7.3 Implementation of the Contract 合同的履行

After the conclusion of a contract, the orders shall be processed. It is important to note that the complex procedures of all sectors shall be followed correctly and in accordance with the terms stipulated in the contract and/or letter of credit.

7.3.1 Export Procedure 出口步骤

Even though it is recognized that there are many

variations in progressing an export contract, there is a general way of doing transaction that could be sought after. As contracts for export in China are mostly concluded under CIF by L/C(Letter of Credit),we will use this type to illustrate the export procedure.

➢ Examining L/C

Under a CIF contract with L/C as its payment term, the importer is required to open the L/C on time, but he may delay for various reasons. With a view to making collection of payment safe, the exporter should urge the importer to expedite the opening of L/C. Upon receipt of the relevant L/C, the exporter then must check the L/C against the sales contract carefully to ensure all terms and conditions in the L/C are in strict conformity with those in the sales contract. All documents involved in the transaction should be made out in accordance with what has been stipulated in the L/C instead of those in the sales contract.

审核信用证

▲对开证银行资信的审核

▲对信用证性质的审核：国外来证必须是不可撤销的、无追索权的信用证，否则会影响到出口商的收汇安全。

▲对信用证所列商品及货币和金额的审核。

▲对信用证装运期、有效期和有效地点的审核。

▲对单据要求的审核。

▲对特殊条款及批注的审核。

➢ Getting goods ready

If the exporter is supposed to produce the goods for shipment, this stage may take place well before the examination of the letter of credit. However, if the exporter is to purchase the goods for shipment, he will normally start the preparation of goods after or slightly before the L/C is ready, depending on the time involved to prepare the goods and the shipping schedule stipulated in the contract. The exporter shall prepare the goods in line with the name, quality, quantity, packing and marking required in the contract. If any certificate (e.g. Certificate of Origin) is required in the contract, the exporter also has to get it ready as stipulated.

备货

▲备货前应仔细确认货物的品质和规格。

▲备交货物的数量应留有余地。

▲根据信用证要求对货物进行包装和刷唛。

▲装运时间应适当留有余地。

▲对须报验的货物，向检验检疫局申请报验。

▲应在检验检疫证书规定的有效期内出运货物。

➢ Applying for mandatory inspection

申请强制检查

If required by the stipulations of the governments

or the contract that goods need to be inspected, the exporter should obtain the mandatory inspection certificates from the authorized institutions before shipping. The exporter should fill out an application form for the inspection of exports and submit it for inspection. At submission, he will be asked to present the following documents: commercial invoice, the copy of sales contract, letter of credit, samples if the goods are sold by sample, as well as the inspection report supplied by the manufacture. If the goods inspected are up to the standard required, the inspection institutions concerned will issue relevant inspection certificates.

若政府或合同中规定要检查货物，则出口商在装运前应向当局申请强制验货证。

➢ Receiving importer's inspection

Although it is not an obligation of the buyer, it is common that the importer always inspects the goods at the port of shipment. This is usually conducted after the necessary mandatory inspection has been completed or after the goods are ready if no such mandatory inspection is required.

来自出口商的检查

尽管不是其义务，但进口商往往也要验货。通常在强制验货后或货物准备装运但无强制验货时。

➢ Booking shipping space

After receiving the relevant L/C, at the time when goods are being prepared, the exporter should contact the shipping company or its agents for the chartering or booking of shipping space. Chartering is required for goods of large quantity which needs full shipload, while for goods in relatively small quantity, booking shipping space would do.

租船订舱

- 各出口公司在货证齐全后，根据外运公司船期表提供的船期情况，填写托运单即订船委托书，并及时送交外运公司。
- 外运公司按照托运单内容会同中国外轮代理公司（外运公司）根据具体情况安排船只或舱位。然后将船名通知托运的进出口公司并签发装货单并作为通知船方收货装运的凭证。
- 外运公司代出口公司向指定的仓库提取货物送至码头仓库。
- 出口货物在装船前都要办理报关手续。对于法定检验商品或信用证规定必须由商检局检验的商品并应事先报请商检局检验出证。待海关查验放行后凭装货单装船。
- 装船完毕后，由船长或大副签发大副收据。托运人凭此向外轮代理公司交付运费并换取正式提单。

➢ Clearing goods for export

After having the goods inspected, before the goods are loaded, the exporters should complete certain customs formalities. He should declare the export goods to the Customs by filling in certain customs forms and submitting appropriate documents such as commercial

出口清关

invoice, export license, copy of sales contract, inspection certificates, shipping order, etc. The Customs will inspect the export goods and decide if the shipment can be cleared through.

在货物检查后，装运前，出口商应完成海关程序，通过填表和提交合适单据进行报关。海关检查后决定是否清关放行。

➢ Getting goods loaded

After that, the exporter may start to prepare for the loading of the goods. Generally speaking, goods can be loaded for shipment only after they are cleared for export. After the completion of the shipment, the exporter will receive the Bill of Lading from the carrier. It is important to note that the date of issuance of bill of lading shall fall within the period allowed in the letter of credit, otherwise it will be refused by the bank for the negotiation of payment.

装货

一般而言，货物清关后就可装船。装船后，出口商可收到承运人签发的提单（Bill of Lading）。提单签发日期应在信用证有效期内，否则银行会拒付。

➢ Obtaining insurance

Under a CIF contract, the exporter should also obtain cargo insurance at his own expense as agreed upon in the contract. Therefore, after loading, he can contact insurance company or his agents to arrange for insurance. According to Incoterms 2010, the coverage on CIF term is the minimum coverage (See Chapter 6). However, if the importer asks for additional insurance coverage, the exporter is expected to effect insurance as required but the expense shall be for the importer's account. This should be made clear in the sales contract.

投保

CIF 合同下，出口商应自付费用对货物投保。根据 Incoterms 2010，仅需按最低险别投保，然而，若进口商要求投保额外险别，额外产生的费用由进口商承担。

➢ Presenting documents for bank negotiation

After shipment is made and insurance is obtained, the exporter should then present all necessary document specified in the L/C for the negotiation of payment within the presentation period required in the contract or the letter of credit. All documents must be made out in accordance with the requirement in the L/C. The document generally include the following: commercial

交单议付

- 货物装船后，出口公司应立即按照信用证的要求，正确缮制各种单据，严格审核无误后，在信用证规定的有效期内送交银行结汇。我国出口结汇目前有下列四种方式。但不论采取那种方式均由结汇银行将应付外汇按当日牌价折成人民币付给出口公司。

invoice, packing list, bill of lading, insurance policy, inspection certificates, etc. Some importing countries may also require such document as the Certificate of Origin, the Consular Invoice, etc. to issue import license or to calculate import customs duty. Under such circumstances, the exporter is expected to obtain these document as required and present them together with other document to the bank for negotiation of payment. If the details in the document presented are in strict conformity with those in the L/C, the exporter will receive payment from the bank as expected.

- 即期结汇指即期信用证如有电报索汇等即期结汇的条款。银行审核单据后于三日内结汇。
- 买单结汇即押汇或议付指银行审核单据无误即以单据作抵押，在扣除邮程利息后垫款结汇。
- 定期结汇指银行结汇期限与押汇规定的邮程期限相同。银行于到期时主动结汇，不扣利息。
- 收妥结汇指银行将单据寄给开证银行并在收到开证银行寄回偿付通知后再予结汇。

7.3.2 Import Procedures 进口程序

Import procedure is closely related to export procedure. Most of the import transactions in our country are under FOB term with payment on L/C. The general procedure of import is:

➢ Opening the L/C

If the payment in the sales contract is to be made by L/C, after signing a contract, the importer should apply for the issuance of an L/C at the issuing bank in time and then forward it to the exporter. The importer has to make sure that the opening of the L/C should be made in time and the terms in the L/C should fit that in the sales contract to avoid future amendments which are costly and time consuming to both parties and may delay shipment. Special attention should be paid to the total sum, description of the goods, validity, documents required, etc.

开立信用证

若合同要求以信用证进行支付，则在签订合同后，进口商应保证及时开证，且依据合同条款开立。特别注意总金额、商品描述、有效期、要求的单据等。

➢ Booking shipping space

Under FOB, it is the importer who must arrange at his own expense for the carriage of the goods from the named port of shipment. After receiving the notice from

租船订舱

FOB 合同下，当收到出口商备货完毕的通知后，进口商应尽快租船订舱，并给予出口商以充分的通知，如船名、

the exporter and knowing that the exporter has got the goods ready for shipment, the importer should charter or book shipping space with the carrier and give the exporter sufficient notice of the information such as the name of the vessel, the name of the loading point and the required delivery time so as to enable the exporter to deliver the goods to the carrier smoothly and without delay.

装货港名称及装货时间等。

➢ Inspecting and supervising at the port of shipment

Before shipment, the importer or his agent will inspect the goods at the port of shipment before loading. If necessary, the importer may also want to supervise the shipment at the loading port.

在装货港检查和监督货物

装船前，进口商或其代理将检查货物。若必要，进口商业希望监督装船过程。

➢ Obtaining insurance

Although under FOB in Incoterms 2010 the importer has no obligation for the contract of insurance, considering the fact that the potential risks threatening the goods in transit are great and the importer is the party who is exposed to these risks, the importer will normally be expected to effect insurance on his own.

投保

虽然2010通则中船上交货术语没有规定进口商投保的义务，但鉴于运输途中潜在的风险巨大，进口商一般会自行办理保险。

➢ Examining documents and making payment

If it is stipulated that the payment should be made by L/C in the sales contract, the importer will be asked to make payment to the issuing bank upon receiving the relevant documents. Even though both the negotiating bank and issuing bank have examined the documents before they make payment to the exporter, it is important for the importer to examine the documents on his own carefully before making payments. If no problem is found with the documents, the importer has to make the payment as has been stipulated in the contract.

审单并付款

当收到相关单据时，应向开证行付款。尽管议付行和开证行已审核，进口方仍需仔细审单，确认无误后再按合同要求付款。

➢ Clearing goods for import

Upon arrival, imported goods from other countries have to be cleared through the Customs. So the importer

进口清关

货物抵达，进口货物应清关放行。

should prepare the necessary documents such as the sales contract, the commercial invoice, packing list, the import license (if any) and inspection certificate while clearing the goods for import. If necessary, the importer also needs to carry out all customs formalities for the transit of his goods through any other country.

进口商应准备相应单据，如销售合同、商业发票、包装清单、进口许可及验货证明进行进口清关。

➢ Taking delivery and inspecting

After making the payment and getting the shipping documents, the importer can take delivery of the goods from the carrier after the arrival of the goods at the destination. However, it should be noted that the importer should inspect the goods to ensure that the goods delivered conform to the description of the goods in the sales contract. Should there be any inconformity, the importer will lodge claim against parties concerned for compensation.

收货和验货

付款并拿到单据后，进口方可收货。为确保货物与合同一致，进口方应验货。若有不符，进口方可进行索赔。

7.4 Breach of Contact 违约

Breach of contract is a legal cause of action in which a binding agreement or bargained—for exchange is not honored by one or more of the parties to the contract by non-performance or interference with the other party's performance. If the party does not fulfill his contractual promise, or has given information to the other party that he will not perform his duty as mentioned in the contract or if by his action and conduct he seems to be unable to perform the contract, he is said to breach the contract.

违约行为（Breach of Contract），是指合同当事人违反合同义务的行为。违约行为是违约责任的基本构成要件，没有违约行为，也就没有违约责任。

Notes

1. Negotiation
交易磋商，又称作贸易谈判，是指在国际货物买卖中交易双方就买卖商品的有关条件进行协商以期达成交易的过程。
2. Enquiry
询盘，也叫询价，是指交易的一方准备购买或出售某种商品，向对方询问买卖该商品的有关交易条件。
3. Offer
发盘，也称报盘、发价、报价。法律上称之为“要约”。
4. Counter Offer
还盘，是指受盘人不同意发盘中的交易条件而提出修改或变更的意见。在法律上叫反要约。
5. Acceptance
接受，是指受盘人在发盘的有效期内，无条件地同意发盘中提出的各项交易条件，愿意按这些条件和对方达成交易的一种表示。
6. Distributive negotiation
分配谈判，是在零和条件下进行的谈判，即以谈判的一方获得收益而另一方付出代价为前提，这是一种非赢即输的谈判。
7. Integrative negotiation
整合式谈判，又称双赢模式，其目的是为了寻找更好的和解方案，并能建立双赢、共赢的局面，也是一种彼此互利的方式。
8. Breach of Contract
违约行为，是指合同当事人违反合同义务的行为。违约行为是违约责任的基本构成要件，没有违约行为，也就没有违约责任。

Exercise

1. Translate the following into Chinese or English.

Negotiation	sign of contract
Inquiry	offer

Counter-Offer

违约 索赔

理赔 救济方法

2. Decide whether the statements are T(True) or F(False).

1) Sometimes when the buyer cannot determine a specific port of discharge, he may require two or three ports to be written on the contract for option.
2) When there are optional ports in the contract, the goods may be unloaded at any one of the ports at the shipping company's disposal.
3) An order bill of lading may be negotiable after being endorsed.
4) According to the UCP 600, a bill of lading which is issued subject to a Charter Party must be accepted unless the Credit stipulates otherwise.
5) When you transport your goods by a Time Charter, you have to pay for loading and unloading.
6) When the ship-owner speeds up his ship and arrives at the destination at an earlier date than is stipulated, he can obtain dispatch money from the shipper.

3. Translate the following sentences into Chinese or English.

1) Please quote the FOB price including delivery charge to Hong Kong.
2) Research foundry market and make product price proposals.
3) 你能给我们寄来一份胶靴的目录并告诉我们付款方式吗？
4) 如果你们的价格优惠，我可以马上订货。

4. Case Analysis.

某年6月13日，中国某公司传真向美国商人发盘供应10 000件瓷器，并列明品名、价格和“牢固木箱”包装等交易条件。美方收到传真后，立即回复表示接受，并要求用“新木箱装运”。我方收到美方回复后，立即着手备货，准备于双方约定的7月份装船。两周后，美方又传真我方称：“由于你方对新木箱包装的要求未予确认，故合同没有成立。”我方则认为合同已成立，双方为此发生争议。该争议应如何解决？

Chapter 8

Methods of International Trade

国际贸易的形式

International trade methods refer to the common practices and channels between countries for the flow of commodities or services. There are many channels of selling goods to the foreign market.

贸易方式（Methods of International Trade），是指国际间进行货物买卖所采取的具体交易做法。即通过什么渠道推销商品、利用什么方法抵偿货款以及采用什么方式进行成交和交易双方之间的关系等几个方面的问题。

☞ **Learning Objectives:**

After learning this chapter, you are expected to:

→ Remember the basic concepts of different methods of international trade;

→ Compare the characteristics of different methods.

8.1 Distribution, Exclusive Sales, Agency 经销、包销、代理

8.1.1 Distribution 经销

Distribution is a channel of allocation of goods from the producer to consumers, which is made up of distributors, wholesalers and retailers besides producers. As marketers well know, distribution is a major

经销（Distribution）是进口商（经销商）与出口商（供货商）达成协议，承担在规定的期限和区域内销售指定商品的一种贸易方式。经销是属于转卖方式的一种贸易方式。

component of the marketing mix, a vital and necessary part of the so-called Four Ps. Distribution involves not one manager, but several in one or more aspects of distribution efficiency.

The distributors buy products from the principals on their own account and take title to them and resell them to their customers in their territory. Therefore, there is no contractual relationship between the principal and the ultimate customer.

The wholesales sell products in large quantities, usually to other distributors. Generally, a wholesale buys large quantities of goods from producers and breaks into bulk deliveries to supply retailers with smaller amounts assembled and sorted to order.

The retailers are distributors who sell goods or services to ultimate consumers. Basically, there are three kinds of retailers: multiple shops, co-operative retailers and independent retailers.

The following five tips may help to avoid risk in doing business with distributors:

- Put the agency agreement in writing. The rights and obligations resulting from a written agreement require no extraneous proof and are all that necessary to record or prove the terms of a contract in most countries.
- Set forth the benefit to both parties in the agreement. Well-balance agreement should not place an excess of profitless burden on one of the parties. Performance of the agreement may be impossible to enforce against a party who has no apparent benefit from it.
- Give clear definition and meaning to all

以下五个建议可有助于避免与经销商交易的风险：

以书面形式订立代理协议。以书面形式记录权利与义务，不再需要其他证据。

在协议中阐明双方的利益。好的协议中，并不会出现一方受益很多，而另一方无明显利益的情况。

对所有合同条件进行清晰的定义和界定。

contract terms. Many English terms that are spelled similarly in the foreign language have entirely different meaning. Require that the English version prevail when there is doubt. To avoid conflict use of Incoterms.

- Expressly state the right obligations of the parties. The agency contract should contain a description of the rights and duties of each party, the nature and duration of the relationship, and the reason for which the agreement may be terminated.

代理商合同应当包含双方权责描述，代理关系性质和持续时间，以及合约可能终止的原因。

- Specify a jurisdictional clause. If local lawsuit will allow, specify in the contract the jurisdiction that will handle any legal disputes that may arise. Where possible, use arbitration. Basic arbitration rules and principles are generally the same anywhere. Clauses in the contract should contain identification of the arbitration body.

如果当地法律允许的话，应在合同中说明可能发生的法律纠纷所属的司法管辖范围。在适当的时候，可提请仲裁。

8.1.2 Exclusive Sales 包销

Exclusive sales are established between a seller and an exclusive distributor by means of an exclusive sales agreement, under which the exclusive distributor is authorized by the seller with an exclusive right to buy and, then, sell the designated goods in the specified area or region within a specified period of time. With such an arrangement the seller should by no means make use of any other channels to market the designated goods to others in the area, and the exclusive distributor, reciprocally, should guarantee to buy a specified amount of the designated goods from the seller within a certain period.

包销（Exclusive Sales）指出口商通过签订协议给国外销售商在一定时期、一定地区经营某一种或某一类商品的专营权利的贸易方式。

Exclusive sales differ greatly from agencies in many ways. Under exclusive sales, the transaction is both a sale and a purchase, and the relationship between the parties concerned is a principal to a principal. The exclusive distributor engages in the purchase and sale of goods at his own cost and risks. In the case of agency arrangements, the relationship between the parties is that a principal to an agent, who, when engaged in the trade, invests no capital, bears no risks of operation, but acts merely on behalf of the principal simply on a commission basis.

8.1.3 Agency 代理

The agency means that the agent signs contracts with a third party on behalf of the principle or does other matters relating to the sales in compliance with the instruction from his principal, while the principal shall be responsible for the agent's business activities and the obligations incurred therein. Meanwhile, an agent is an individual or legal entity authorized to act on behalf of another one. Generally, there are four kinds of agency: broker, sole agent, commission agent and general agent.

代理（Agency）是国际贸易中的一种习惯做法。在国际贸易中，所谓代理商（Agent）是指接受委托人（Principal）的委托向第三者出售商品并办理与交易有关的其他事项的人，通过代理商进行贸易的方式称为代理方式。在代理方式下，委托人（即货主）一般都给予代理人在特定地区和在一定时间内代销指定的商品的权利。他们之间是委托代销关系。代理商有积极推销商品的义务和享有收取佣金的权利。

A broker brings two parties together, enabling them to enter into a contract to which the broker is not a principal. A sole agent, also called exclusive agent, has exclusive rights to sell a product or service in a particular territory for a specified period. A commission agent specializes in buying and selling goods for a principal in another country for a commission. They always execute the orders given by a principal to buy or sell goods on payment of a fee or a commission based on the value of the deal. A general agent is an agent who is authorized to do all acts related to the principal's business, which may include negotiating contract, establishing credit, advertising, arranging for shipping and setting up overseas offices and outlets.

It must be stressed that the agent can't surpass the scope of authority and he can't sign a contract in his own name. That is, the agent is only a middleman and receives commission. It is free from the responsibilities of the contract.

8.2 Auction, Consignment, Fairs and Sales 拍卖、寄售、展卖

8.2.1 Auction 拍卖

In an auction, goods are sold to the party who submits the highest bit. Auctions, broadly defined, are used to allocate significant economic resources, from works of art to short-term government bonds to offshore tracts for oil and gas exploration to the radio spectrum. They take many forms. For example, bids may be called out sequentially (as in auctions for works of art) or may be submitted in sealed envelopes; the price paid may be the highest bid, or some other price; if more than one unit of the goods is being sold, bids may be taken on all units simultaneously, or the units may be sold sequentially.

拍卖（Auction）是由专营拍卖业务的拍卖行接受货主的委托，在一定的时间和地点，按照一定的章程和规则，以公开叫价的方法，把货物卖给出价最高的买主的一种贸易方式。

The mainly features of auction are as follows:

- It is processed in an organization.
- It has its particular law and regulations.
- It is the spot transaction.

8.2.2 Consignment 寄售

The consignment means that the consignor delivers the goods to the place of consignment abroad first, then

寄售（Consignment）是一种委托代售的贸易方式。寄售人先将准备销售的

entrusts the consignee with the task to sell the goods according to the conditions and methods stipulated in the agreement of consignment.

货物运往国外寄售地，委托当地代销人按照双方商定的条件，由代销人为其销售，所得货款扣除佣金及有关费用后，交付给寄售人。

The seller (consignor) retains title to the goods during shipment and storage of the product in the warehouse or retail store. The consignee acts as a selling agent, selling the goods and remitting the net proceeds to the consignor. Like open-account sales, consignment sales can also be risky, and they lend themselves to only certain kinds of merchandise. Great care should be taken in working out this contractual arrangement.

寄售贸易是根据寄售协议进行的。寄售协议属于信托合同性质。寄售人与代销人之间是委托代售关系，而不是买卖关系。

Moreover, the features of consignment are as follows:

- The consignor shall first deliver the goods to the agent or consignment agent.
- Before the commission agent sells out the goods, the title to the goods still belongs to the consignor.
- The commission agent is commissioned to sell the goods for the consignor and he will deal with the goods according to the order of the consignor only.
- The consignment agent will not under any risks and expenses and he only charges commission for his service.

寄售的特点:

- 寄售是一种现货交易。寄售人先将货物运往国外，然后由代销人在当地销售。
- 货物在售出前，其所有权属寄售人。
- 寄售人与代销人之间是委托代售关系。代销人只为寄售人提供服务并收取佣金，其责任只限于在货物抵达后照顾货物，尽力推销，并依照寄售人的指示处置货物。
- 货物售出前的一切费用和风险由寄售人承担。

8.2.3 Fairs and Sales 展卖

Fairs and sales mean showing and selling goods by taking advantage of exhibitions, trade fairs or other forms of goods display. When entering into a fair, the companies have to choose the proper commodities,

展卖（Fair and Sales）是指利用各种形式的展览会和博览会对商品实行展销结合的一种贸易方式。

good partners, proper places to exhibit the goods and good opportunities to exhibit the goods.

8.3 Invitation to Tender and Submission of Tender 招标和投标

A tender is a formal proposal to buy a specified quantity of goods at a specified price. Generally, a tender involves the procedures as invitation to tender, submission of tender, bid opening, tender discussion and decision, establishment of contract and execution of contract.

投标（Tender）是投标人根据招标人（Inviter to Bid）的招标条件，应邀发出实盘，以期达成交易的一种贸易方式。这里提到的招标人是购买商品的人，投标人是供货人。

8.3.1 Invitation to Tender 招标

Invitation to tender is the initiating step of a competitive tendering process in which qualified suppliers or contractors are invited to submit sealed bids for construction or for supply of specific and clearly defined goods or services during a specified timeframe. It is also called request for tenders.

招标（Invitation to Tender）是指招标人预先发出招标公告或招标单，提出拟购商品的品种、数量和有关买卖条件或拟建项目的各种条件，邀请投标人在规定的时间和地点投标的行为。招标实际上是竞卖的交易方式。

Sometimes, it may be replaced by invitation for bid. However, there is a little difference between them. Invitation for bid (IFB), or invitation to bid (ITB), is a part of the sealed bid process. Companies or government organizations give in-depth specifications for projects and invite contractors to bid their proposals for various projects. The sealed bids are opened at the predetermined time and recorded. A contract is awarded to the best bid. It is also called request for quote.

If not stated otherwise, the contractor or supplier with the lowest bid is awarded the contract, provided that they meet the minimum criteria for the bid. This is in contrast to a request for proposal (RFP), in which case other reasons (technology used, quality) might cause or allow choice of the second best offer. An RFP is a request for a price from a buyer but the buyer would also expect suggestions and ideas on how the project work should be done. RFPs are thus focused on more than just pricing/cost, they entail a bit of consulting from the contractor or vendor.

8.3.2 Submission of Tender 投标

Submission of tender means that the bidder makes a formal statement of promise, usually in response to the request for quotation, to supply the goods or services required by a tenderer, at specified prices, and within a specified period.

投标（Submission of Tender）是指投标人根据招标公告或招标单规定的条件，在指定的时间内向招标人递盘的行为。投标相当于磋商中的发盘。

8.4 Countertrade 对销贸易

Counter trade is a mode of trade which makes use of the agreed commodity or service as a mode of payment for the equipment, technology imported from abroad. It has many forms including barter trade, compensation trade, counter purchase, offset trade, switch trade and etc.

对销贸易（Counter Trade）是指在互惠的前提下，由两个或两个以上的贸易方达成协议，规定一方的进口产品可以部分或全部以相对的出口产品来支付。

The reasons why countertrade is adopted can be summed up in four parts:

- Some people can't pay in the currency that you want. This may occur as a result of a nonconvertible currency, a shortage of foreign exchange or a lack of commercial credit.
- To stimulate or protect the output of domestic industries of the buyer's country.

- To gain a competitive advantage over competing suppliers.
- To cope with the rules and regulations in the buyer's country, which are aimed at planning and balancing overseas trade.

8.5 Futures Trading and Hedging 期货交易与套期保值

In the last decades derivatives have become increasingly important in the world of finance. Futures and options are now traded actively on many exchanges throughout the world. Forward contracts, swaps and many different types of options are regularly traded outside exchanges by financial institutions, fund managers and corporate treasurers in what is called the over-the-counter market. Derivatives are also sometimes added to a bond or stock issue.

8.5.1 Futures Trading 期货交易

A derivative can be defined as a financial instrument whose value depends on (or derives from) the value of other, more basic underlying variables. As mentioned above, futures contract is a particularly simple derivative. The derivatives exchange is the market where individuals trade standardized contracts that have been defined by the exchange. The over-the-counter market is an important alternative to exchanges and, measured in terms of the total volume if trading, has become much larger than the exchange-trade market.

金融衍生产品（Derivative），也称金融衍生工具、金融衍生产物，是指其价值依赖于标的资产（Underlying Asset）价值变动的合约。这种合约可以是标准化的，也可以是非标准化的。标准化合约是指其标的资产（基础资产）的交易价格、交易时间、资产特征、交易方式等都是事先标准化的，因此此类合约大多在交易所上市交易，如期货。非标准化合约是指以上各项由交易的双方自行约定，因此具有很强的灵活性，比如远期合约。

8.5.1.1 Concept

期货交易（Futures Trading）期货交易

The futures trading are organized markets at which

futures contracts of particular commodities are sold according to its regulations at a stipulated time. A future contract is an agreement between two parties to buy or sell an asset at a certain future time for a certain price. It can be contrasted with a spot contract, which is an agreement to buy or sell an asset today.

是按照交易所的规定，由买卖双方在交易所内达成远期交割的贸易方式，交易所的期货交易，在资本主义国家多数是属于买空卖空的业务，便于投机商利用不同时间价格的涨落，买进卖出赚取价格差额。因此，交易所的期货交易量很大。但订约双方大多数不是交割实际货物，而是用货币支付价格变动的差额。

There are differences between futures contract and forward contract. Basically, futures contract are traded on an organized exchange, and the contract terms are standardized by the exchange. By contrast, forward contract are private agreements between two financial institutions or between a financial institution and one of its corporation clients. Besides, one way in which a futures contract is different from a forward contract is that an exact delivery date is usually not specified.

期货合同与远期合同不同。期货合同在规范化的交易所中交易，合同条件是标准化的。远期合同是两个金融机构之间私人协议而成。此外，期货合同中交货日期不确定。

One of the parties to a futures contract assumes a long position and agrees to buy the underlying asset on a certain specified future date for a certain specified price. The other party assumes a short position and agrees to sell the underlying asset on the same date for the same price. Actually, the vast majority of futures contracts do not lead to delivery. The reason is that most traders choose to close out their positions prior to the delivery period specified in the contract. Closing out a position means entering into the opposite types of trade from the original one.

期货合同中一方看涨，同意在未来某一日期以某一价格买某资产。另一方看跌，同意在未来同一日期以同价卖某资产。实际上，大量期货并不真正交货。许多交易商在合同中具体交货日期前买/卖出期权。

8.5.1.2 Specification of the Futures Contract

When developing a new futures contract, the exchange must specify in some detail the exact nature of the agreement between the two parties. In particular, it must specify the asset, the contract size (exactly how much of the asset will be delivered under one contract), where delivery will be made, and when delivery will be made. Sometimes alternatives are specified for the grade of the asset that will be delivered or for the delivery locations.

Generally, it is the party with the short position (the party that has agreed to sell the asset) that chooses what will happen when alternatives are specified by the exchange. When the party with the short position is ready to deliver, it files a notice of intention to deliver with the exchange. This notice will indicate selections it has made with respect to the grade of asset that will be delivered and the delivery location.

8.5.1.3 Types of Traders

There are two main types of traders executing trades: commission brokers and local. Commission brokers are following the instructions of their clients and charge a commission for doing so. Locals are trading on their own account.

Individuals taking positions, whether locals or the clients of commission brokers, can be categorized as hedgers, speculators, or arbitrageurs.

Hedgers use futures, forwards and options to reduce the risk that they face from potential future movements in a market variable. Note that if the companies choose not to hedge, they might do better than if they do hedge. Alternatively, they might do worse.

Speculators use futures, forwards and options to bet on the future direction of a market variable. Whereas hedgers want to avoid an exposure to adverse movements in the price of an asset, speculators wish to

经纪人（Broker）是指为市场上买卖双方提供中介服务从中收取佣金的人。经纪人可分交易商经纪(inter-dealer brokers)和代理经纪(client or agency brokers)两大类，前者只为专业的做市商服务，后者则为机构或个人投资者服务。

自营商（Local）是证券业内以本金买卖而非代理买卖证券的个人或公司。自营商的利润或损失来自于同一证券的买卖价差。在不同时期，同一个人或公司可能会分别充当经纪商或自营商的角色。

套期保值者（Hedger）是指那些把期货市场作为价格风险转移的场所，利用期货合约作为将来在现货市场上进行买卖的商品的临时替代物，对其现在买进（或已拥有，或将来拥有）准备以后出售或对将来需要买进商品的价格进行保值的机构和个人。这些套期保值者大多是生产商、加工商、库存商以及贸易商和金融机构，其原始动机是期望通过期货市场寻求价格保障，尽可能消除不愿意承担的现货交易的价格风险，从而能够集中精力于本行业的生产经营业务上，并以次取得正常的生产经营利润。

投机者（Speculator），投机者是指在期货市场上通过“买空卖空”、“卖空买空”，希望以较小的资金来博取利润的投资者。投机者愿意承担期货价格变动的风险，一旦预测期货价格将上涨，投机者就会买进

take a position in the market. Speculators can be classified as scalpers, day traders or position traders. Scalpers are watching for very short term trends and attempt to profit from small changes in the contract price. They usually hold their positions for only a few minutes. Day traders hold their positions for less than one trading day. They are unwilling to take the risk that adverse news will occur overnight. Position traders hold their positions for much longer periods of time. They hope to make significant profits from major movements in the markets.

Arbitrageurs are the third important group of participants in futures, forward, and options markets. Arbitrage involves locking in a risking profit by simultaneously entering into transactions in two or more market.

8.5.2 Hedging 套期保值

Hedging is a way of reducing risk. Many of the participants in futures markets are hedgers, and their aim is to use futures markets to reduce a particular risk that they face. This risk might relate to the price of oil, a foreign exchange rate, the level of the stock market, or some other variables.

When an individual or company chooses to use futures markets to hedge a risk, the objective is usually to take a position that neutralizes the risk as far as possible. A perfect hedge is one that completely eliminates the risk. However, perfect hedges are rare in practice.

A short hedge is a hedge that involves a short position in futures contracts. A short hedge is appropriate when the hedger already owns an asset and expected to sell it at some time in the future. A short hedge can also be used when an asset is not owned right

期货合同；一旦预测期货价格将下降，投机者就会卖出期货合同，待价格与自己预料的方向变化一致时，再抓住机会进行对冲。通常投机者在期货市场上要冒很大的风险。

套利者（arbitrager，arbitrageur），是指利用“股指期货市场和股票现货市场（期现套利）、不同的股指期货市场（跨市套利）、不同股指期货合约（跨商品套利）或者同种商品不同交割月份（跨期套利）”之间出现的价格不合理关系，通过同时买进卖出以赚取价差收益的机构或个人。

套期保值（Hedging）是指交易者配合在现货市场的买卖，在期货市场买进或卖出与现货市场交易品种、数量相同，但方向相反的期货合同，以期在未来某一时间通过卖出或买进此期货合同来补偿因现货市场价格变动带来的实际价格风险。

套期保值的理论基础：现货和期货市场的走势趋同（在正常市场条件下），由于这两个市场受同一供求关系的影响，所以二者价格同涨同跌；但是由于在这两个市场上操作相反，所以盈亏相反，期货市场的盈利可以弥补现货市场的亏损。

卖出套期保值（Short Hedge），又称“空头套期保值”，是为了防止现货价格在交割时下跌的风险而先在期货市场卖出与现货数量相当的合约所进行的交易方式。持有空头头寸，来为交易者将要在现货市场上卖出的现货而从进行保值。因此，卖出套期保值又称为“卖空保值”或

now but will be owned at some time in the future.

Hedges that involve taking a long position in a futures contract are known as long hedges. A long hedge is appropriate when a company knows it will have to purchase a certain asset in the future and wants to lock in the price now. Long hedges can also be used to partially offset an existing short position.

"卖期保值"。卖出套期保值目的在于回避日后因价格下跌而带来的亏损风险。

买入套期保值(Buying Hedge 或 Long Hedge)，又称"多头套期保值"，是在期货市场购入期货，用期货市场多头保证现货市场的空头，以规避价格上涨的风险。持有多头头寸，来为交易者将要在现货市场上买进的现货商品保值。因此又称为"多头保值"或"买空保值"。买入套期保值的目的是为了防止日后因价格上升而带来的亏损风险。这种用期货市场的盈利对冲现货市场亏损的做法，可以将远期价格固定在预计的水平上。买入套期保值是需要现货商品而又担心价格上涨的投资者常用的保值方法。

8.6 Processing Trade and Leasing Trade 加工贸易与租赁贸易

8.6.1 Processing Trade 加工贸易

The process industries are those industries where the primary production processes are either continuous, or occur on a batch of materials that is indistinguishable. For example, a food processing company making sauce may make the sauce in a continuous, uninterrupted flow from receipt of ingredients through packaging. Or batches may be produced depending on the cook kettle sizes but immediately combined and re-routed. In either case, there is no concept of a unit of sauce while it is being processed. Examples of the process industries include food, beverages, chemicals, pharmaceuticals, petroleum, ceramics, base metals, coal, plastics, rubber, textiles, tobacco, wood and wood products, paper and

加工贸易（Processing trade），包括来料加工（Processing with Given Materials）与来件装配（Assembling with Provided Parts）。前者指是指由出口人提供原材料、辅料、包装物料，或部分有关的机器设备、仪器、工具、模具等，委托进口方有关工厂加工成所需要的成品出口。后者指出口方提供零件、部件和元器件以及装配所需的设备和技术，交进口方有关工厂按对方提供的图纸或样品进行组装，成品全部交给出口方自行销售，进口方只收取组装费用。

paper products, etc.

Applying industrial engineering tools in the process industries can vary greatly from applying these same tools in discrete parts manufacturing. The Process Industries Division is a forum for the exchange of ideas in theory and practice of industrial engineering techniques applied to process industries; facilitating greater interactions among industry and academic professionals by organizing.

8.6.2 Leasing Trade 租赁贸易

Leasing is a process by which a firm can obtain the use of a certain fixed assets for which it must pay a series of contractual, periodic, tax deductible payments. The lessee is the receiver of the services or the assets under the lease contract and the lessor is the owner of the assets. The relationship between the tenant and the landlord is called a tenancy, and can be for a fixed or an indefinite period of time (called the term of the lease). The consideration for the lease is called rent. A gross lease is when the tenant pays a flat rental amount and the landlord pays for all property charges regularly incurred by the ownership from lawnmowers and washing machines to handbags and jewelry.

租赁贸易（Leasing Trade）也称“租赁信贷”（Lease Credit），是信贷和贸易相结合的一种贸易方式。它是由租赁方（出租人 Leasor）根据租赁契约，将设备出租给租借方（承租人 Lessee）在一定期限内使用，并收取租金，设备仍属出租人所有。凡分别在不同国家的出租人，承租人之间进行的租赁贸易即为国际租赁。

Under normal circumstances, a freehold owner of property is at liberty to do what they want with their property, including destroys it or hand over possession of the property to a tenant. However, if the owner has surrendered possession to another (the tenant) than any interference with the quiet enjoyment of the property by the tenant in lawful possession is unlawful.

Similar principles apply to real property as well as to personal property, though the terminology would be different. Similar principles apply to sub-leasing, that is the leasing by a tenant in possession to a sub-tenant. The right to sub-lease can be expressly prohibited by the main lease.

8.7 Electric Commerce and Paperless Business 电子商务与无纸化办公

International trade today is being conducted in an era of electric commerce (E-commerce) embracing paperless trading. Its benefits are intrinsic and wide ranging. It is reducing the trade cycle and opening up new market. Moreover, it is being greatly facilitated by the International Agencies who have formulated the mechanism under which international trade transactions may be conducted with complete confidence.

8.7.1 Electric Commerce 电子商务

Electronic commerce, commonly known as E-commerce, is a type of industry where buying and selling of product or service over electronic systems such as the Internet and other computer networks. Electronic commerce draws on such technologies as mobile commerce, electronic funds transfer, supply chain management, Internet marketing, online transaction processing, electronic data interchange (EDI), inventory management systems, and automated data collection systems. Modern electronic commerce typically uses the World Wide Web at least at one point in the transaction's life-cycle, although it may encompass a wider range of technologies such as e-mail,

电子商务（Electronic Commerce，E-commerce）通常是指是在全球各地广泛的商业贸易活动中，在因特网开放的网络环境下，基于浏览器/服务器应用方式，买卖双方不谋面地进行各种商务活动，实现消费者的网上购物、商户之间的网上交易和在线电子支付以及各种商务活动、交易活动、金融活动和相关的综合服务活动的一种新型的商业运营模式。电子商务是利用微电脑技术和网络通讯技术进行的商务活动。

mobile devices social media, and telephones as well.

Electronic commerce is generally considered to be the sales aspect of E-business. It also consists of the exchange of data to facilitate the financing and payment aspects of business transactions.

Generally, E-commerce can be divided into:

- E-tailing or "virtual storefronts" on Web sites with online catalogs, sometimes gathered into a "virtual mall".
- The gathering and use of demographic data through Web contacts and social media.
- Electronic Data Interchange (EDI), the business-to-business exchange of data.
- E-mail and fax and their use as media for reaching prospects and established customers (for example, with newsletters).
- Business-to-business buying and selling.
- The security of business transactions.

电子商务一般可分为：

- 电子零售，又称虚拟店面
- 通过网络联系和社交媒介进行人口统计数据的收集和使用。
- 电子数据互换，B2B 数据交换
- 通过电子邮件和传真来达到目的或搭建客户平台。
- B2B 的买卖
- 交易的安全

In addition, there are many types of E-commerce transactions:

ABC (Agents to Business to Consumer)
B2B (Business to Business)
B2C (Business to Consumer)
C2C (Consumer to Consumer)
B2M (Business to Manager)
B2G (Business to Government)
M2C (Manager to Consumer)
O2C (Online to offline)
C2B (Customer to Business)
B2B2 (Business to Business to Consumer)
B2T (Business to Team)

Some common applications related to electronic commerce are: document automation in supply chain and logistics, domestic and international payment systems, enterprise content management, group buying, automated online assistants, instant messaging, newsgroups, online shopping and order tracking, online banking, online office suites, shopping cart software, tele-conferencing, electronic tickets, and etc.

8.7.2 Paperless Business 无纸化办公

The paperless business is aimed at eliminating or greatly reducing the use of paper in the process of business. This is done by converting documents and other papers into digital form. Proponents claim that "going paperless" can save money, boost productivity, save space, make documentation and information sharing easier, keep personal information more secure, and help the environment. The concept can also be extended to communications outside the office.

无纸化办公（Paperless Business）是指利用现代化的网络技术进行办公。主要传媒工具是计算机等现代化办公工具，可以实现不用纸张和笔进行各种业务以及事务处理。

Notes

1. Distribution
   经销，是进口商（经销商）与出口商（供货商）达成协议，承担在规定的期限和区域内销售指定商品的一种贸易方式。经销是属于转卖方式的一种贸易方式。
2. Exclusive Sales
   包销是指出口商通过签订协议给国外销售商在一定时期、一定地区经营某一种或某一类商品的专营权利的贸易方式。
3. Agent
   在国际贸易中，所谓代理商是指接受委托人（Principal）的委托向第三者出售商品并办理与交易有关的其他事项的人。
4. Auction
   拍卖是由专营拍卖业务的拍卖行接受货主的委托，在一定的时间和地点，按照一定的章程和规则，以公开叫价的方法，把货物卖给出价最高的买主的一种贸易方式。

5. Consignment

寄售是一种委托代售的贸易方式。寄售人先将准备销售的货物运往国外寄售地，委托当地代销人按照双方商定的条件，由代销人为其销售，所得货款扣除佣金及有关费用后，交付给寄售人。

6. Tender

投标是投标人根据招标人（Inviter to Bid）的招标条件，应邀发出实盘，以期达成交易的一种贸易方式。

7. Counter Trade

对销贸易是指在互惠的前提下，由两个或两个以上的贸易方达成协议，规定一方的进口产品可以部分或全部以相对的出口产品来支付。

8. Futures Trading

期货交易是按照交易所的规定，由买卖双方在交易所内达成远期交割的贸易方式。

9. Hedge

套期保值是指交易者配合在现货市场的买卖，在期货市场买进或卖出与现货市场交易品种、数量相同，但方向相反的期货合同，以期在未来某一时间通过卖出或买进此期货合同来补偿因现货市场价格变动带来的实际价格风险。

10. Leasing Trade

租赁贸易，也称“租赁信贷”（Lease Credit），是信贷和贸易相结合的一种贸易方式。

11. Electronic Commerce (E-commerce)

电子商务通常是指是在全球各地广泛的商业贸易活动中，在因特网开放的网络环境下，基于浏览器/服务器应用方式，买卖双方不谋面地进行各种商务活动，实现消费者的网上购物、商户之间的网上交易和在线电子支付以及各种商务活动、交易活动、金融活动和相关的综合服务活动的一种新型的商业运营模式。

12. Paperless Business

无纸化办公是指利用现代化的网络技术进行办公。主要传媒工具是计算机等现代化办公工具，可以实现不用纸张和笔进行各种业务以及事务处理。

Exercise

1. Translate the following into Chinese or English.

Distribution	Futures
Consignment	hedging

Tender	E-commerce
投标	对销贸易
远期合同	加工贸易
无纸化办公	

2. Translate the following sentences into Chinese or English.

1) Intermediaries are companies (such as wholesalers and retailers) that help move godsend and services between procedures and consumers. There are companies that make things and then sell those things to wholesalers, there resell them to retailers, which sell them to consumers.
2) Hedging is a two-step process. Depending upon a hedger's cash market situation, the hedger would either buy or sell futures as the first position. Then, at a later date, before the futures hedger would take a second position opposite the opening transaction. The opening and closing positions of the hedge must be for the same commodity number of contracts, and delivery month.
3) 一般来说，批发商所经营的是通过零售商再次转卖给消费者的商品。直接销售渠道则是由制造商直接把商品卖给消费者。
4) 合同价格只根据合同规定并在中标函中写明为工程的设计，实施与完成以及对任何缺陷的修补，而应支付给承包商的金额。

3. Group Discussion

Form teams of five and discuss the E-commerce revolution. How many students now shop for goods and services online? What are their online shopping experiences? What do you see as the future for such purchases? Then, prepare a three-minute summary for the class.

Appendix

Key to Exercises

Chapter 1

2. Match each one on the left with its correct meaning on the right.

1. J 2. A 3. E 4. B 5. C 6. D 7. I 8. G 9. F 10. H

3. Fill in the blanks

1) Export goods are tangible goods sent out of countries.
2) Trade in services are international earnings other than those derived from the exporting and importing of tangible goods.
3) Import goods are tangible goods brought in.
4) International trade is all business transactions that involve two or more countries.
5) Investment is used primarily as financial means for a company to earn more money on its money with relative safety.

4. Translation

1) There is no country in the world that can produce all the products it needs. Thus countries join in international division of labor for effective production and reproduction. Sometimes a country can buy goods and services from abroad on a barter basis. Barter means doing business by exchanging goods of one sort for goods of another sort without using money. Barter trade itself is not enough to meet a country's import needs. But as a form of international trade, it is still attractive in developing countries where foreign exchange is in short supply and inflow of foreign funds is far from sufficient to meet their obligations in external trade.
2) The different kinds of trade nations engaged in are varied and complex, a mixture of visible and invisible trade. Most nations are more dependent on exports than on any

other activity. The earnings from exports pay for the imports that they need and want. A nation's balance of payment is a record of these complex transactions. By reflecting all of these transactions in monetary terms, a nation is able to combine the income it receives, for example, from exports, tourists' expenditures, and immigrant remittances. This combined incomes is then spent on such items as manufactured goods from other countries, travel for its citizens to other countries, and the hiring of construction engineers.

Chapter 2

2. Translation

1) 两者在质量上无显著差异。
2) 我们真诚希望质量与合同规定相符。
3) 包装材料的选用和装潢设计要考虑到商品的质量和价格。
4) 我们不仅要考虑商品的内在质量与外观形态，也要考虑顾客的品位要求。
5) 对危险品和有毒的货物，应在每件货物上明显印刷出有关标记和性质说明。
6) The inner packing that catches the eye must help us push sales.
7) A topper, matched with the superior-grade packing, speaks itself for its high quality and preciousness.
8) We must improve the quality of the export goods so as to strengthen its competitiveness in the international market.

4. Two columns are given for you to decide which method is best suited for a certain commodity. Please match them.

1) A 2) C 3) D 4) E 5) B 6) G 7) F 8) H

5. Calculation

1. 1lb =0.453,58kg, so 40lb=18.144kg

Maximum: [10×1,000kg×(1+5%)]/18.144
= 578.7 (Attention: 0.7should be deleted here)
= 578cartons

Minimum: [10×1,000kg×(1–5%)]/18.144
= 523.6 (Attention: 0.6should be deleted here)
= 524cartons

Answer: 1) At most, Company A can deliver 578cartons of Seafood.

2) At least, Company A should deliver 524cartons of Seafood.

2. 1) 100=x (1+11%)÷(1+9%)   x=98.198

2) 98.198×(1+5%)=103.107,9<104

所以，104 公吨不符合合同规定。

3) 取出 104–103.107,9=0.892,1（公吨）。

Chapter 3

2. Multiple Choices

1) C 2) A 3) A 4) C 5) B 6) C 7) A

4. Judge whether the following statements are true (T) or false (F).

1\. T 2. T 3. F 4. F 5. F 6. F 7. F 8. T

5. Translate into English the Chinese in the parentheses with given English word or phrase.

1) please refer to Incoterms 2010
2) In reference to the consignment of June 5
3) you must load the goods on board in accordance with the stipulations of the Incoterms
4) but our business is on cash payment whether the customs are new or old
5) Because of the frequent change of the market prices, it is not possible for us to keep the prices open for a whole week.
6) Our prices are subject to change without notice
7) meeting each other halfway and allowing you a 10% discount
8) to receive your cable offer of July 15 for 300 dozen shirts of sample No.1302 CIF New York at USD 35 per dozen
9) the lowest FOB Liverpool prices of the following articles
10) As this is a big order, we hope you can make a 5% discount off the list price

Chapter 4

2. Judge whether the following statements are true (T) or false (F).

1) T 2) F 3) T 4) T 5) T 6) F 7) F 8) T 9) F 10) T

Chapter 5

2. Translation

1) 除开证行费用外的所有其他银行费用由受益人支付。
2) 一式五份签署的商业发票应标明信用证号、合同号和运输标志。
3) 只有在获得进口许可并在我方电传通知后此信用证才生效。
4) We hope you can ship immediately as so as you receive our L/C.
5) L/C should remain effective within 15 days after shipment.
6) We can give you some discount if you use L/C.
7) In the collection on the documentary bill, bank plays an intermediary role, passing the remittance documents to the collecting bank and receiving the payment from the collecting bank.
8) When settled, the exporter shall submit all documents needed by L/C to the negotiating bank.

Chapter 6

3. Translation

1) 由于公认的不可抗力导致延迟交货或无法交货的，出口商可以免责。
2) 仲裁裁决是终局性的，对双方当事人均有约束。
3) 任何与本合同无关或相关的争议应最终通过仲裁解决，而不是上诉法院。
4) 证书应当标明装运前已经检验。
5) 我们非常遗憾地通知你：当你的货物到达时有 15 箱损坏，且明显是由于你方包装不善引起的。
6) We hope to place the arbitration in the import country.
7) This is the inspection report provided by a very famous London notary.
8) We do not assume liability for any loss incurred in transportation.
9) Wrong number of item let you receive wrong goods. We apologize for it and accept your claim.

Chapter 7

1. 交易磋商/贸易谈判　　签合同　　询价/询盘
发盘/报盘/发价/报价　　还盘　　Breach of Contact
claim　　claim settlement　　remedies

2. 1) T 2) T 3) F 4) T 5) T 6) F
3. 1) 请报香港价船上交货价，包括到香港的运费。
   2) 市场调研并提出产品的价格方案。
   3) Could you please send us a catalog of your rubber boots together with terms of payment?
   4) If your prices are favorable, I can place an order right away.
4. 提示：买方对卖方的发盘表示接受，虽在其接受发盘时对包装条件提出了新的要求，但非属实质性的修改，并且卖方对此未表示反对，而且着手备货，这就表示合同已按原发盘内容及接受中的某些修改为交易条件成立。

Chapter 8

2. Translation

1) 中介机构是指帮助商品和劳务在生产者和消费者之间流动的企业（如批发商和零售商）。有些企业生产商品卖给批发商，批发商再卖给零售商，零售商卖给消费者。
2) 套期保值可分为两个阶段。套期保值者根据自己在现货市场的处境，可通过买进或卖出期货合约来建立第一个期货市场头寸。然后，在近期某一日，保值者通过做一相反的交易而对原头寸进行对冲。针对原持有的多头或空头期货头寸进行的两手交易的商品必须完全一致，无论合约数量还是交割数量都必须一致。
3) Generally speaking, the wholesalers operate the products that resold to consumers via retailers. Direct sales channel is to sell the goods directly from manufacturers to consumers.
4) Contract price, referring to the contract, is the amount of money that should be paid to the contractor for the designing, implementation and accomplishment of projects and for the revision of any defection.

Glossary

Abandonment: 索赔/权利的放弃

The act of relinquishing claim or right to property.

About: 大约，约

“About”. ”Approx”, and “Circa” are terms which when used in a letter of credit, are construed to allow a difference not to exceed 10% more or 10% less than the monetary amount, or the quantity, or the unit price stipulated in the letter of credit

Absolute Advantage: 绝对成本

An advantage of one nation or area over another in the costs of producing an item in terms of used resource

Acceptance: 承兑

Acceptance is the act, by the drawee, of writing down “accepted” on the bill, signing his name and dating it. It represents a formal promise by the drawee to pay the bill when it matures. If the acceptor refuses to pay when the bill matures, the payee is entitled to sue him.

Acceptance Letter of Credit: 承兑信用证

A letter of credit which instead of agreeing to pay the beneficiary immediately upon presentation of documents requires presentation of a time draft drawn by the beneficiary upon the issuing bank or another bank. However, the beneficiary may, in effect, obtain prompt.

Accepted Draft: 已承兑汇票

A draft or a bill of exchange accepted by the drawee (acceptor) by putting his signature and “accepted” on its face. In doing so, he commits himself to pay the bill upon presentation at maturity

Accepted Bank: 承兑银行

A bank which by signing "accepted" on a time draft accepts responsibility to pay when the draft becomes due.

Acceptor: 承兑人
The party that signs "accepted" on a draft or obligation, agreeing to pay the stated sum at maturity

Accession: 加入
Accession is process by which a country becomes a member of an international agreement (usually an agreement that has already been accepted by other countries).

Accommodation: 通融
An arrangement or engagement made as a favor to another, not dependent upon a consideration received.

Accommodation Note or Paper: 通融票据，欠单
A bill of exchange or bank's acceptance which is endorsed, accepted, or drawn by one party (the accommodating party) to benefit another party. The accommodating party generally does not charge or seek compensation for this act.

Account Number: 账户编号，账号
An identification number assigned in its records for purposes of faster and more accurate accounting and record keeping, by banks, institutions, and business of all kinds to their depositors, users, members, subscribers, customers, vendors, or other entities

Account Party: 开证申请人
Same as Applicant, the party at whose request a bank issues a letter of credit.

Account Payable: 应付账款
A current liability representing the amounts owed to creditors for merchandise or services purchased on open account.

Accounts Receivable: 应收账款

The amount of money a business expects to receive for merchandise or services furnished by it to others on open account.

Acquisition: 收购
The act of becoming owner of a property. In finance, it is the purchase of a company's assets or its common stock

Act of God: 不可抗力
A violent act of nature such as lightning, flood, earthquake or hurricane which man can neither cause nor intervene with.

Actual Total Loss: 实际全损
Actual total loss means the insured goods upon arrival are badly damaged, or have been lost or found valueless.

Ad Valorem Duty: 从价税
Duty calculated on the basis of value (usually a percentage of the value).

Advance Arrangements: 事先联系，预先安排
In transportation, advance arrangements must be made for certain kinds of cargo which require special handling: hazardous cargo, over weight, over sized, over normal quantity, time sensitive, shipped unpacked, live animals, etc. Not every carrier can or will transport every kind of cargo.

Advice: 通知，装运通知，托收/收款通知，信用证条款通知
① A report from one party to another informing them of an occurrence with regard to some business transaction: a shipment, a collection, a manufacture, etc. ② A notification by an advising bank on behalf of the issuing bank to a beneficiary informing them of the terms of a letter of credit.

Advising Bank: 通知行
The advising bank is the bank to which the Issuing Bank sends the Letter of Credit with instructions to notify the exporter (Beneficiary).

Afloat: 已经装船，在运输途中 Refers to shipment of cargo which is currently on board a vessel between ports.

After Date: 开票日后（……天付款）
A notation used on financial instruments (such as drafts or bills of exchange) to fix the maturity date as a fixed number of days past the date of drawing of the draft.

After Sight: 见票后（……天付款）
A notation on a draft that indicates that payment is due a stated number of days after the draft has been presented to the drawee.

Agent: 代理人
A person or legal entity authorized to act on behalf of another.

Agent Bank: 代理银行
① A bank acting on behalf of another bank. ② A bank acting for lenders and bondholders, similar to an indenture trustee.

Aggregated Valuation: 协定价值
The value of a shipment that is agreed upon by both the shipper and the carrier to define the freight rate and/or the liability of the carrier.

Air Cargo: 空运货物
Property of any kind that is transported by aircraft (excluding passenger baggage and mail).

Air Express: 特快空运
Expedited air freight service.

Air Post Parcel: 航空邮包
Parcels shipped through the mails to be transported by air

Air Waybill: 空运提单
The shipping document used for the transportation of air freight: includes conditions,

limitations of liability, shipping instructions, description of commodity, and applicable transportation charges. It is generally similar to a straight non-negotiable bill of lading and is used for similar purposes.

Allowance: 折让，折扣，减价
A deduction or discount from the price permitted by a seller.

Alternative Tariff: 选择关税
In transportation, a tariff with two or more rates for the same goods, to and from the same points, with the opportunity available to the shipper to use the lowest of the charges.

Amendment: 修改
An addition, deletion, or modification of a document.

Antidumping Duties: 反倾销关税
Additional duties which are assessed on imported goods when whose goods are sold to the importing country at price that is less than "fair value"("fair value" usually being defined as the price on the exporting country's domestic market or to third countries), and when those imported goods are found to cause or to threaten material injury to industry of the importing country.

Applicant: 申请人
The applicant applies to his bank to open a letter of credit for the seller. The bank will normally require the applicant to have sufficient funds on deposit in the bank to cover at least a part of the amount covered by the L/C.

Appreciation: 升值
An increase in the value of something, of goods, of currency, of shares of stock, etc
Apron: 停机坪，前沿码头，岸边装货场 ① Area of the airport where planes are parked, used for loading and unloading of aircraft. ② Area along waterside edges of a pier, not under cover, used for loading and unloading of vessels.

Arbitrage: 套购，套利，套汇

A method of taking advantage of the fact that there may be different prices in different markets for identical goods such as gold, foreign exchange or commodities. Simultaneously, one buys in the lower prices market and sells in the higher one.

Assessment: 财产价值评定，估价，税额评定
① The valuation or determination as to value, of property. ② The act of apportioning amounts to be paid. ③ An amount assessed or charged, for example: taxes or dues.

At Sight: 即期，见票即付
A notation on a draft which indicates that payment is due upon its presentation.

Automated Commercial System (ACS): (美国海关)电子数据自动采集、控制和处理系统
(USA) The comprehensive electronic data system of U. S. Customs for tracking, controlling, and processing commercial importations.

Automated Information Exchange System (AIES): (美国海关)电子数据自动交换系统
(USA) A module of the Automated Commercial System of U.S. Customs which provides an automated method of exchanging information between Field Import Specialists and National Import Specialists.

Avoidance of Contract: 撤销合同
The legal cancellation of a contract because an event occurs that makes performance of the contract terms impossible or inequitable and that releases the parties from their obligations.

Back Order: 延期交货
The portion of an order that cannot be delivered at the scheduled time, but will be delivered at a later date when available

Bad Faith: 恶意
The intent to mislead or deceive. It does not include misleading by an honest, inadvertent or uncalled or misstatement.

Balance of Payments: 国际收支，国际收支差额

A statement summarizing all the economic and financial transactions between companies, banks, private households and public authorities of one nation with those of the other nations of the world over a specific time period. It includes merchandise trade payments, payments and receipts on account of shipping services, tourist services, financial services, government expenditures, short-and long-term capital movements, interest and dividends, gold movements, etc

Balance of Trade: 贸易平衡，贸易差额
The difference in value between a country's total imports and exports over a specific time period.

Bale: 大包，捆包
A large bundle or package of compressed and bound goods, usually with an outer covering, often of burlap.

Bale Cargo: 捆包货物
Cargo shipped in bales.

Bank Acceptance: 银行承兑（汇票）
A draft drawn on and accepted by a bank.

Bank Draft: 银行汇票
A form of check drawn by a bank against its account in another bank.

Bank Guarantee 银行保函
A bank guarantee is an undertaking by a bank to settle a debt in the event that the debtor fails to do so. A bank guarantee serves as security for loan. However, the bank will require the goods cover in cash or counter-indemnity before they issue a guarantee.

Bank Holding Company: 银行持股公司
(USA) Any company which directly controls, with power to vote, more than five percent of voting shares of two or more banks (as defined by the Bank Holding Company Act).

Bank Holiday: 银行假日
A day on which banks are closed.

Bank Notes: 银行本票
A promissory note having the appearance of currency, issued by a bank or banker authorized to do so, payable to bearer on demand, and intended to circulate as money.

Banker's Bank: 中央银行
A bank that is established by mutual consent by independent and unaffiliated banks to provide a clearinghouse for financial transactions.

Banker's Draft: 银行汇票
A draft payable on demand and drawn by, or on behalf of, a bank upon itself or upon another bank, sometimes a foreign bank, where it maintains an account or a relationship.

Bankers Acceptance: 银行承兑汇票
A draft calling for payment at a future date on which the drawee is a bank, and the bank has agreed to pay by signing "accepted" on the draft.

Bareboat Charter: 光船租赁
The term bareboat means a ship without crew and ship's master. The charterer (shipper) crews and operates the shipments within a period of time, usually a number of years.

Bearer: 持票人，持有人
The person in possession of negotiable instrument, document of title, or security marked "payable to bearer", or the person in possession of one of these documents endorsed in blank.

Beneficiary 受益人
The beneficiary is the party that has contracted to sell goods. It is usually the exporter in the Letter of Credit process.

Berth: 泊位
The place beside a docking area where a ship is secured and cargo can be loaded or unloaded.

Bid Bond: 投标押金 A type of indemnity bond. A surety guarantee often required to be established by a bidder to guarantee fulfillment of his offer if accepted.

Bilateral Trade: 双边贸易
The commerce between two countries.

Bill: 汇票，发票
① A "Bill of Exchange" or "Draft" (same thing). ② The word "Bill" has many other international trade connotations, e.g. "Invoice".

Bill of Exchange: 汇票
A bill of exchange is an unconditional order in writing, addressed by one person (the drawer) to another (the drawee) and signed by the person issuing it. It requires the drawee to pay on demand, or at a fixed or determinable future time, a specified sum of money to, or to the order of, a specified person the payee) or to the bearer.

Bill of Lading: 提单
A document issued by a carrier which is evidence of receipt of the goods, and is a contract of carriage. It describes the goods, the detail of the intended voyage, and it specifies the conditions of transportation. If issued in negotiable form, i.e. "to order", it becomes documentary evidence of title to the goods.

Booking: 订舱位
The making of arrangements for a shipment with the representatives of a vessel or airline.

Box: 盒式拖车/集装箱，盒，箱
① Term referring to trailer, semi-trailer, or container used in transportation. ② A type of package of wood, cardboard, metal, plastic or other material.

Box Car: 篷车
A closed railroad freight car.

Breakage: 破损津贴，零数金额，破碎

① A monetary allowance that a manufacturer allots for compensation to a buyer for breakage to goods (usually fragile) while in shipment. ② A fractional amount due either party in a transaction, for example in computing interest. ③ In marine insurance, "breakage" refers to breakage of fragile goods such as glass and china.

Breakbulk: 杂货船，卸货
① A breakbulk ship is one which transports cargo which is packed in cases, bales, cartons, drums, carboys, etc., and this cargo is carried in the ship's cargo holds rather than in containers (although some loaded containers may be carried). ② "To breakbulk" is to unload packaged cargo from a "breakbulk ship" or from a container and to distribute it.

Breakbulk Cargo: 杂货，普通货物
Cargo that is shipped in packing units such as cartons, cases, crates, bales, or drums, but not containerized.

Broker: 经纪人
One that acts as an agent for others, as in negotiating contracts, purchases, or sales in return for a fee or commission.

Bulk Cargo: 散装货
Cargo that is made up of an unpacked commodity; example include grain, oil, an ore.

Bulk Carrier: 散装船
A vessel designed for the shipment of bulk cargo.

Bulk Freight: 散装货
Cargo not in packages or containers.

Bulk Sales: 成批销售
The transfer or sales of substantially all of an inventory of an enterprise in a single transaction not in the usual course of business.

Call: 催缴

① A demand for early repayment of an obligation, or for the performance of a specific act under a contract. ② A demand for the payment of money. ③ The act of redeeming a bond earlier than the full term. ④ Short for "Call Option", a contract giving the holder the right to receive from the issuer a specified amount of security at a specified price on or before a certain date. ⑤ Short for "Margin Call"-a call by a future or an options exchange, or by a broker to its clients, for additional collateral to that previously posted when the futures, options, or securities were purchased without posting their full value.

Call Money: 活期借款
Money lent by banks on a short-term basis which the bank, as lender, can "call" (demand payment at any time, usually on 24 hours notice)

Capital Marker: 资本市场
The market for long-term investment funds in the form of stocks bonds, commercial paper, etc

Captain's Protest: 海损异议书，海难证明书
A written sworn statement of the master of a vessel to the effect that damage suffered by the ship during the voyage was caused by storm or other peril of the sea without any negligence or misconduct on his own part.

Cargo: 货物，船货
Merchandise hauled by transportation lines.

Cargo Manifest: 货运舱单
A list of cargo being transported or warehoused.

Cargo Tonnage: 载货吨位
The weight of a shipment or ship's total cargo expressed in tons.

Carrier: 承载人
A legal entity that is in the business of transporting passengers or goods for hire.

Cash Against Documents (CAD): 凭单付款

A term used in collections supported by shipping documents which are released to the buyer only against payment. Same as Documents Against Payment (D/P)

Central Bank: 中央银行
An institution with the sole right to issue bank notes and power to dictate the monetary policy for a currency zone.

Certificate of Inspection: 检验证明书，检查书
A certificate issued by an independent third party verifying the condition of cargo or of property.

Certificate of Manufacture: 制造证明，厂方证明书
① A certificate sometimes required from a manufacturer to attest that goods have been manufactured according to the contract; for example, to support payment under a letter of credit. ② (USA) A form required to support a claim for duty drawback based on manufacture in the United States.

Certificate of Weight: 重量证明书
A document certifying to the weight of a shipment.

Certification: 证明书
① Official proof of authenticity ② The formal assertion of some fact in writing.

CFR 成本加运费
Cost and Freight. The exporter pays costs and freight to deliver the goods to named port of destination. This term can be used only for sea and inland waterway transport.

Chargeable Weight: 计量重量
The weight or volume of a shipment used in determining freight charges.

Charter Party: 租船合同
A charter party—charter party contract—is a written contract between the ship operator and charter (shipper). The contract normally includes details of ports of loading and discharge,

freight rate and time involved in voyage (s).

Charter Services: 包租
Temporary hiring of an aircraft or vessel for the transportation of cargo or passengers.

Charter Shipping: 租船运输
Charter shipping is a tramp service. The term tramp, as used in ocean shipping, refers to a cargo ship that is not operating on regular routes and schedules. A tramp picks up cargo only when it is chartered (hired) from the ship operator.

Check: 支票
A check is a preprinted form on which instructions are given to a banker to pay a stated sum of money to a named recipient. It represents an unconditional order by the drawer to his bank to pay some amount of money to named recipient.

CIP (Carriage an Insurance Paid To…named place of destination): 运费和保险费付至（……制定目的地）
The seller has the same obligations as under CPT but with the addition that the seller has to procure cargo insurance against the buyer's risk of or damage to the goods during the carriage. The seller pays the insurance premium and is only required to obtain minimum coverage.

Claim: 债权，索赔，赔偿
① A demand of payment ② In insurance, a demand for payment of money or property as the result of an insured loss. ③ In transportation, a demand for return of overpaid charges. Also, a demand for reimbursement of losses due to loss or casualty to cargo or failure to deliver.

Clean Bill of Lading: 清洁提单
The clean bill of lading bears an indication that the goods were received without damage, irregularities or short shipment, usually the words "apparent good order and condition", "clean on board" or the like are indicated on the B/L.

Clean Draft: 光票，不附单据
A draft with no commercial documents attached.

Clearance: 出港手续，通关，结关

① The completion of governmental requirements so that a carrier may arrive in a port and unlade cargo and passengers, or may lade cargo and passengers and depart for a foreign destination. ② The accomplishment of the customs formalities necessary to allow goods to be imported or be exported.

CIF: 成本加保险运费

Cost, Insurance and Freight. The exporter pays costs, insurance and freight to deliver the goods to named port of destination.

Collection: 托收，收款，收集

① The presentation for payment of an obligation and the payment thereof. ② A gathering of similar goods. Under a collection, the seller ships the goods, and submits the draft and/or shipping documents to seller's local bank to collect the proceeds through its branch or corresponding bank in the buyer's country.

Combine Bill of Loading: 联运提单

A bill of loading covering a shipment of goods by more than one mode of transportation.

Combined Transport: 联合运输，联运

Consignment sent by means of various modes of transport.

Commercial Bank: 商业银行

In the USA, a bank that is authorized to accept demand deposits. It may also receive time deposits, make loans, engage in rust services, issue letter of credit, accept and pay drafts, rent safe deposit boxes and engage in many other similar activities.

Commercial Documents: 商业票据

Documents exchanged between the buyer and the seller such as commercial invoices or shipping documents that give detailed information about the goods and/or services contracted.

Commercial Invoice: 商业发票

A document which details the transaction between a seller and a buyer. It minimally should give the name and address of the seller and of the buyer, the date of the sale, a description of the goods sold, the quantity, the unit price, the terms of sale, and the total money amount due. If it is an invoice between buyer and seller of different countries it should also indicate the kind of currency.

Commercial Letter of Credit: 商业信用证
An instrument by which a bank substitutes its credit for that of a customer to enable him to finance the purchase of goods or goods or to incur other commitments. The bank issues a letter (or document) on behalf of its client to supplier and agrees to pay them upon presentation of documentary evidence that the supplier has performed in accordance with the term of the letter of credit.

Commercial paper: 商业票据，商业文件
Negotiable instruments used in commerce. Usually they are short-term, unsecured, promissory notes issued by highly rated entities and are traded on the money markets.

Commercial Treaty: 商务条约
An agreement between two or more countries that establishes the conditions under which business may be conducted between their citizen within their countries.

Commission: 佣金
When selling through an agent, the commission may be included in the quoted price. The commission may reflected using "&C" {+ the percentage rates of commission} or "C" {+ the percentage rates of commission} after the trade term. For example, CIF & C5 Bangkok (or CIF5 Bangkok) means that the quoted price includes a 5% commission.

Competitive Rate: 竞争性运费率
Rate determined by one transportation line to compete with the rate of another transportation line.

Conditioned weight: 公量
Conditioned weight is the weight obtained by deducting the actual moisture content of a commodity and adding the standardized moisture content. Conditioned weight is applied

chiefly to commodities that have a high unit value and tend to absorb moisture from the air.

Conference Shipping: 班轮公会运输

Conference shipping is provided by the conference carrier or by a member of a freight conference. The freight conference—conference or steamship conference or liner conference—is a group of vessel operators who operate on the same routes and cooperate on shipping schedules at the standardized freight rates between ports.

Confirmed Letter of Credit: 保兑信用证

A Letter of Credit where a Confirming Bank, usually located in the exporter's country，has guaranteed payment under the Letter of Credit assuming that all terms and conditions of the Letter of Credit have been met. With a Confirmed Letter of Credit, the payment risk is assumed by both the Confirming Bank and the Issuing Bank. Thereby it provides more protection to the exporter.

Confirming Bank: 保兑银行

The confirming bank is the bank, at the request of the Issuing Bank，which adds its confirmation to the Letter of Credit. In doing so, the Confirming Bank undertakes to make payment to the exporter upon presentation of documents under the Letter of Credit assuming all terms and conditions of the Letter of Credit have been met.

Confirming sample: 确认样品

In the case of a sale by buyer's sample, the seller will send to the buyer a sample equivalent to that supplied by the buyer for the buyer's confirmation and approval. When the buyer accepts the sample made by the seller, it will replace the buyer's sample as the sample for sale. The sample made by the seller based on the buyer's sample is called a counter sample or confirming sample.

Consignment: 寄售

① Goods or property sent by the aid of a carrier from one person (the consignor) to another (the consignee) ② Entrusting of goods to another to sell as agent for the sender.

Constructive Total Loss 推定全损

Constructive total loss occurs when the actual loss of the insured goods is unavoidable, or when the ship or the consignment has to be abandoned because the cost of salvage or recovery will exceed the value of the ship and the consignment in sound condition upon arrival.

Consular Invoice: 领事发票

An invoice covering a shipment of goods usually required to be certified by the counsel of the country for which the merchandise is destined. It may be required to be on special fees.

Consulate: 领事馆

An office of a country within another country (often there are several, located in the larger commercial centers). These offices represent the commercial interests of citizens of their country.

Containers: 集装箱

The practice of packing goods in large metal containers, although relatively expensive, has become increasingly popular. Advantages include the reductions in water damage, in handling damage, and in pilferage. And today most ports and ships are equipped to handle container.

Container Vessel: 集装箱船

An ocean going vessel designed specifically to handle the loading, carriage and removal of standard freight containers.

Contract Carrier: 契约承运人

Excluding common carriers, any person who under contract will transport passengers or goods for agreed upon compensation.

Contract Negotiation: 合同谈判

Contract negotiation is the process by which the seller and the buyer negotiate the terms and conditions of a transaction with the intent of arriving at the agreement. The purpose of contract negotiation is to conclude a sales contract. It can take two form: oral negotiation and written negotiation.

Cost-plus Method of Pricing: 成本加利定价法

In the cost-plus method of calculation, the exporter starts with the domestic manufacturing cost and adds administration, research and development, overheads, freight forwarding, distributor margins, customs charges and profit.

Convertibility: 可兑换性
The attribute of being exchangeable, such as a currency freely able to be exchanged for another, or as preferred stock or bonds to be exchanged for common stock.

Cost Plus: 成本加利
A pricing method where the purchaser agrees to pay the production cost of the goods plus a fixed percentage to the seller for profit.

Country of Departure: 启运国
The country from which a shipment of goods, a carrier, or a passenger has or his scheduled to depart.

Country of Destination: 到达国
The country that is the ultimate destination for a shipment of goods. For a carrier, it is the country in which it intends to complete its current voyage or flight.

Country of Dispatch: 发货国
The country from which a cargo is shipped.

Country of Origin: 原产国，出产国
The country in which goods were produced, mined, grown or manufactured.

CPT (Carriage Paid To…named port of destination): 运费付至（……指定目的地）
The seller pays the freight for the carriage of the goods to the named destination. The risk of loss of or damage to the goods, as well as any additional costs due to events occurring after the time the goods have been delivered to the carrier, is transferred from the seller to the buyer when the goods have been delivered into the custody of the carrier.

Customs: 海关
The customs is a governmental organization which checks and supervises the import and

export for a nation.

CY versus CFS: 堆场与中转站

The CY and CFS terms apply to the manner and location of cargo delivery and receipt in a container service. The CY is the delivery (or receipt) of a whole container from (or at) the shipper's or the forwarder's (or the consignee's) cargo yard or premises. CFS is the delivery (or receipt) of loose cargo from (or at) the carrier's container freight station.

DAF (Delivered At Frontier… named place): 边境交货（……指定地点）

The seller fulfils his obligation to deliver when the goods have been made available, cleared for export, at the named point and place at the frontier, but the customs border of the adjoining country.

Damage: 损失，损害，损失赔偿（金）

① A loss or harm to a person or their property. ② The pecuniary or indemnity which may be recovered by any person who has suffered loss, detriment or injury to his person, property or right through the unlawful act, omission, or negligence of another.

Dangerous Goods: 危险货物

Good which are capable of posing a health or safety risk.

Date Draft: 定期汇票

A draft which matures a specified number of days after the date it is issued.

Date of Issue: 开证日

The arbitrary date on a contract or on a financial instrument fixed as the date from which the term runs. (Neither the actual date on the instrument, nor the date was actually signed, nor the date the instrument was executed, nor the date the instrument was delivered, are considered to be the "date of issue" or the "issuance date".)

DDP (Delivered Duty Paid…named place of destination): 完税后交货（……指定目的地）

The seller fulfils his obligation to deliver when the goods have been made available at the named place in the country of importation. The seller has to bear the risks and costs, including duties, taxes and other charges of delivering the goods thereto, cleared for importation.

DDU (Delivered Duty Unpaid...named place of destination): 未完税后交货（……指定目的地） The seller fulfils his obligation to deliver when the goods have been made available at the named place in the country of importation. The seller has to bear the costs and risks involved in bringing the goods thereto (excluding duties, taxes and other official charges payable upon importation as well as the costs and risks of carrying out customs formalities) The buyer has to pay any additional costs and bear any risks caused by his failure to clear the goods for import in time.

Dealer: 商人，代销商
An individual or firm who purchases goods for resale.

Deck Cargo: 舱面货物，甲板货物
Cargo that is shipped on the deck of a vessel rather than in holds below.

Declared Valued For Carriage: 运费申报价值
The value of goods declared to the carrier by the shipper for the purposes of determining charges and establishing the liability of the carrier.

Deferred Payment Letter of Credit: 延期付信用证
A letter of credit that allows the buyer to take possession of goods by agreeing to pay the issuing bank or the confirming bank at a fixed future date.

Delivery: 送货，交货
① In the case of transportation, the act of transferring physical possession. ② The act of actually or of constructively placing goods or property within the possession or control of another.

Delivery Order: 提送单
A document from the consignee, shipper, or owner of freight ordering the release of freight to another party.

Demurrage: 延滞费，滞留费

① In international transportation, a charge for the failure to remove cargo from a terminal within the allowed free time. Also, a charge for failure to load or unload a ship within the allowed period. ② (USA) In domestic transportation, a penalty charge against users for use of carriers' equipment beyond the allowed free time.

DEQ (Delivered Ex Quay Duty Paid…named port of destination): 目的港码头交货（……指定目的港）

The seller fulfils his obligation to deliver when he has made the goods available to the buyer on the quay (wharf) at the named port of destination, cleared for importation. The seller has to bear all risks and costs including duties, taxes and other charges of delivering the goods thereto. (Note: If the parties wish the buyer to clear the goods for importation and pay the duty, the words "duty unpaid" should be used instead of "duty paid", and other costs of importation can also be excluded from the seller's obligations if this is made clear by adding words to this effect.)

DES (Delivered Ex Ship…named port of destination): 目的港船上交货（……指定目的港）

The seller fulfils his obligation to deliver when the goods have been made available to the buyer on the board the ship uncleared for import at the named port of destination. The seller must bear all the costs and risks involved in bringing the goods to the named port of destination.

Destination: 目的地

The place to which a shipment or person is going.

Developed Countries: 发达国家

The place to which a shipment or person is going.

Developing Countries: 发达中国家

A term used to describe countries that lack strong amounts of industrialization, infrastructure, and sophisticated technology, but are beginning to build these capabilities.

Differential: 差量

An amount added to or deducted from a base shipping freight rate between two given locations to determine a new rate to or cargo from a vessel, vehicle, or aircraft.

Discharging: 卸货
The unloading of cargo from a carrier, or of the contents from a container.

Discount: 贴现
Discounting the bill means that the bank or discount house will purchase the bill and pays the holder of bill an amount of money less than the face value of the bill.

Discounted Bill: 已贴现票据
An accepted draft against which a loan is made and the interest is deducted immediately.

Discrepancies: 不符点
Any inconsistencies found in documents presented, or failures to comply with, the terms and conditions of the Letter of Credit.

Discrimination: 歧视
A failure to treat all persons or parties equally where no reasonable distinction can be found between those favored and those not favored. It mat be reflected in treatment, service or rates.

Dishonor: 拒付
Dishonor means the payer refuses to pay or accept the bill when it is presented for payment or acceptance.

Dispatch: 速遣费，急件，发运
① An amount paid by a vessel's operator to a charterer if loading or unloading is completed in less time than stipulated in the charter agreement. ② A message or report to a newspaper from a correspondent, or between government services such as state or military. ③ To send to a destination.

Distributor: 经销商
An agent who sells for a supplier at wholesale and usually maintains an inventory of the

supplier's products.

Diversion: 转向，绕航

Any change in the routing of a shipment once it has been received by the carrier at point of origin and prior to delivery at destination.

Dock: (码头)装卸站台，船坞，泊位

① A loading or unloading platform at an industrial location or carrier terminal. ② A ship's berth or wharf.

Documents against Acceptance: 承兑交单

Documents against acceptance means the collecting bank will release the document to the importer after the time draft is accepted. When the time draft matures, the importer will make the payment.

Documents against Payment: 付款交单

Documents against payment means the documents can be released to the importer only after he makes payment.

Door-to-Door: 门对门服务

Shipping service from shipper's door to consignee's door.

Draft 汇票

An unconditional order in writing addressed by one person to another, signed by the person giving it, requiring the person to whom it is addressed to pay, on demand or at a fixed or determinable future time a certain sum of money to or to the order of a specified person or bearer. Also referred to as a Bill of Exchange.

Drawee Bank 受票银行

The bank named in the Letter of Credit on which the drafts are to be drawn.

Dry Cargo: 干货

Cargo which is of solid, dry material. It is not liquid or gas, and generally the term exclude cargo requiring special temperature controls.

Dry-Bulk Container: 散装干货创

A shipping container designed to carry unpackaged free-flowing dry exclude cargo requiring special temperature controls.

Dry-Bulk Container: 干货集装箱

Any shipping container designed to transport goods other than liquids or gases.

Dumping: 倾销

The sale of goods in a foreign country at less than "fair value" (a price lower than that at which it is sold within the exporting country or to third countries), and which thereby materially injures, or threatens to materially injures, that industry in the foreign country.

Dunnage: 垫衬物

Materials placed around cargo to prevent shifting or damage while in transit.

Durable Goods: 耐用品

Any product which is not consumed through use.

Duplicate Sample: 复样

In the case of a sale by seller's sample, the seller should keep one or more equivalent samples for himself when delivering a sample to the buyer. The sample kept by the seller is called a duplicate sample.

Duty: 关税

A tax levied bya government on the import or export of goods. (Note: The U.S.Constitution forbids the levying of taxes by the U.S. on exports.However, most foreign governments do not have this restriction)

Electronic Commerce: 电子商务

A system of integrated communications, data management, and security services that allow business applications within different organizations to automatically interchange information.

Electronic Data Interchange (EDI): 电子数据交换
Electronic transmission of data and information according to particular protocols.

Embargo: 禁运
A government prohibition of exports or imports with respect to specific products or specific foreign countries.

Endorsement: 背书
The endorsement is added when the holder of the bill signs his name on the back of the bill or when the holder writes on the bill the name of the person to whom the bill is transferred.

En Route: 在途中
In transit (referring to goods, passengers, or vessels)

Entry: 报关单，报关
① That documentation required to be filed with the appropriate customs officer to secure the release of imported merchandise from customs custody. ② The act of filing that documentation.

ETA: 预计抵达日
The expected date and time of arrival of a carrier.

ETD: 预计离港日
The expected data and time of departure of a carrier.

Ex Factory: 工厂交货（……指定地点）
This term is still widely used but it is being replaced by the Incoterm EXW-Ex Works. It is a sale term where the title to goods passes to the buyer when they leave the bendor's dock and consequently at that point the liability for loss or damage and the expenses of shipment also pass from vendor to buyer.

Exchange Rate: 汇率
The price of one currency expressed in terms of another.

Expiry Date: 到期日

The "End",specifically: the cessation;termination by lapse of time as the expirarion of a lease, insurance policy, or statute;coming to a close or termination. The expiry date is the date on which these events occur. It is the last date that options or warrants can be executed.

Export: 出口

To send or transport goods abroad out of a customs territory;to sever them from the mass of things belonging to one country with the intention of uniting them to the mass of things belonging to a foreign country.

Exporter: 出口商

The party that has contracted to sell the goods. Also known as the seller or beneficiary.

Export Broker: 出口经纪人

A firm that specializes in bringing foreign buyers and domestic sellers together for a fee but usually does not participate in the actual business transaction.

Export Control: 出口管制

The establishment of procedures for the governmental control of export for statistical or strategic purposes.

Export Duty: 出口税

A tax imposed by some nations on their exports.

Export License: 出口许可证

A license issued to exporters by governments to permit them to export certain goods to certain countries. Such goods may be of strategic importance, or simply in short supply, or are controlled to comply with foreign agreements.

Export Merchant: 出口贸易商

A company that buys domestic and foreign products and sells to foreign purchasers. Usually an export merchant is able to compete because of specialized knowledge of the products in which they deal, detailed knowledge of foreign markets, and expertise in international trading techniques.

Export Mix: 出口商品结构
Export mix means the composition of exported goods. From its export mix we can see the competitive advantages and disadvantages of a nation. For example, the export mix of the U. S. A. and China is quite different.

Export Quotas: 出口配额
Specified maximums which a nation places on the value or volume of certain of its exports.

EXW (Ex Works...named place): 工厂交货（……指定地点）
The seller fulfils his obligation to deliver when he has made the goods available at his premises (i.e.works, factory, warehouse, etc.)to the buyer. In particular, he is not responsible for loading the goods on the vehicle provided by the buyer or for clearing the goods for export, unless otherwise agreed. The buyers bears all costs and risks involved in taking the goods from the seller's premises to the desired destination.

Factoring: 保理
A factoring contract is a contract in which a supplier assigns his accounts receivable to a factor for collecting the proceeds and/or for protecting bad debts.

FAS: 装运港船边交货
Free Alongside Ship. The exporter delivers the goods alongside the vessel on the quay or in the lighters at the named port of shipment

FCA (Free Carrier...named place): 货运承运人（……指定地点）
The seller fulfils his obligation to deliver when he has handed over the goods，cleared for export，into the charge of the carrier named by the buyer at the named place or point.

FCL: 整箱货
The FCL means the load reaches its allowable maximum (or full) weight or measurement. In practice, however, the FCL in ocean freight does not always mean packing a containerto its full payload or full capacity. For example, an exporter books a 20'container that is intended for

a consignee at the FCL flat rate of US $1, 500. If the consignment occupiesonly 500 cu. ft. and weighs 5,000 kgs.，the case is still FCL and the exporter has to payUS $1,500.
FDA: (美国)食品药物管理局
(USA) Food And Drug Administration.

Financial Documents: 金融票据
Documents used in international transactions that are directly related to payment. E, g.drafts.

Financial Instrument: 有价证券票据
A document which has a monetary value or is evidence of a monetary transaction，such as drafus，bills of exchange，checks and promissory notes.

Financial Market: 金融市场
Market for the exchange of capital and credit in an economy.

Fixed Charges: 固定费用
① Charges which do not increase or decrease with a change in volume. ② Expenses that have to be borne whether any business is done or not.

Flag: 旗，船籍
A reference to the country of registry of a vessel

Floating: 浮动的
Free determination of rates based on supply and demand，for example，exchange rates or interest rates.

FOB: 装运港船上交货
Free On Board. The exporter delivers the goods on board the vessel or at the airport at the airport at the named port/airport of shipment.

Force Majeure: 不可抗力
Force majeure (French: superior force) means an event outside the control of either party to a contract (such as a strike, riot, war) that may excuse either party from fulfilling his contractual

obligation in certain circumstances, provided that the contract contains a force majeure clause. According to international trade practice, a contract may be suspended or terminated as a consequence of the force majeure.

Forfeiting: 福费延

“Forfeiting”is the act of purchasing an exporter’s receivables unconditionally at a discount by paying cash.

Foreign Currency: 外币

The currency of any foreign country which is authorized by that country as the medium of circulation.

Foreign Exchange: 外币兑换

Currency of countries exchangeable for other currencies according to their relative values based on supply and demand.

Foreign Exchange rate: 汇率

The rate or price of the currency of one country in terms of the currency of another.

Foreign Investment：国外投资

The purchase of assets which are abroad.

Forward Foreign Exchange: 远期外汇

An agreement to purchase or sell an amount of foreign currency at a future date at a predetermined price.

Free In and Out (F. I. O): 船方不负责装卸货费用

A pricing term indicating that the vessel operator is not responsible for the cost of loading and unloading.

Free Port: 自由港

An area where imported goods may be brought without payment of duies.

Free Trade Theory: 自由贸易理论

Free trade theory advocates the free flow of goods and services between nations. Protectionism holds that governments should intervene in trade to prevent the free flow of foreign products into their domestic markets.

Freight: 货运，运费

① All merchandise, goods, products, or commodities shipped by rail, air, road, or water, other than baggage, express mail, or regular mail. ② The compensation paid for the transport of goods/

Futures Contract: 期货契约

A contract for the future delivery of a specified commodity, currency or security on a specific date at a rate determined in the present.

General Agreement on Tariffs and Trade (GATT): 关税与贸易总协定

Both a multilateral trade agreement aimed at expanding international trade and the organization which oversees the agreement. The main goals of GATT are to liberalize world trade and place it on a secure basis thereby contributing to economic growth and development and the welfare of the world's people. The organization. GATT, has been succeeded by the World Trade Organization (WTO).

General Average: 共同海损

General average is the partial loss resulting from a deliberate act of the ship's master, such as throwing overboard all or part of the cargo to save the ship. In this case, all parties involved will share the loss of the specific consignor.

General Cargo Rate: 普通货运费率

The rate a carrier charges for the transportation of cargo which does not qualify for a lower special class or commodity rate in the carrier tariff.

General Cargo Vessels: 普通货船，杂货船

A vessel designed to handle breakbulk cargo such as bags, cartons, cases, crates and drums, either individually or in unitized or palletized loads.

General Extraneous Risks: 一般外来风险

General extraneous risks are risks due to theft, rain, leakage, shortage, breakage, dampness, mildewing, heating, taint of odor, hooking and rusting.

General Tariff: 普通税则

A tariff that applies to countries that do not enjoy either preferential or most favored nation tariff treatment.

Generalized System of Preferences (GSP): 普惠制

A program providing for free rates of duty for merchandise from beneficiary developing independent countries and territories to encourage their economic growth.

Goods: 货物

Merchandise;suppies;raw materials;wares;commodities;or products. The meaning may vary in various situations but for purposes of a contract for storage or transportation, or with reference to collateral for security, it means all things treated as movable.

Gross: 12 打，总

① 12 dozen or 144 articles. ② Total (as in "Gross W eight").

Gross Domestic Product: 国内生产总值

A measure of the market value of all goods and services produced within the boundaries of a nation. It excludes income from external enterprises or investments.

Gross National Product: 国民生产总值

A measure of the market value of all goods and services produced within the boundaries of a nation plus receipts from foreign business activities and investments beyond the national boundaries.

Gross Weight: 毛重

Gross weight is the total weight of the commodity and the tare, i.e. the package weight.

Hard Money: 硬通货币

Currency of a nation having stability in the country and a reputation abroad for economic strength, and as a result it has wide and ready acceptability on world markets.

Heavy Lift: 重件
Any article deemed by rules in a vessel's tariff to be beyond a certain weight. It may be too heavy for the ship's tackle and requires special equipment such as a floating crane.

Heavy Lift Charge: 超重费
In a maritime tariff, a charge made for lifting heavy articles to load or unload them.

Heavy Lift Vessel: 超重起吊船只
A vessel with heavy lift cranes and other equipment designed to be self-sustaining in the handling of heavy cargo.

Hedge: 套期保值
To reduce one's risk of loss but compensating transactions on the other side. For example, buy goods for future delivery priced in a foreign currency. Hedge by buying the foreign exchange needed at the rate then in effect. Or, another way of hedging is to buy a forward exchange contract. In both cases the buyer will have a known cost in its own currency. This is a hedge against the risk of foreign exchange fluctuation;it is not a hedge against a change in the price of the goods.

Hold: 船舱，延迟，暂留，保持，持有，拥有
① The interior of a vessel below deck where cargo is carried. ② To delay;to pause (verb); a delay;a purse (noun). ③ A verb with multiple other meanings than those noted above such as: to retain, to contain, to maintain, to bind, to bear, to own.

Honor: 承兑
To accept a bill of exchange;or to pay a note check or draft at maturity.

House-to-House: 户到户，厂到厂
A shipping term indicating that a container will be offered by the carrier for use by the shipper and the receiver for the transport of the contents from the from the domicile of one to be

domicile of the other, but the carrier only contracts to transport the loaded container from terminal at origin to terminal at destination (usually called C/Y to C/Y -container yard to container yard).

Immigration: 移民
The entry of foreign nationals into a country for the purpose of establishing permanent residence..

Import: 进口
The act of bringing or causing any goods to be brought into a customs territory.

Import Duty: 进口关税
Customer duty which is collected on in connection with the importation of goods.

Importer: 进口商
The party that has contracted to buy the goods. It is also known as the buyer or applicant.

Import License: 进口许可证
An import license (or import permit)is an authorization by a competent authority for the importation of goods which are subject to restriction.

Import Quota: 进口配额
A protective device establishing limits on the quantity of a particular product that may be imported into a country.

Import Restrictions: 进口限制
Any one of a series of tariff and non-tariff barriers imposed by an importing nation to control the volume of goods coming into the country from other countries.

Imports: 进口货
Goods brought into a customs territory.

Income: 收入

Money or its equivalent earned or accrued, arising from the sale of goods or services.

Incoterms: 国际贸易术语解释通则
An abbreviation of "International Commercial Terms"published by the International Chamber of Commerce. It is a set of rules for the interpretation of the most commonly used trade terms in foreign trade which parties to a contract can agree upon to avoid misunderstandings, disputes and litigation.

Indemnify: 赔偿，保障
① To compensate for actual loss sustained. ② To give a security for the reimbursement of a person in case of an anticipated loss falling upon him.

Indemnify: 赔偿，赔偿协议/保证
① A compensation to make a person whole from a loss already sustained. ② A contract or assurance by which one engages to secure another against an anticipated loss.

Infant Industry Argument: 幼稚工业保护说
The view that "temporary protection" for a new industry or firm in a particular country through tariff and non-tariff barriers to imports can help it to become established and eventually competitive in world markets, in which case the protective measures will no longer be needed.

Inflation: 通货膨胀
Loss of purchasing power of money caused by growth of the amount of money in circulation and reflected in a rise in prices without a proportionate increase in value of the things purchased.

Inland Bill of Lading: 内陆提单
A bill of lading used in transporting goods overland.

Inland Carrie: 内陆承运人
A transportation line which hauls cargo inland: truck rail, barge, inland waterways, or domestic airline flights.

Inner Packing: 内包装

Inner Packing, or immediate packing or packaging helps promote the merchandize, which is highly appreciated in the school of marketing.

Inspection Certificate: 检验证书

A document describing the condition of goods and confirming that they have been inspected.

Insurance Policy: 保险单

The insurance policy is the contract made between the insurer and the insured.

Insured Amount: 投保金额

The insured amount is the amount of money the insurer agrees to pay in the event of damage to, or loss of the insured goods. In other words, the insured amount is the upper limit of compensation payable to the insured in case of loss. In international trade, the insured amount is often the CIF value of the consignment plus 10%, the additional 10% plus compensating for the loss of expected profit from transaction.

Insured: 被保险人

The insured is the party insured against loss and to whom compensation is made. In foreign trade, the buyer is most often the insured. The insured may sometimes be the seller who effects the insurance.

Insurer: 保险人

The insurer is the party providing insurance service and who makes the payment in case of loss. For example, PICC，the People's Insurance Company of China, is the biggest insurer in China.

Intellectual Property: 知识产权

Non-tangible property that is the result of creativity such as copyrights and patents.

Intermodal Transport: 协调联运，联运

Coordinated transport of freight using multiple methods of transportation.

Invisible Trade Balance: 无形贸易差额

The balance of trade reflecting the import and export of services.

Invoice: 发票

A written account or itemized statement, usually on a printed form with the name and address of the seller, listing merchandise sold or shipped to a purchaser, consignee, factor, etc. showing their name and address, and containing a description of the merchandise, the quantity, values or prices and charges, and other significant details of the transaction such as the term of sale and the currency of the purchase.

Issuance: 保险

① The execution, validation, and tender of delivery of a contract or financial instrument to the appropriate party. ② The act of sending forth, promulgating, or the giving of a thing its first inception. The first delivery of an instrument to a holder or remitter.

International Trade: 国际贸易

International trade is the exchange of commodities or services between different nations. Foreign trade is the exchange of goods or services between one nation or area with other nations or areas. All foreign trades together form international trade.

Irrevocable Letter of Credit: 不可撤销信用证

A Letter of Credit that cannot be canceled or changed without the consent of all patties, especially the consent of the seller. Unless otherwise stipulated，all Letters of Credit are irrevocable.

Issuing Bank: 开证行

The bank issuing the Letter of Credit at the request of its customer the importer (Applicant)in favor of the exporter (Beneficiary)，guaranteeing payment under the Letter of Credit if all terms and conditions are met.

Jettison: (船遇难时把货物)投弃

The act of throwing overboard at sea part of a vessel's paraphernalia or cargo or hull-usually in hopes of saving the ship from sinking.

Joint Venture: 合资企业，合资经营

A combination of two or more individuals or legal entities who undertake together a transaction for mutual gain or to engage in a commercial enterprise together with mutual sharing of profits or losses.

Key Currency: 基本货币，（国际）主要货币

A major currency in the global economy. Key currencies include the U.S. dollar, the British pound sterling, the German mark, the Swiss franc, the Dutch guilder, the Japanese yen and the Canadian dollar.

Laissez-faire: 自由放任，自由贸易

A term used to describe minimal governmental involvement in an economy, allowing market forces and individuals to make their own decisions, with little or no regulation.

Landing Quality, Landing Weight or quantity: 到岸质量，到岸重量或数量

In this mode of inspection，the seller and the buyer agree that the quality and quantity of the commodities are inspected at the place of destination, and that the inspection certificate，issued by the inspection institution at the place of destination, is the final proof of quality and quantity of the commodities. In this case, any loss in quality and quantity during transit is borne by the seller, to the disadvantage of the seller.

LCL: 拼箱货

If an exporter intends to pack a container to full capacity or full payload with consignments for the same destination for two or more consignees, the case is LCL and the carrier will charge the LCL freight rate on each consignment..In LCL arrangement, the shipper is required to deliver the cargo to the carrier's container freight station for containerization. Thus there is no guarantee that the two or more consignments from the same exporter will share the same container. In some case，an exporter is allowed to pack a container at his premises in the LCL arrangement. In this case，the carrier will use the same container to pack in more cargo from other shipper (s) to make a full container load at the container freight station.

Legal Inspection: 法定检验

Legal inspection is the compulsory inspection of imported and exported goods. The purpose of legal inspection is to insure the quality of exported goods and protect the safety and health of the people. Import and export commodities which are included in the List of Commodities and import and export commodities subject to inspection by the commodity inspection authorities under other laws or administrative rules and regulations must be inspected by the commodity inspection authorities or inspection organizations designed by the State Administration for Commodity Inspection.

Letter of Credit: 信用证
A written instrument issued by a bank at the request of its customers, the importer (Applicant), whereby the bank promises to pay the exporter (Beneficiary) for goods or services provided that the exporter presents all documents called for, exactly as stipulated in the Letter of Credit, And meets all other terms and conditions set out in the Letter of Credit. It is also referred to as a Documentary Credit.

Letter of Intent: 意向书
A document that describes the preliminary understanding between parties who intend to make a contract or join together in another action.

Lighter: 驳船
A barge towed by a tugboat and used mainly in harbors and island waterways for the transport of cargo to and from ships. Some may be self-powered.

Lighter Aboard Ship: 字母船，载驳船
Some ships are constructed to carry special barges (lighters). These barges can go to smaller docks, go into inland waterways, load cargo at those places, and then carry it back to the ship which lifts the barges abroad, with their cargo, and their cargo, and transports them overseas. Discharge of cargo is accomplished in the same manner.

Lighterage: 驳船费，驳船装卸
Some ships are constructed to carry special barge (lighters). These barges can go to smaller docks, go into inland waterways, load cargo at those places, and then carry it back to the ship which lifts the barges aboard, with their cargo, and transports them overseas. Discharge of cargo is accomplished in the same manner.

Line Haul: 长途运输
The direct movement of freight between two major ports by a single ship.
Liner: 定期班轮
A vessel carrying passengers and cargo that operates with a fixed schedule on a particular route.

Liner Terms: 班轮条件
Conditions under which a shipping company will transport goods, including in the amount payable for freight the cost both for loading and discharge of the cargo from the vessel.

Lloyds of London: (伦敦)劳埃德公司
An English association of insurance underwriters, the oldest of its kind in the world. Not in itself an insurance company.

Loading: 装货
The physical placing of cargo into a truck, a shipping container, or onto a vessel.

Long Form Bill of Lading: 全式提单
In a long form bill of lading the terms and conditions of carriage are printed on the reverse (back) of the bill of lading. The long form bill of lading is commonly used in international shipping.

Mail Transfer/ Telegraphic Transfer: 信汇/电汇
The remitting bank notifies the paying bank in the seller's country of the remittance by mail or by telegraphic means. In the former case it is called mail transfer, in the latter case it is called telegraphic transfer.

Manifest: 载货清单
① A document listing and describing the cargo contents of a carrier, container or warehouse.
② Evident to the sense, especially to the sight, obvious to the understanding, evident to the mind, open, clear, visible, unmistakable, indubitable, indisputable, and self-evident.

Margin: 成本与卖价的差额，毛利，保证金

① In commercial terms the difference between the cost of goods sold and the total net sales prices. ② The purchase of a stock or a commodity with payment of only part of the purchase price in cash (called the margin) and the balance by loan (usually made by the broker).

Marginal Cost: 边际成本
The increase in the total costs of a producer of producing one more unit of output, or the decrease in producing one less unit of output.

Maritime: 海事，海运
Business pertaining to commerce or navigation by sea.

Market Access: 市场准入
The openness of a national market to foreign products and services.

Market Economy: 市场经济
An economic system where resource are allocated and production of goods determined by market forces rather than by government decree.

Market Price: 市场价格
The price established in the market where buyers and sellers compete with each other to negotiate the best prices and terms.

Mate's Receipt: 大副收据，收货单
A declaration issued by an officer of a vessel stating that certain goods have been received on board his vessel.

More or Less Clause: 溢短装条款
More or less generally includes the quantity allowance percentage; which party determines the quantity allowance; and the price of the exceeding quantity.

Most Favored Nation: 最惠国
A trade policy commitment on the part of one nation to expend to another nation tariff rates as low as applies to any other "most favored nations", and to treat imports from that nation

without discrimination.

Multilateral Agreement: 多边贸易
An agreement among more than two persons, firms, or governments.

Multi-modal Transport: 多式联运
Transportation which includes at least two modes of transport, such as shipping by rail and by sea.

Multinational Corporation: 跨国公司
A corporation having subsidiaries in more than one country.

NAFTA: 北美自由贸易协定
North American Free Trade Agreement

National Treatment: 国民待遇
National treatment afford foreign individuals and firms the same competitive opportunities, including market access, as are available to domestic parties.

Nationalization: 民族化
Takeover by a government of a public or private activity.

Negotiable: 可转让的，可议付的
Legally capable of being transferred by endorsement or delivery.

Negotiable Bill of Lading: 可转让提单
A bill of lading transferable by endorsement by virtue of its terms which make the goods which it covers deliverable to "bearer", or to the order of a named party, or to assigns.

Net Price: 净价，实价
Price after all deductions, discount, rebates, etc. have been taken.

Net Weight 净重

Net weight is the weight of the commodity excluding the tare. Unless otherwise specified the weight of commodity usually refers to the net weight of it.

Notify Address: 受通知地址
Address of the party mentioned in the transport document to which the carrier is to give notice about the arrival of the shipment.

Notify Party:（到货）受通知人
Name and address of a party indicated in the transport document to be notified by the shipping company of the arrival of a shipment.

Ocean Bill of Lading: 海运提单
A receipt for the cargo and a contract for transportation issued by an ocean carrier. When issued in negotiable form, it is also instrument of title.

Ocean Freight: 海洋运输
Large items, bulk commodities and items that do not require fast delivery can be shipped economically by sea.

Offer: 发盘
According to the United Nations Convention on Contracts for the International Sale of Goods, proposal to conclude a contract addressed to one or more specific persons constitutes an offer if it is sufficiently definite and indicates the intention of the party making the offer to be bound in case of acceptance

On Board Bill of Lading: 已装船提单
The on board bill of lading—shipped bill of lading—proves that goods have been shipped, as evidenced by the pre-printed wording or the on board notation (e. g. “on board”, “laden on board” or “shipped on board”)on the bill of lading.

On Deck Bill of Lading: 舱面提单，甲板提单
An ocean bill of lading containing the notation that the goods have loaded on the deck of the vessel.

Order Bill of Lading: 指示提单

In an order bill of lading—negotiable bill of lading—the title to the goods is conferred to the order of shipper or to the order of a named party in the letter of credit (the issuing bank usually)·An order bill of lading provides the shipper or the named party with the title to the goods. The title to the goods is transferable to another party by endorsement, usually on the reverse (back)of the bill of lading (B/L) by the bona fide holder of the B/L. If an endorsement of the B/L is required in the letter of credit (L/C), all the originals of the B/L must be endorsed.

Outer Packing: 外包装

Outer packing or big packing is mainly employed against the shipping hazards.

Packing List: 装箱单

A document listing the merchandise in a particular shipment indicating the kind and quantity in each package.

Pallet: 托盘，垫板

A platform with or without sides, on which a number of packages or pieces may be loaded to facilitate handling. Usually the pallet is constructed so that it has space underneath it to permit lifting by mechanical equipment.

Par: 票面金额，面额，平价

Equal. An equality between the face value of a bill of exchange, share of stock, etc., and its actual market value. If it can be sold for more, it is "above par", if for less, it is "below par".

Par Value: 票面价值，平价

① The official fixed exchange rate between two currencies or between a currency and a specific weight of gold. ② "Par Value" of a currency is its official rate of exchange. ③ "Par Value" of a share of stock is the value declared on its face. ④ As to a mortgage or a trust deed, it is the balance owing, without discount.

Particular Average: 单独海损

Particular average is a partial loss suffered by the party whose consignment is partially lost or damaged.

Payee: 收款人，受款人

① The person or organization to whose order a check or draft or note is made payable. ② One to whom money is paid or is to be paid.

Payer: 付款人

One who pays or is to pay, particularly the person who is to make payment of a check, bill, note, or account.

Penalties: 处罚，罚金

① Punishment, corporeal or pecuniary, or civil or criminal, although its meaning is generally confined to pecuniary punishment for doing an act that is prohibited or failing to do one which is required. ② The sum of money which the obligor of a bond undertakes to pay in the event of his failure to perform his obligations under the conditions of the bond.

Performance: 履行

The proper fulfillment of a contract or obligation according to its terms.

Pier-to-Pier: 码头到码头

Shipment of cargo with carrier responsibility from origin pier to discharge pier.

Pilferage: 偷盗，小偷小摸

Taking of property by stealth or clandestine theft, usually in small quantities.

Pilot: 飞机驾驶员，领航员

① A person who flies an airplane. ② A person whose occupation is to guide ships, particularly along a coast, or into and out of harbor.

Point of Origin: 启运地，启运站

The location at which a shipment is received by a transportation line from the shipper.

Port: 港口

① A place intended for loading and unloading the cargo or passengers of vessels- it may be within a natural harbor on a coast, or on a river, or within sheltered water produced by artificial jetties. ② A place where customs officers are stationed for the collection of duties and the control of imports and exports.

Port Charge: 港口费，入港费
A charge made for various services performed at ports.

Port of Discharge: 卸货港
The port at which a shipment is off loaded by a transportation line.

Port of Entry: 出口港
A place where Customs is stationed to control departures of carriers, passengers, and goods to foreign countries.

Portfolio Investment: 证券投资
In investment, the collective term for all the securities held by one person or institution.

Preferential Tariff: 优惠关税，特惠关税
A tariff which imposes lower rates of duty on goods imported from some countries.

Premium: 保险金
The premium is the money paid to the insurer for providing the insurance service. The premium is always a percentage of the insured amount.

Presentation: 提示
Presentation is the act, by the holder of the bill of exchange, of taking the bill to the drawee and demanding that he make payment or accept the bill of exchange.

Procurement: 采购
The act of obtaining; attainment; acquisition; purchasing; or buying.

Pro Forma Invoice: 形式发票
The term pro forma is from Latin and means “as a matter of form”. The pro forma invoice Is a very important document in the quotation process and a company will often include it in

A response to a potential buyer's enquiry,

Promissory Note: 本票
A promissory note is a negotiable instrument that contains a promise to pay a certain sum money to a named person, to order, or to the bearer on demand or at a fixed or determinable future time. It is unconditional, signed by its maker, and is delivered to the payee or bearer.

Protectionism: 保护主义
The deliberate use or encouragement of restrictions on imports to enable relatively inefficient domestic producers to compete successfully with foreign producers, or to protect and preserve those industries and producers considered of critical national interest.

Protective Tariff: 保护性关税
A duty or tax on imported products to make them more expensive in comparison to domestic products.

Quality Latitude: 品质机动幅度
Quality latitude means that the seller and the buyer both agree that the quality of the goods delivered can vary within an agreed range.

Quality of Commodity: 商品的品质
The quality of commodity is a combination of intrinsic attributes and the outer from or shape of a commodity.

Quantitative Restricions: 数量限制
Explicit limits, or quotas, on the physical amounts of particular commodities that can be imported or exported during a specified time period, usually measured by volume but sometimes by value. The quota may be applied on a selective basis, with varying limits set according to the country of origin or destination, or on a quantitative global basis that only specifies the total limit and thus tends to benefit more efficient supplies.

Quantity Allowance: 数量机动幅度
Quantity allowance is the allowed deviation in quantity on delivery from that stipulated in the

contract. The quantity clause in a sales contract usually specifies the quantity allowance. The purpose of the quantity allowance is to convenience delivery，shipment or preparation of goods. We can stipulate the quantity allowance in two ways: the more or Iess clause or using approximate quantity.

Quay: 停泊码头
A structure built for the purpose of mooring a vessel; also called a pier.

Quota: 配额
A limitation on the quantity of goods that may be imported into a country from all countries or from specific countries during a set period of time. Export quotas have similar parameters.

Quotation: 报价
A quotation describes the product, states price, sets the time of shipment, and specifies terms of sale and terms of payment.

Rail Waybill: 铁路运单
A document used to control the transportation of a shipment of goods via rail. It is similar in content to an inland hill of lading, with freight and other charges, and routing.

Receipt: 收据；签收
① Any written acknowledgment of value received. It is a mere admission of a fact without containing any affirmative obligation. ② Receipt of goods which means taking possession of goods

Received Bill of Lading: 已收待运提单
The received bill of lading does not prove that goods have been shipped, It only acknowledges that goods have been received by the carrier for shipment. Therefore, the goods could be in the dock or warehouse.

Reciprocal Trade Agreement: 互惠贸易协定
An international agreement between two or more countries to establish mutual trade concessions that are expected to be of equal value

Reciprocity: 互惠

The process by which governments extend similar concessions to each other.

Reimbursing Bank: 偿付行

The bank designated in the Letter of Credit to reimburse the "available with" bank which submits payment claims under the Letter of Credit.

Remittance: 汇付

Funds forwarded from one person to another. Remittance means to make payment through bank transfer. In remittance, there are four parties involved: remitter, remitting bank, paying bank and beneficiary.

Revocable Letter of Credit: 可撤销信用证

A revocable Letter of Credit can be revoked without the consent of the exporter, meaning that it may be canceled or changed up to the time the documents are presented

Right of Subrogation 代位权

After paying a claim to the insured, the insurer is subrogated to all rights and claims the insured has against the third party that caused the damage to the goods. The insured, after receiving the indemnity, will commonly sign a letter of subrogation to the insurer.

Roll on, Roll off: 滚装滚卸船

A category of ships designed to load and discharge cargo which rolls on wheels, and as the name says is driven onto the decks of the vessel and driven off.

Rollover Credit: 展期信用，滚动贷款

Short-term notes or loans which may be extended after the initial due date

Route: 航线；路线

① A customary or regular line of passage or travel. ② The course or direction that a particular shipment moves. ③ To direct the routing of a shipment (and whose services shall be employed).

Sale by Sample: 凭样品买卖

Sale by sample means a sale made on the basis of a sample, that is the quality and condition of the bulk of the goods will be at least as good as that of the sample.

Sale by Seller's Sample: 凭卖方样品买卖

When the seller supplies the sample, it is sale by seller's sample. When the buyer offers the sample, it is sale by buyer's sample.

Sales Agreement: 销售合同

A written document (a contract) by which a seller agrees to convey property to a buyer for a stipulated price under specified conditions.

Sales Tax: 销售税

A tax placed by a state or municipality on items at the time of their sale usually a percentage of the purchase price.

Salvage: 救助费，救助，救出残货

① Compensation paid for the rescue of a ship, its cargo or passengers from the perils of the sea. ② Or, the act of saving a ship or its cargo from possible loss. ③ Or, property saved from a wreck or fire

Sample 样品

A sample is a product, which is selected from a large consignment which is specially designed and processed.

Seal: 印章

A mark or sign that is used to attest the execution of an instrument, contract, or other document.

Seaworthiness: 适航性

The fitness or safety of a vessel for its intended use.

Security: 抵押品，担保，抵押证券

① Property pledged as collateral to a debt. ② Protection; assurance; indemnification. A document that indicates evidence of indebtedness or of equity interest—including notes, bonds, debentures, stocks, certificate of interest, etc, which may be traded on an exchange.

Settlement Date: 交割日
The date on which payment for a transaction must be made.

Shipment: 发货，装运，装运的货物
① Delivery of cargo to a carrier for transportation ② The transportation of goods. ③ The property which is the subject of transportation.

Shipped on Deck: 装载于甲板上
Goods shipped on the deck of a vessel. The bill of lading covering goods shipped on deck must be annotated to that effect.

Shipper: 托运人，发货人，装货人
① One who transports goods for a charge. In normal usage, such a person would be called a carrier, but carriers are also called "shippers". ② One who tenders goods to a carrier for transportation. ③ The sender of goods to be transported as distinct from the receiver or the consignee.

Shipping Marks: 运输标记
The marks and numbers on a shipment identify the cargo in the same way as an ID card identifies a person. The exporter, customs, carriers, and importers rely on them to distinguish one consignment from another. The marks and numbers identify the cargo, not the consignee, and they must he easily identifiable.

Shipping Order: 装货单，装运通知
Instructions from a shipper to a carrier for the transportation of goods.

Shipping Quality and Quantity for negotiation. Re-Inspection at Destination: 装运港性检验，目的港复验
In this mode of inspection，the seller and the buyer agree to inspect the quality and quantity of

the commodities at the place of shipment, and the inspection certificates issued at the place of shipment can be used by the seller as negotiation documents. The seller and buyer also agree that the buyer has the right to re-inspect the quality and quantity of the goods at place of destination and make a claim for compensation. This mode of inspection is relatively fair to both the seller and the buyer and is most widely used in international trade.

Shipping Quality, Shipping Weight or Quantity: 离岸质量，离岸数量
In this mode of inspection, the seller and the buyer agree that the commodities are inspected before shipping, at the place of shipment, and the resulting inspection certificate serves as final proof of the quality and quantity of the commodities shipped. The inspecting institution is usually a third party agreed upon by the two parties. This kind of inspection deprives the buyer of the right to re-inspect the goods upon arrival and so is disadvantageous to the buyer.

Short Form Bill of Lading: 简式提单
A bill of lading on which the detailed conditions of transportation are not listed in full, but instead there is a statement which declares them to be incorporated by reference, and states the place where they are available.

Shortage: 短缺，短量
A deficiency in quantity shipped, stored, or received.

Soft Currency:（不易兑换的）软通货，软性货币
The currency of a country that is not readily accepted by other countries and is not readily converted into currencies which arc readily acceptable (hard currencies).

Special Extraneous Risks: 特别外来风险
Special extraneous risks are risks such as on deck, war strikes, failure of delivery and rejection, etc.

Spot Exchange: 现汇
The purchase and sale of foreign exchange for delivery and payment at the time of the transaction.

Spot Exchange Rate: 即期外汇汇率
The price of one currency expressed in terms of another currency at a given moment in time.

Spot Market: 现货交易市场
The market for a commodity or foreign exchange available for immediate delivery.

Spot Price: 现货价格
The selling of goods or commodities for immediate delivery.

Standby Letter of Credit: 备用信用证
A written instrument issued by a bank (Issuing Bank)at the request of its customer (Applicant) on behalf of a beneficiary, whereby the Issuing Bank agrees to provide financial remedy in the event that the applicant defaults on any terms and conditions specified under the Standby Letter of Credit. Standby Letters of Credit are often issued at the request of importers in favor of exporters as financial security for goods purchased on Open Account.

Storage: 仓储
The keeping of goods in a warehouse or other repository.

Storage in Transit: 运输途中的储存
The stopping of freight traffic at a point located between the point located between the point of origin and destination to be stored and re-forwarded at a later date.

Stowage: 理仓
The arranging and packing of cargo in a vessel for shipment.

Straight Bill of Lading: 记名提单
In a straight bill of lading—non-negotiable bill of lading—the title to the goods is conferred directly to a party named in the letter of credit (the importer usually), as such title to the goods is not transferable to another party by endorsement. In other words, the bill of lading is not negotiable.

Strike Clause: 罢工条款

An insurance clause which may be included in policies to cover against losses as a result of strike, riots and civil communication.

Subsidiary: 子公司

Any organization more than 50 percent of whose voting stock is owned by another firm.

Swap (transactions):（汇兑期货）掉期

A kind of financial transaction which has many variations, usually highly complex. They generally involve a simultaneous exchange of assets (the swap) by counter-parties for other different assets of comparable value. The assets may be commodities or they may be financial instruments involving interest rates, cash flows, foreign exchange, debts or equities. In addition to financial profits, the swaps have many purposes such as limiting risks, overcoming restrictions in certain markets, or balancing portfolios.

Switch: 转手贸易

A form of counter-trade in which the seller sells on credit and then transfers the credit to a third party at a discount. Or, in another type of switch, the rights to purchase certain goods, resulting

From a counter-trade operation, are sold to a third party at a discount.

Tare Weight: 皮重，自重

The weight of a container and/or packing materials, but without the goods be shipped

.The gross weight of a shipment less the net weight of the goods being shipped (in other words, the weight of the packing).

Tariff: 关税

① A comprehensive list or "schedule" of merchandise with applicable duty rates to be paid or charged for each listed article; together with governing rules and regulations (a "customs" tariff) ② A schedule of rates and charges applied by a business, especially a common carrier, together with a description of the services offered and the rules and regulations applicable.

Tariff Rate Quotas: 税率配额

(Customs) Application of a higher duty rate to imported goods after a specified quantity of. the item has entered the country at a lower prevailing rate.

Tariff Schedule: 关税率表
(Customs) A comprehensive list of the goods which may be imported into a. country, and the import duties applicable to each product.

Tender: 小船（大船的服务船），投标书，投标，煤水车
① An offer of money. An offer to supply something. An offer to present something. ② To satisfy a claim, an unconditional offer to perform coupled with a manifest ability to carry out the offer. ③ A small vessel which serves a large vessel is a port for the purpose of supplying provisions and carrying passengers to and from ship to shore. ④ A car connected behind a steam railroad locomotive to carry coal and water (almost obsolete).

Tenor: 汇票期限
The term fixed for the payment of a draft or debt.

Terminal: 装卸区，集散站
An facility which is used by a rail, ship, air, or truck line as a place for receiving and delivering cargo; loading; unloading; transferring; temporarily storing; and similarly handling freight; and repairing and servicing equipment.

Terminal Charge: 终点站服务费
A charge made for services performed at transportation terminals.

Terms of Trade: 进出口货价比率，贸易条件
The ratio of the index of export prices to the index of import prices. (Note the difference from "Trade Terms")

Theoretical Weight: 理论重量
If the weight of each item is approximately the same, the total weight of a consignment can be considered as the product of the individual weight of one item time, the number of items. The weight got in this way is called the theoretical weight.

Through Bill of Lading: 全程提单，联运提单

A single bill of lading covering receipt of cargo at a point of origin for delivery to an ultimate consignee, usually involving multiple carriers and multiple modes of transport.

Time Charter: 期租船

A ship is chartered for a period of time. This type of charter shipping is similar to a voyage charter in the crewing and operating of the ship. The contract may call for a specific or unlimited number of voyages within the agreed time..

To Order: 指定收货人

A term on a financial instrument or title document indicating that it is negotiable and transferable.

Trade Deficit: 贸易赤字

A nation's excess of imports over exports over a period of time.

Trade Surplus: 贸易顺差

A nation's excess of exports over imports over a period of time.

Trade Terms: 贸易术语，贸易条款

The setting of responsibilities of the buyers and sellers in a sale including sale price, the payment of costs such as shipping, insurance and customs; the arranging of the performance of these activities; and the determination of risks when title passes (Note the difference from "Terms of Trade").

Trailer: 拖车

A vehicle without motor power designed to be drawn by another vehicle.

Tramp Line: 不定期航线

A transportation line operating tramp steamers in waterborne commerce.

Tramp Steamer: 不定期货船

A vessel which does not operate under any regular schedule from one port to another, but calls at any port where cargo may be obtained and charges a negotiated amount of freight. Usually they transport break-bulk or bulk cargo.

Transferable Letter of Credit: 可转让信用证
A Letter of Credit that allows the beneficiary (Exporter) to instruct its bank to transfer the credit in part or in whole to a Secondary Beneficiary.

Trans-ship: 中转，转运，过境运输
① To transfer goods from one transportation line to another, or from one ship to another, or from one airline to another in order to complete a delivery. ② To ship to one country, and then to re-export to another. (Sometimes the second exporting country may be incorrectly represented as the country of origin.)

Transfer (mail, wire, cable): 汇兑，转账
A transfer is the remittance of a sum of money to a party in another place. This may be accomplished by mailing cash or drafts or using the services of a commercial bank or a wire transfer company for a fee.

Transparency: 透明度
The extent to which laws, regulations, agreements, and practices affective international trade are open, clear, measurable, and verifiable.

Transport Documents: 运输单据
All types of documents evidencing acceptance, receipt and shipment of goods.

Trust Receipt: 信托收据
A written declaration by a customer to a bank that ownership in goods released by the bank is retained by the bank, and that the client has received the goods in trust only. Such a trust receipt may be given by the customer to the bank to induce the bank to issue a letter of indemnity to a carrier to release a shipment.

Turnkey: 统包方式，“交钥匙”方式
A term for a method of construction whereby the contractor assumes total responsibility from

design through completion of the product and release to the client in a stage to complete that the buyer need only to turn the key to open the door and walk into a facility that is ready to seprate.

Turnkey Contract: 统包式合同，“交钥匙”合同
An agreement under which a contractor agrees to complete a product to that it is ready for use when delivered to the other contracting party.

Uruguay Round: 乌拉圭回合
The eighth round of multilateral trade negotiations under the General Agreement on Tariffs and end Trade (GATT). The Uruguay Round (so named because meetings began in Punta De Este, Uruguay in 1487) concluded in December, 1993 after seven years of talks between 117 member nations. From those negotiations the World Trade Organization came into being.

Uniform Customs and Practices for Documentary Credits (UCP) 跟单信用证统一惯例
A set of guidelines, rules and definitions governing Letters of Credit published by the International Chamber of Commerce. For those banks that subscribe, UCP facilitates the standardization of Letters of Credit.

Usance: 远期汇票期限
The common period fixed for payment by usage, custard, or habit of dealings between the country where a bill of exchange is drawn and that where it is payable. It varies according to the countries involved.

Validity: 合法性，有效期
① Validity—Legal sufficiency More regularity in the execution of documents may not be enough for “legal sufficiency” ② The time period for which a letter of credit is valid.

Valuation: 估价，估值
The act of ascertaining the worth of a thing. The estimated worth of a thing.

Value Added: 增值
The amount by which the value of an article is increased at each stage of items they purchase

and resell.

Voyage Charter: 程租船
A ship is chartered for a single journey that may involve more than one port of call. The ship operator crews and operates the ship and the operator's own ship's master is in control of the ship.

War Clause: 战时自动终止条款
A marine insurance provision excluding the liability of an insurer if a loss is caused by war or hostile action. Bills of Lading and charter parties may contain a "War Clause" giving the vessel options to maintain it's safety in case of hostilities.

War Risk: 战争险
The risk to a vessel, its cargo and passengers by aggressive actions of a hostile nation or group.

War Risk Insurance: 战争险
Insurance covering loss or damage caused by war or other hostile actions. Usually a separate policy from a marine insurance policy, or a special attachment to it.

Warranty: 保证书，保证
A promise by a contracting party that the other party can rely on certain facts or representations as being true

Waybill: 运货单
A document prepared by a transportation line at the point of shipment for use in the handling of the shipment showing the point of origin, destination, route, consignor, consignee, description of shipment and amount charged for the transportation service and other services connected with the transport. It is similar in point of information to a bill of lading.

Wharfage: 码头费
A charge assessed by a pier or dock owner for handling incoming or outgoing cargo.

Without Reserve: 无保留条件

A term applied to a sale by auction indicating that no price is reserved (there is no minimum price).

World Bank: 世界银行

The International Bank for Reconstruction and Development (IBRD) commonly referred to as the World Bank, is an intergovernmental financial institution located in Washington, D. C. Its objectives are to help raise productivity and incomes and reduce poverty in developing countries through the granting of loans.

World Trade Organization: 世界贸易组织

The international organization which resulted from the Uruguay Round of GATT negotiations. It is intended to promote world trade and to settle disputes member nations.

Yen: 日元/日本货币

The currency of Japan.

Yuan: 元/中国货币

The currency of China.

Zip Code: 划分美国邮区编号 (USA)

A numerical code, established by the U. S. Postal Service, used for the purpose of routing mail and to identify delivery zones. Some foreign countries have a similar system. Carriers often apply this code in the same manner in the handling of freight and the determination freight charges.

Reference

1. 吴百福，徐小薇. 进出口贸易实务教程. 上海：上海人民出版社，2011.
2. 国际商会中国国家委员会. 2000年国际贸易术语解释通则. 上海：中信出版社，2000.
3. 国际商会中国国家委员会. 2010国际贸易术语解释通则（英汉对照）. 北京：中国民主法制出版社，2011.
4. 帅建林. 英汉对照国际贸易惯例案例解析——Case Study of International Trade Customs and Practices. 北京：对外经济贸易大学出版社，2006.
5. 帅建林. 国际贸易实务（英语版）. 北京：对外经济贸易大学出版社，2007.
6. 黎孝先. 国际贸易实务. 北京：对外经济贸易大学出版社，2000.
7. 冷柏军. 国际贸易实务. 北京：北京大学出版社，2009.
8. 熊伟，陈凯. 国际贸易实务英语. 武汉：武汉大学出版社，2007.
9. 陈胜权. 国际贸易实务经典教材习题详解. 北京：对外经济贸易大学出版社，2005.
10. 易露露，陈原. 国际贸易实务双语教程. 北京：清华大学出版社，2006.
11. 易露霞，方玲玲，尤彧聪. 国际贸易实务案例教程: 双语. 北京：清华大学出版社，2010.
12. 姚新超. 国际贸易实务. 北京：对外经济贸易大学出版社，2011.
13. 张炳达. 国际贸易实务. 上海：立信会计出版社，2009.
14. 周瑞琪，王小欧，徐月芳. 国际贸易实务（英文版）. 北京：对外经济贸易大学出版社，2011.
15. ALI M. EL-AGRAA. International Trade. New York: St. Martin's Press, Inc., 1983.
16. BRANCH, A E. Export Practice and Management, 5th edition，Business Press, Thomson Learning, 1987.
17. BRENTON PAUL. International Trade. Oxford University Press, 1997.
18. WILEY. International Trade: Theory and Practice. New York: John Wiley &Sons, 1987.
19. MARK ELIS and CHRISTINE JOHNSON, Teaching Business English, Oxford: Oxford University Press, 1994.
20. NELSON A CARL. Import /Export，How to Take Your Business Across Borders. McGraw-Hill Education and Posts & Telecom Press, 2009.